SERMONS.

Printing Statement:

Due to the very old age and scarcity of this book,
many of the pages may be hard to read due to the
blurring of the original text, possible missing pages,
missing text and other issues beyond our control.

Because this is such an important and rare work, we
believe it is best to reproduce this book regardless of
its original condition.

Thank you for your understanding.

SERMONS

PREACHED BEFORE THE

UNIVERSITY OF OXFORD,

IN THE

CATHEDRAL OF CHRIST CHURCH,

FROM 1836 TO 1847.

BY

R. D. HAMPDEN, D.D.,

(LATE REGIUS PROFESSOR OF DIVINITY,)

BISHOP OF HEREFORD.

LONDON:

B. FELLOWES, LUDGATE STREET.

M.DCCC.XLVIII.

PRINTED BY RICHARD AND JOHN E. TAYLOR,
RED LION COURT, FLEET STREET.

MOST of the Sermons included in this Volume have already appeared in print. One or two of them have passed through several Editions. But as they are all closely connected in their bearing on points recently brought into prominent discussion, it has been thought desirable to collect them, with others also preached before the University on the same points, in the present form. The whole, it is humbly hoped, will, through Divine grace, serve to a sound knowledge of the Gospel of our Blessed God and Saviour, and to the edification of the Church founded on Him.

CONTENTS.

b 2

SERMON VI.

THE ONE SACRIFICE FOR SIN.

Heb. ix. 27, 28.

SERMON VII.

THE WAY, THE TRUTH, AND THE LIFE.

John xiv. 6.

SERMON VIII.

THE FAREWELL CHARGE.

2 Tim. iv. 1–5.

I charge thee therefore before God, and the Lord Jesus
Christ, who shall judge the quick and the dead at his
appearing and his kingdom; preach the word; be instant in season, out of season; reprove, rebuke, exhort
with all long-suffering and doctrine. For the time will
come when they will not endure sound doctrine; but
after their own lusts shall they heap to themselves
teachers, having itching ears; and they shall turn away
their ears from the truth, and shall be turned unto
fables. But watch thou in all things; endure afflic-

SERMON IX.

CHRIST SANCTIFYING HIS CHURCH.

JOHN xvii. 17–21.

Sanctify them through Thy truth : Thy word is truth. As
Thou hast sent Me into the world, even so have I also
sent them into the world. And for their sakes I sanctify Myself, that they also might be sanctified through
the Truth. Neither pray I for these alone, but for them
also which shall believe on Me through their word ; that
they all may be one ; as Thou, Father, art in Me, and I
in Thee, that they also may be one in Us : that the
world may believe that Thou hast sent Me. 283

SERMON X.

THE FAITHFUL STEWARD.

1 COR. iv. 1, 2.

Let a man so account of us, as of the ministers of Christ,
and stewards of the mysteries of God. Moreover it is
required in stewards that a man be found faithful 327

SERMON XI.

THE INCARNATION A REALITY.

2 COR. xi. 2, 3.

But I fear, lest, by any means, as the serpent beguiled
Eve through his subtilty, so your minds should be cor-

SERMON I.

WHAT THINK YE OF CHRIST?

PREACHED AT THE CATHEDRAL OF CHRIST CHURCH,

On SUNDAY, October 15, 1837.

SERMONS.

SERMON I.

WHAT THINK YE OF CHRIST?

MATT. XXII. 42.

What think ye of Christ?

THE question contained in these few words is
the most important that was ever put to man.
It is not one of this particular time or place, but
of all times and places. There is no one that
has ever lived, or ever will live, in the world,
but must feel an interest in it. But the particular occasion on which it was uttered, as related
by the Evangelist, was one of eminently surpassing interest. Here was our Lord Himself
in the midst of captious opponents of his teaching,—persons who had gathered themselves to-

B 2

gether, having " taken counsel how they might entangle him in his talk,"—persons desirous rather of checking inquiry into the truth, than of learning the truth,—our Lord Himself, I say proposing to such persons the pregnant question —" What think ye of Christ?" What think ye, that is, of Him who is now addressing you? What expectation concerning Him have you formed from the prophetic revelations of his person in your sacred books? You are busy in scrutinizing my pretensions to the office of the Christ; you think you are able to confute me out of my own mouth—to prove to the world that I understand not the counsel of the Father —that I have not the skill to solve the perplexities which disputers of the world may raise as to the interpretation of the divine oracles. Let me hear, therefore, how you have read and applied the word of God. And that I may judge of this by a sure test, tell me, what think you of Him of whom Moses wrote, and to whom all the Prophets bear witness? What think ye of Christ? whose Son is He?

The character of the persons to whom the question was put on this occasion adds to the interest of it; for who were they? They were the very persons to whom it especially belonged to be able to give a right answer to it. They were Scribes and Pharisees—doctors of the Law —men who made it their profession to expound the Scriptures—who sat in Moses' seat, and claimed a deference to their expositions as authoritative and binding on the people—who prided themselves on their knowledge of the sacred law as righteousness in themselves, and accounted the people at large as " sinners " not knowing the law. From such, a wise answer to the question might surely have been expected, if from any. Who but those who were reputed the masters in Israel, were the men to whom others might look for a reason of the hope of Israel ?

And how was the expectation gratified ? Truly, they were not slow in giving an answer to the question. They were not so wanting to their profession, as not readily to give some account of the Scripture testimony to the Christ. And they answered truly when they said of him,— He is the Son of David. At the same time how little were they aware of the full import of that testimony of the Scripture concerning Christ ! Had this declaration of holy prophecy been rightly

viewed and appreciated, they would have surmised at least the mighty mystery veiled in the
simple description of the Son of David. They
might have seen that this Son of David was a
Son of prayer, and covenant, and prophecy,—
not of mere flesh and blood alone ; but that whilst
He should come in the line of natural descent of
the seed of David, He should be born in a way
in which no Son of David had ever before been
born, and his throne established as no throne of
David's family had ever been established. For
God had sworn in his Holiness that he would not
" fail David : " " David shall never want a man
to sit upon the throne of the house of Israel *."
He had said, " Behold a Virgin shall conceive
and bear a Son, and shall call his name Immanuel † ;" that " the government should be
upon his shoulder, and his name should be called
Wonderful, Counsellor, the Mighty God, the
Everlasting Father, the Prince of Peace ;" and
that " of the increase of his government and
peace there should be no end, upon the throne
of David, and upon his kingdom, to order it, and
to establish it with judgement and with justice,
from henceforth, even for ever." So that in the

* Jer. xxxiii. 17.   † Isaiah vii. 14.

very acknowledgement of Christ as the Son of David was implied an acknowledgement of "God made man"—that high truth wrapped up in all God's earlier dispensations, but at length fully revealed in his last message by the Son Himself coming in the name and authority of the Father, bearing the fulness of the Godhead bodily, and, in his own person, at once paying the price and granting the forgiveness of sins.

The learned Scribe and Pharisee might well, I say, have surmised this mystery of the Son of David, and, like the devout Simeon and Anna, have returned thanks to God that their eyes had seen *his* salvation. But no; their hearts were hardened, and their eyes were holden that they should not behold *their Lord* and *David's Lord* in the lowly Son of David who then stood before them. Therefore He stood in the midst of them, and they knew Him not. They read the Scriptures—they discoursed on the Scriptures—they had the word of God fluent on their tongue—they were expert at untying the knots of the Scripture-language, and commenting on the text; but "going about to establish their own righteousness," they knew not the Lord their Righteousness. The veil was on their hearts. They

were not prepared, accordingly, to meet the next
question which our Lord proposed to them on
their own answer: "How then doth David in
spirit call Him Lord, saying, The Lord said unto
my Lord, Sit thou on my right hand, till I make
thine enemies thy footstool? If David then call
Him Lord, how is He his Son?"

This further question was indeed a trial of their
spirit. It called upon them either to confess that
they knew not the bearing of the prophecies on
the person of the Messiah, or candidly to examine
his pretensions to the twofold character of David's
Son and David's Lord. It was quite needless for
our Lord to press his searching inquiry further.
It was vain to teach those more fully who had
not ears to hear his doctrine, and who were per-
versely wise in their own conceits. He contents
Himself, therefore, with having scattered the
seeds of the truth, and leading the mind that
would receive them to ripen them into fruit.

This, we may observe, is our Lord's usual
manner when He addresses his teaching to the
people at large. He drops hints and suggestions
of mighty truths, or gives popular representations of them under some familiar image, as in
the case of his parables, which the humble and

docile hearer might apply by his own religious meditation to the improvement of his knowledge and conduct, or the inattentive and worldly might slight if he would. To his intimate disciples,— those who had proved their attachment to his person and doctrine by their constancy of faith under all the discouragements of his personal ministry,—to them He explains Himself more distinctly; as in regard to his parables He expounds their application which He had withheld from the multitude—assigning, as a reason of his conduct, " It is given unto you to know the mysteries of the kingdom of heaven, but to them —' them that are without*'—it is not given; for whosoever hath, to him shall be given, and he shall have more abundance : but whosoever hath not, from him shall be taken away even that he hath. Therefore speak I to them in parables : because they seeing see not; and hearing they hear not, neither do they understand." " But blessed are your eyes, for they see; and your ears, for they hear†."

The reason here given concerning his use of parables applies generally to his teaching; and it is only what we find to be the method of the

* Mark iv. 11.   † Matt. xiii. 11—16.

Holy Spirit in his proceedings with men. He communicates instruction, and gives grace to the willing open mind. He calls to the self-willed and insensible, and knocks even at the door which is shut against Him. But He comes not in, *if the door be not opened to Him.* It is only, " if any man *hear my voice*," He says, " and *open the door,* 'that' I will come in to him, and will sup with him, and he with Me*."

And this difference in his teaching is shown in his further asking the disciples themselves, on an occasion when He had already learnt from them what the people thought of Him, " But whom say ye that I am?" He expected clearly to receive a more spiritual acknowledgement of Him, from those who had enjoyed a more intimate communion with Him. And when He heard from the lips of the devout Peter the true Gospel-confession, " Thou art the Christ, the Son of the living God!" He declared, that this was no knowledge for the ears of the carnal man, or which could be learned in the school of worldly wisdom, but the fruit of God's special blessing, —God's own revelation to the heart of his faithful disciple,—by saying, " Blessed art thou, Simon

* Rev. iii. 20.

Bar-jona : for flesh and blood hath not revealed it unto thee, but my Father which is in heaven." And he further marked the importance,—not indeed of reserving or concealing the truth—but of duly considering how it might effectually be imparted, by forbidding them to tell any man that He was Jesus the Christ* ; forbidding them, that is, to attempt to enlighten the minds of a corrupt world by laying suddenly before them a truth to which they had nothing congenial,— which they would only hear to blaspheme, and so harden themselves the more against the means of future conviction.

I do not presume to say that this is the whole account of our Lord's gradual method of teaching. In this point, as in others relating to Scripture-truth, we may, by comparing passages together, humbly discern a ground of propriety in the method of God's proceeding, and avail ourselves of it in the interpretation of God's word, without intruding into reasons which God has in his own keeping, or measuring his plans by the span of our judgement. With this understanding, I say there is a peculiar propriety in the mode in which our Lord reproved the self-righteous Scribe on

* Matt. xvi. 20.

the occasion to which the words of the text introduce us, by withholding from one in that state
of mind a more distinct instruction in the great
mystery of godliness.

He was *Himself*, indeed,—his nature, and office,
and character, and doctrine,—the great Mystery,
which Prophets and Evangelists and Apostles
were raised up at successive periods and inspired
to preach; and until his mission therefore was
accomplished, a full information of the Truth as
it is in Him could not be given to the world.
His own teaching was the last solemn introduction to the full disclosure of the mystery which
had hitherto been hidden or only dimly seen.
For even his chosen Apostles did not receive
from Him during his personal ministry their
whole instruction in the Gospel. He had many
things to say unto them; but they could not bear
them then. It was during the forty days that
He was seen of them after his resurrection, that
He taught them " things pertaining to the kingdom of God." Still it was not until the Comforter
came, that even these chosen vessels received
fully the vital truth,—" I am in my Father, and
ye in me, and I in you*." And at length being

* John xiv. 20.

illumined by the Comforter, "and having all things brought to their remembrance, whatsoever He had said unto them*," they were thus richly instructed and qualified for the work of their ministry ; being enabled to set forth the saving truths of the Gospel in that breadth and height and depth, in which the Christian now reads them in the Bible.

This full revelation of the truth as it is in Jesus, we, Christian Brethren, now enjoy. By his word, written in the Old and New Testament, our Lord now puts to us the question of the text,—" *What think ye of Christ?*" Our trial, too, is strictly analogous to that to which the Jewish Scribe was subjected on the occasion when the words were uttered by our Lord Himself. We have the Scriptures before us, as the Jew had. We, as Christians, plume ourselves on our peculiar knowledge of the ways of God. We take to ourselves a conscious satisfaction, that from the least to the greatest of us we all "know the Lord†." For if we change only the term Jew for Christian, the following words of St. Paul apply to us no less than to those to whom he addressed them : " Behold, thou art

* John xiv. 26.   † Jer. xxxi. 34.

called a Jew, and restest in the Law, and makest thy boast of God, and knowest his will, and approvest the things that are more excellent, being instructed out of the Law ; and art confident that thou thyself art a guide of the blind, a light of them which are in darkness, an instructor of the foolish, a teacher of babes, which hast the form of knowledge and of the truth in the Law*.'' We think ourselves able, too, like the Scribe and the Pharisee, to dispute out of the Scriptures,— to point out the grounds of catholic and orthodox belief, and silence the heretic and gainsayer by proving out of the Scripture that Jesus is the Christ.

And whilst Christians at large (and Christians especially of our own Church, referred as they are for all matter of doctrine to the warrant of the Bible, and so enjoined by their Church to prove all things by the Bible,) claim to be able to give a reason of the hope that is in them, we of such a place as this, in particular, being for the most part devoted, beyond most other Christians, to the study and exposition of God's word, correspond in this respect very closely to the Scribes and Doctors of the Law under the old

* Rom. ii. 17.

dispensation. Of us, therefore, it cannot be doubted, that our Lord especially asks for an answer to his question,—*What think ye of Christ?*

But it is not to us *solely*, though it may be *chiefly*, that he now puts the question. We shall do well to take it ourselves, as what principally concerns us ; that we may examine ourselves as to our faithfulness in studying and expounding the Scriptures, and teaching others out of them without hypocrisy, and proving to them that we have found the Christ, and fully " believe and are assured " that He is the Saviour of the world. But it does not concern us alone, as I have said ; nor must we apply it to ourselves solely in our capacity of ministers or students of God's word. The question is put to us *as Christians*, and we are strictly concerned to answer it *as Christians*. " *What think ye then*, Brethren, *of Christ ?*"

It is not then, be it observed, to obtain a speculative answer to the question, that the Gospel would have us apply it to ourselves. Our Lord Himself clearly did not put it to the learned Scribe with this view. He knew that the Scribes sat in the seat of Moses, and might well be expert in questions of the Law and points of abstract argument. It had been their education, and their practice, to sit in the Temple, hearing and asking questions; and doubtless they had all been " taught (as St. Paul speaks of himself) according to the perfect manner of the Law of the Fathers." Nor can it be supposed that, because they returned no answer to our Lord's further question, " If David then call him Lord, how is he Son ?" they could give no solution whatever of the difficulty. They could not answer further without committing themselves at least to *inquiry* concerning the claims of Jesus to be the Christ. But they saw to what point the examination was tending, and therefore did not answer, nor dare to ask him any more questions.

Nor is it to be supposed of any of us who have been brought up in the Church of Christ, baptized in the true faith, and instructed in the faith in which we were baptized, that we should not know what we ought to think of Christ, or that our opinions respecting his person and office are yet to be formed. We are happily guided in this respect by the sound scriptural views which our Church has set forth in its formularies. The question then—*What think ye of Christ?* abstractedly viewed—considered, that is, as leading to a general statement of our doctrines on the subject—is already satisfactorily answered by us who are here assembled. God forbid that any of us should be hypocrites in such a matter, or *profess in words* what we do *not really hold* !

Let it be presumed, then, that we all do indeed confess with sincerity that our Lord Jesus Christ is perfect God and perfect man,—uniting mysteriously in his one Person the Divine and the human natures,—equal to the Father as touching his Godhead, inferior to the Father as touching his manhood,—the true Immanuel by nature as well as by designation of his office : so that not only is Salvation by Him, but that there is *none other Name* given under Heaven whereby we can be saved. So far I trust we do know what to think of Christ ; so far we do know " in whom we have believed." And each of us, according to the talents which God has given him, is able, it may be hoped, to show by the sure testimony of the Bible that we have undoubted authority for thus thinking of Christ.

But this is not all. The question for us to answer is,—What is the *state of our hearts* towards Christ ? What is the *effect on* our feelings and conduct of those right thoughts of Him which the scriptural teaching of the Church puts into

c

our mouths? Are we able, in reviewing our system of faith, to make the answer of a good conscience, that we do indeed know the Christ, the Saviour of the world? "The natural man" may speak in exact words of the things of God; but we have it affirmed by divine authority, that "the natural man receiveth not the things of the Spirit of God; for they are foolishness unto him: neither can he know them, because they are spiritually discerned*." And again, "no man can say" (say, that is, with a real and full meaning,) "that Jesus is the Lord but by the Holy Ghost†." So our Lord Himself in the passage already quoted: "Flesh and blood hath not revealed it" (the true doctrine of the Christ) "to thee, but my Father which is in heaven." If, therefore, we know the truth of Christ in its vitality, we are acting under the gracious influences of the Holy Spirit. That Blessed Comforter is *now to us* as He was to the Apostles, the Teacher who guides us to the truth, filling us with all joy and peace in believing, and bringing all things to our remembrance whatsoever Christ has said unto us.

What fruits, then, we must ask ourselves, are

---

* 1 Cor. ii. 14.   † 1 Cor. xii. 3.

we giving that the Holy Spirit is working in our hearts, and carrying us as sincere believers to Christ? Do we find ourselves becoming more and more familiar with the things pertaining to the kingdom of God, having more and more effectually brought to our knowledge and remembrance all things whatsoever Jesus Christ, and his Prophets, Evangelists, and Apostles, have said unto us? Here is our real test,—here is the secret but sure answer to be obtained to the question—" What think ye of Christ?" Take the question simply as our Lord put it; and it may perhaps be answered by a full account of what the Scriptures have said of the nature and character and office of Jesus Christ. Take it however as the Holy Spirit, following up the teaching of the Lord Jesus, applies it to our hearts and minds; and what is it short of a trial of our spirit—an examination of the faith that is in us—whether it be such as Christ Himself would own to be the faith of his true disciples? It is an awful warning which our Lord has bequeathed to his Church, in saying even of those twelve whom He had chosen as his peculiar disciples, " Have not I chosen you twelve, and one

c 2

of you is a scandalous accuser*?" They had all been ready to declare their faith in Him as the Christ, the "Son of the living God." The words were Peter's, but they were said in the name of all. We hear of no exception: yet one of those very confessors of their Lord was an accuser and a betrayer. Ought we not to take warning therefore from this appalling example, in what temper of mind we make our good confession of the truth as it is in Jesus? How should we not search into ourselves, lest a spirit of covetousness, or ambition, or concupiscence, or party, or any other worldly unchristian motive, profane the sanctuary of our faith, and banish the Holy Spirit from our hearts!

There is indeed a peculiar temptation to those who make Christianity their professional study, to rest in mere *thoughts* of Christ and the Gospel, —to regard the truth simply *as truth*,—instead of going on to perfection by further receiving it as the means of personal justification and personal sanctification. I do not say there is any tendency

---

* John vi. 70. This is clearly the proper meaning of the word here rendered "devil" in our translation, and *diabolus* in the Vulgate.

in such study to withdraw us from personal religion; on the contrary, the study of the truth naturally conspires with the love and practice of it. But to the mind which is not deeply imbued throughout its study of the truth with the feeling, that, "to win Christ and to be found in him," is above the understanding of all mysteries and the possession of all knowledge, that study may prove a dangerous seduction. The heart may be hardened in going over the doctrines of the Gospel as it is in the mere "going over the theory of virtue *," if there be no accompanying endeavour to enforce those doctrines as matter of discipline on the heart,—if there be no lifting up of the devout feelings to that Holy Spirit with whose ways we are then seeking to acquaint ourselves.

Persons, therefore, whose calling it is to speak or write on the subject of religion, and to instruct others in it, ought to be especially on their guard against mistaking *advocacy* of the truth for *personal adoption* of it, or taking up low unchristian views of what it is to be " wise unto salvation." May those of us who are ministers of the Word,—for as our privilege in thus continually handling

* Butler's Analogy.

divine things is greater, so is our responsibility greater in the use of them,—be kept from this fatal delusion!

Let us all know then, Brethren, that the question—*What think ye of Christ?* is one which not only meets our eye at the door of the school of Christ, but one which must accompany all our learning there. We are to labour so to " know Christ," that we may " be known of Him." For consider what it was that kept the learned Jews from acknowledging Jesus to be the Son of God no less than the Son of David. It was what they *thought of themselves,*—their self-righteousness—their repugnance to deny themselves—their seeking to be justified by their observance of the Law,—and not casting themselves in humble confidence on the Righteousness of God in Christ. See how many admonitions our Lord addresses to them, to the effect, that he came not to call the *righteous,* but *sinners* to repentance and faith in Him. See also how St. Paul, in his Epistles to the Romans and the Galatians, strives to wean his countrymen from their presumptuous dependence on any merits of their own, and to persuade them to follow the example of faithful Abraham, by looking simply and unreservedly to the promises of God, and leaning on Divine Grace for pardon and acceptance. Hear again what our Lord himself says :—" If any man will come after me, let him take up his cross,"—" let him deny himself ;" let him, that is, put self entirely out of view—account himself as "dust and ashes" —as nothingness, before God, and so " let him follow me." Let the question, therefore, *What think ye of Christ ?* be accompanied by the question of each to his own conscience,—What think ye *of yourselves ?* Have you that humiliation of soul which the Gospel requires of you ? Do you regard the doctrine of Christ Crucified as a doctrine not only true, but absolutely and indispensably *needful for you ?* For it is one thing to say, in general terms, all men are sinners, and therefore the vicarious sacrifice of the Redeemer is necessary for all men, and another thing for each man to smite upon his own breast and say, " God be merciful through Christ to *me a sinner.*" A heartfelt conviction of sin is a work of no easy accomplishment. It is, like every other part of our Christian conduct, the effect of the gracious operation of the Holy Spirit on our hearts. It is He who must enable us not to think more highly of ourselves than we *ought* to think. The love of self,—the clinging to the notion of personal merit in some low degree at least,—is so natural to the corrupt heart, that it cannot be expelled but by invisible succour and strength. The very external respectability and moral propriety of some men's lives induce an unscriptural satisfaction with themselves. They mourn over the sins of an apostate world, but they are content with *themselves* that they go not to the same excess of riot as others. They begin to think that they *were* sinners, but that they *are now no longer so.* They seem to apply to themselves tacitly the words of St. Paul to the Romans, " God be thanked, that ye *were* the servants of sin, but ye have *now* obeyed that form of doctrine which was delivered unto you* ;" whereas the Apostle clearly does not encourage any such idea, as that Christians had passed from sinfulness in embracing the Gospel, but simply praises God that a sense of the pollution and guilt of sin had been wrought in their minds,—that they had repented, —renounced their former sinful course—and turned to Christ. In one sense, indeed, those who do really flee to the hope of the Gospel do also cease to be sinners ; that is, God no longer

* Rom. vi. 17.

treats them as sinners, but " accepts them in the Beloved,"—accounts them righteous for Christ's sake, and fully acquits them of the guilt and punishment of sin. To such also He gives grace to hate and forsake sin, raising them up from the death of sin, and making them holy by the gift of his Spirit. Still a constant conviction of sin is a necessary accompaniment of a living faith in every heir of corruption. Nay, it is most necessary to him who is well grown in grace, and has made most progress in Christian holiness, lest at any moment he should be high-minded and cast off fear,—lest at any time he should account himself to have " apprehended," and forget that, though justified, he needs to be justified *still*.

Finally, Brethren, let the conduct of the Scribes and Pharisees be a solemn lesson to us, *how* we handle the word of God, how we say with them, " *We see* ;" whilst He talks with us by his Spirit, and calls upon us to learn, that it is He who opens the eyes of the blind, and gives light to them that are sitting in darkness and the shadow of death. "For judgement," he says, " I am come into this world, that they which see not might see, and that they which see might be made blind." Are we ever tempted to answer with the Pharisees, "Are we blind also?" Hear then our Lord's reply :—" If ye were blind, ye should have no sin: but now ye say, We see ; therefore your sin remaineth*."

Here were persons eminently zealous of the divine Law, eminently religious in their profession, —no despisers of authority,—no profane livers, —yet was iniquity found even in their holy things. Our Lord declares of them that their " sin remained." Even such could read of Christ, —could converse with Him,—could acknowledge his mighty works, and his wisdom more than human,—and yet come away from these sacred thoughts with their " *sins remaining*," justified in their own eyes, but *not justified in the sight of God.*

O may we, whilst we think of Him, lift up our hearts to Him, as the Son of man who is also the Son of God, who gave himself for us, and ever liveth to make intercession for us ! May we say, not only with the understanding but from the bottom of our hearts, " O Son of David, have mercy upon us !"   " Graciously hear us, O Christ ! graciously hear us, O Lord Christ !"

* John ix. 41.

Pray we, therefore, " that the God of our Lord Jesus Christ, the Father of glory, may give unto us the spirit of wisdom and revelation in the knowledge of Him : the eyes of our understanding being enlightened ; that we may know what is the hope of his calling, and what the riches of the glory of his inheritance in the saints, and what is the exceeding greatness of his power to us-ward who believe, according to the working of his mighty power, which He wrought in Christ, when He raised Him from the dead, and set Him at his own right hand in the heavenly places, far above all principality, and power, and might, and dominion, and every name that is named, not only in this world, but also in that which is to come ; and hath put all things under his feet ; and gave Him to be the Head over all things to the Church, which is his body, the fulness of Him that filleth all in all*."

* Eph. i. 17, &c.

SERMON II.

FILLING UP THE AFFLICTIONS OF CHRIST.

PREACHED AT THE CATHEDRAL OF CHRIST CHURCH,

On SUNDAY, February 13, 1838.

SERMON II.

FILLING UP THE AFFLICTIONS OF CHRIST.

COL. I. 24.

Who now rejoice in my sufferings for you, and fill up that which is behind of the afflictions of Christ in my flesh for his body's sake, which is the Church.

THE continual presence of Christ with his Church, and the sustaining and strengthening of it as his body by his abiding influence, are truths which form a grand subject of Christian interest and edification. The subject however is one to which, I fear, we do not sufficiently recur for support and encouragement in our Christian course. And yet the truth of this his constant abiding in us and with us, so far as we really belong to Him, —so far as we are members of that his mystical body which is the company of all faithful people, —is as plainly written in the page of Scripture, and as strongly urged on our notice, as is that of his eternal presence with the Father and the

Holy Spirit in Heaven, there to plead the merits of his Sacrifice in behalf of his Church.

For what are all those striking declarations of his own mouth? " I will not leave you comfortless : I will come to you. Yet a little while, and the world seeth me no more ; but ye see me : because I live, ye shall live also. At that day ye shall know that I am in my Father, and ye in me, and I in you*." " If a man love me, he will keep my words : and my Father will love him, and we will come unto him, and make our abode with him†." " I am the true vine, and my Father is the husbandman. Every branch in me that beareth not fruit, He taketh away : and every branch that beareth fruit, He purgeth it, that it may bring forth more fruit." "Abide in me, and I in you. As the branch cannot bear fruit of itself, except it abide in the vine ; no more can ye, except ye abide in me. I am the vine, ye are the branches : he that abideth in me, and I in him, the same bringeth forth much fruit : for without me ye can do nothing. If a man abide not in me, he is cast forth as a branch, and is withered ; and men gather them, and cast them into the fire, and they are burned‡." And

* John xiv. 18—20.   † John xiv. 23.   ‡ John xv. 4—6.

to show further that these promises of his presence are not to be restricted to the Apostles or
to Apostolic times,—besides the general promises
of being "always" with his disciples "to the
end of the world," and in the midst of any who
should be gathered together in his name,—He
expressly says, "Neither pray I for these alone,
but for them also which shall believe on me
through their word; that they all may be one;
as Thou, Father, art in me, and I in Thee, that
they also may be one in Us: that the world may
believe that Thou hast sent me. And the glory
which Thou gavest me I have given them; that
they may be one, even as We are one; I in them,
and Thou in me, that they may be made perfect
in one *." "And I have declared unto them
Thy Name, and will declare it: that the love
wherewith Thou hast loved me may be in them,
and I in them†." What, again, says his beloved
disciple, speaking in his own person? "That
which we have seen and heard declare we unto
you, that ye also may have fellowship with us:
and truly our fellowship is with the Father, and
with his Son Jesus Christ‡." "If that which
ye have heard from the beginning shall remain

* John xvii. 20–23.   † John xvii. 26.   ‡ 1 John i. 3.

D

in you, ye also shall continue in the Son, and in
the Father *." " And he that keepeth his commandments dwelleth in Him, and He in him,
and hereby we know that He abideth in us by
the Spirit which He hath given us†." " Hereby
know we that we dwell in Him, and He in us,
because He hath given us of his Spirit." " Whosoever shall confess that Jesus is the Son of God,
God dwelleth in him, and he in God." " God
is love, and he that dwelleth in love dwelleth in
God, and God in Him ‡." Such is the testimony of our Lord himself, and of that disciple
who,—from the long period of his Apostolic life
and the fervour of his Christian love,—knew by
the fullest experience the blessedness of Christ's
presence with his Church, to the truth of this
doctrine of our faith.

From St. Paul, however, the chosen vessel,
whom the Holy Spirit appears to have especially
commissioned to give a fuller exposition on many
points of Gospel truth beyond the other inspired
ministers of the Word, we should naturally expect a more explicit statement on the subject of
this holy truth in particular. Accordingly this
Apostle has, we find, set forth the truth of

* 1 John ii. 24.   † 1 John iii. 24.   ‡ 1 John iv. 16.

" Christ's dwelling in the hearts of his disciples by faith*," in a manner forcibly to teach and enforce its vital importance. If we are to take our estimate of its importance from the view presented by this Apostle, it is a truth which should never be lost sight of in our Christian exertions. It ought to circulate, if I may so express it, through all our faith. He has pointedly set forth to us Christ as the " Head over all things to the Church, which is his body, the fulness of Him that filleth all in all †"—" the Head, from whom the whole body fitly joined together and compacted by that which every joint supplieth, according to the effectual working in the measure of every part, maketh increase of the body unto the edifying of itself in love ‡." He has further depicted the intimacy and inseparableness of the union subsisting between Christ and the Church, after the analogy under which the Old Testament exhibits God's love for Israel, by referring us to the first holy marriage, when the woman was formed from the side of the man. " For no man," he says, " ever yet hated his own flesh ; but nourisheth and cherisheth it, even as the Lord the Church : for we are members of his

---

* Eph. iii. 17.　　† Eph. i. 22.　　‡ Eph. iv. 16.

body, of his flesh, and of his bones.   For this
cause shall a man leave his father and mother,
and shall be joined unto his wife, and they two
shall be one flesh.   This is a great mystery: but
I speak concerning Christ and the Church*."

Enforcing the same divine truth, the Apostle
further expands it into particulars.   He tells us
how entirely the sons of God in Christ are united
to Him in all the holy principles and acts of their
Christian life,—how He is their Christ in all that
He has done and suffered for the sake of sinful
man ; the life and death of Christ being the great
realities which impart a Christian efficacy to the
life and death of every action of his disciple.
Thus he speaks of the Christian as " buried with
Christ in baptism, wherein also ye are risen," he
adds, " with Him, through the faith of the operation of God, who hath raised Him from the dead.
And you, being dead in your sins and the uncir-
cumcision of your flesh, hath He quickened together with Him†."   And again, " If ye then be
risen with Christ, seek those things which are
above, where Christ sitteth on the right hand of
God.   Set your affection on things above, not on
things on the earth.   For ye are dead, and your

* Eph. v. 29.   † Col. ii. 12.

life is hid with Christ in God*." And again, "Whether we live, we live unto the Lord, or whether we die, we die unto the Lord ; so that both living and dying we are the Lord's."

But whilst Scripture thus teaches us the holy truth, that Christ is ever present with the body of his faithful people, and regards them as " bone of his bone, and flesh of his flesh," there is one point of view of the subject which it brings before us especially, and labours as it were to inculcate on us. It is that in which the Christian is represented as suffering with Christ —as a partaker of the sufferings of Christ—as " always bearing about in the body the dying of the Lord Jesus†," —as " knowing the fellowship of his sufferings, being made conformable unto his death‡ ;" and more explicitly in the words of the text, where St. Paul, having touched on his labours in preaching the salvation of the Gospel to the Gentiles amidst persecutions from his Judaizing brethren, takes comfort to himself from the thought, that he was filling up on his part the afflictions of Christ,—or that in his station as a disciple and minister of Christ he was a faithful counterpart of his suffering Lord. " But now," he says, " I

* Col. iii. 1–3. † 2 Cor. iv. 10. ‡ Phil. iii. 10.

rejoice in my sufferings for you, and fill up that which is behind of the afflictions of Christ in my flesh for his body, which is the Church."

The words themselves are not without their difficulty as we first read them. But when we come to the closer consideration of them, they are found clearly to convey the sense to which I have applied them,—to signify, that is, that the disciple of Christ has his Lord with him in the moments of his sufferings and trials in the world, and so present with him that his afflictions are appropriated by his Lord to Himself,—his afflictions are Christ's afflictions; what he endures as a member of the body of Christ, and for the sake of that body,—for the maintenance and extension of the faith,—so corresponds with the afflictions of the Saviour himself, that He sanctifies and blesses them as His own,—vouchsafes to regard them as filling up that which is behind of his own afflictions,—as if they were a continuance and furtherance of those sufferings which He underwent in his own person in the flesh for his Church. Thus are afflictions for the Gospel's sake, truly Christian afflictions—truly afflictions of Christ.

This is an interpretation of the passage which, while it carries out the doctrine of Christ's pre-

sence with his faithful disciple to a subject of the
deepest interest to every Christian soul, is free
from the very serious error which these words
have been sometimes supposed to countenance.
By those who overlook the whole tenor of our
Scriptural instruction concerning the benefit of
Christ's sufferings in our behalf, and the strong
language of St. Paul himself describing the perfection and all-sufficiency of those sufferings, the
passage may be construed to imply an *efficacy* in
the sufferings of the disciple of Christ correspond-
ing to that which really belongs, and belongs *exclusively*, to the meritorious passion and death of
the Redeemer. The labourer in the service of
Christ,—the martyr to his efforts in the cause of
his holy faith,—may thus be exalted to the condition, not of a fellow-labourer with Christ and
worker together with the Spirit (which is a perfectly Scriptural view of the subject), but to that
of a co-mediator with Christ—of one who con-
tributes something by his own sufferings to propitiate the wrath of God. Such is the un-evan-
gelical sense which some may draw out of the
expression of " filling up what is behind of the
afflictions of Christ."

They may not, indeed, go so far as to say that

the sufferings of St. Paul had any efficacy *in themselves* originally and independently of the Sacrifice of Christ. The Church of Rome, when it imputes a power of Satisfaction to the sufferings and intercession of saints, does not go so far as to *separate* that power from the Satisfaction made on the Cross. But, at the same time, that Church seriously impairs the doctrine of Christ's Satisfaction by thus adding to it a *human* satisfaction, however subordinate and dependent.

So it is with those who think there is any mystic remedial efficacy in the afflictions which the Christian undergoes in his conflict with the world. They may not intend to deny the primary efficacy of the One Satisfaction made for sin, but they do in effect annul the truth by the unscriptural merits with which they overlay it. Christ is then no longer all in all. It is no longer in such a view of the matter, Christ working in his disciple, that we contemplate in the Christian wrestling with temptation and resisting it successfully, but it is rather man working out the passion of Christ, and completing what Christ has begun.

Such, I am persuaded then, is not the meaning of the passage of the text. The " filling up that

which is behind of the afflictions of Christ " is
not the supplying what Christ has left undone
in the way of satisfaction or remedy for sin, but
simply the going through that work which He
has laid on all his disciples as the followers of a
suffering crucified master. " If they have persecuted me, they will also persecute you*," he
said to his first chosen disciples. " If they have
called the master of the house Beelzebub, how
much more shall they call them of his house-
hold†?" " If any man will come after me, let
him deny himself, and take up his cross and follow me‡." So clearly has he forewarned us all,
that if we would be *His*, we must be like him ;
if we would be partakers of his glory, we must
be partakers also of his suffering.

These labours, then, to which we are called,
are the afflictions of Christ, to which the Apostle
alludes in the text. The "filling up," for our
parts, " what is behind " in them, is the steady
perseverance in that course of Gospel-patience
on which we have entered. For such it was
clearly in the case of St. Paul. He had for
many years been bearing his cross ; he had been
long fighting the good fight ; he was now ready

* John xv. 20.   † Matt. x. 25.   ‡ Matt. xvi. 24.

to depart and be with Christ; but it was more needful for the brethren that he should continue his labours. He knew that his course of Christian endurance was not yet finished; and he was willing to go through it,—to fill up what was yet wanting in that measure of affliction which his Lord had appointed him. Therefore it is he speaks of himself as " filling up what was behind of the afflictions of Christ in his flesh for the sake of his body, which is the Church." His afflictions were afflictions of Christ, because he had Christ with him strengthening him, and bearing them with him; and because, too, they were afflictions laid on him by Christ, and undergone for the sake of Christ and Christ's body —the Church. And the filling up, accordingly, was the filling up—*not* of anything left undone by Christ, but of *his own* as yet imperfect work; —*his own*, I say, and yet *not* his own, because it was not himself really working, but Christ working in him both to will and to do, and consecrating his labours to the service of his Lord.

That this is the proper construction of the passage appears from other passages of Scripture, and in particular of the Apostle's writings, in which the same idea is clothed in expressions not involving the same ambiguity as those of the text. Thus, when St. Paul was checked in his career of persecution, our Saviour owns the persecution of his saints as a persecution of himself. " Saul, Saul," he cried out, " why persecutest thou me ? " " *I am Jesus* whom thou persecutest *.*" He does not say, Why persecutest thou *mine?*—They are *my saints* whom thou persecutest ;—but he at once takes their troubles to *himself* as *his own.* It is *Jesus himself* who is afflicted ; the afflictions of his saints are the *afflictions of Christ.* In like manner, St. Paul himself writing to the Corinthians, and expressing the comfort which he experienced under tribulation, and which he desired to impart to others, attributes the whole to Christ himself. " For as the sufferings," he says, " of Christ abound in us, so our consolation also aboundeth by Christ †." In the following passages he further declares how Christ carries on in his faithful disciples his own concern and sympathy for those whom he had saved by suffering. " We are troubled," exclaims the Apostle, " on every side, yet not distressed ; we are perplexed, but not in despair ; persecuted, but not forsaken ;

* Acts ix. 4, 5.   † 2 Cor. i. 5.

cast down, but not destroyed ; always bearing about in the body the dying of the Lord Jesus, that the life also of Jesus might be made manifest in our body. For we which live are alway delivered unto death for Jesus' sake, that the life also of Jesus might be made manifest in our mortal flesh. So then death worketh in us, but life in you*." Lastly, when he speaks of himself to the Galatians, as "bearing in his body the marks of the Lord Jesus†,"—whether we interpret this of the stripes which he had received after the manner of his Lord's indignities, or as an allusion to the punctures imprinted on the flesh of the slave,—he pointedly identifies his afflictions for the sake of the Gospel with those of his Master, when he thus characterizes them as "*the marks*" of the Lord himself.

Let us take, then, this doctrine of Scripture, this holy and comforting truth, this strengthening assurance, that the sufferings of the Christian in the flesh are the sufferings of Christ, inasmuch as he is present with his suffering disciple, and appoints to him a course of endurance in conformity with his own trials on earth, that "though Christ has finished his own sufferings for the ex-

---

* 2 Cor. iv. 8–12. † Gal. vi. 17.

piation of the world, yet there are ὑστερήματα
θλίψεων, portions that are behind of the sufferings
of Christ, which must be filled up by his body,
the Church*:" and let us apply it, as all Scripture is capable of being applied, to our instruction
and furtherance in righteousness.

I said at the commencement of this discourse,
that Christians in general do not sufficiently bear
in mind in their conduct the remembrance of
Christ's constant presence with them.   If they
were never forgetful that the bond which unites
them as members of the Church is Christ Himself,—that their whole Christian life is *in Him*
and *by Him*,—their whole sufficiency of that
Blessed Spirit which proceeds from the Father
and Himself, the gift of his prayers and intercession and sacrifice for them, and uniting them to
Him, and breathing the "sweet savour of Christ"
over all they think or do in the name of Christ;
—if Christians, I say, were never forgetful of
this,—what a purity and holy fervour would it
not impart to all their conduct!   Then indeed
would the blessedness of being a Christian fully
appear; then would it be manifested to the world

* Bishop Taylor's Sermons.   Works, vol. v. p. 532.

that *it is a privilege* to belong to Christ,—that
there is *a joy* and *a peace* in believing.

But the view of this holy state to which my
present observations more particularly call your
attention is,—the sustaining power under trials
which may be drawn from the Christian's trust,
that he is filling up by his sufferings, and patience, and resignation, and constancy, *what is
behind of the afflictions of Christ.*

The application is strong and immediate to
those, in the first place, who, like the Apostle,
are specially delegated to minister for the sake
of the body of Christ. How impressive and animating to them is the thought, that by their labours in the Gospel they are set forth as an
example to the world of the suffering Saviour
whom they preach! There are many of those
present here this day, who have thus been called
to preach and exemplify the Cross of Christ.
May I avail myself of the occasion to address to
them a word of exhortation on this view of our
holy calling, and admonish them—of what I myself feel, corrupt and frail human nature cannot
be too often admonished,—that we are not our
own, but His, to whom we have given ourselves ;

that we are not doing our own work, but His ; that our very sufferings for the Gospel's sake, or exertions in preaching and spreading it and increasing its influence,—so far as they are faithful exertions, bearing on them the marks of Christ, the symbols of his passion, and truly representing to the world the doctrine of the Cross,—are the afflictions of Christ Himself.

We sometimes magnify our office, and justly : for what can be a greater dignity than to be called to so high a charge, as to be trustees and almoners of God's bounty through Christ to a poor fallen world? But to rise to a due estimate of the sacred importance of our duties, we must think of those duties as representing the cares and labours of Him who is from first to last the Author and Finisher of our Salvation. In that work He stands alone. He trod the wine-press alone. None entered, or ever can enter, into his sorrow. The work of propitiation was finished when He declared it finished on the Cross. What we do, therefore, by his commission and authority in preaching Him crucified, is his doing in us. And can any other consideration inspire us with such high conceptions of our ministerial duties ? It at once takes from us any confidence in ourselves, any arrogance on account of the high function with which we are invested, and stimulates us to a holy energy beyond ourselves.

There is, however, a view of our office which magnifies it unduly: and it arises from a want of right consideration of the truth of Scripture which I am now endeavouring to present to your notice. It is the regarding ourselves as a vicarious interceding body between Christ and his people, and thus detaching our ministerial services from his, as if they possessed an intrinsic holiness *apart from Him*—apart from his vital presence, influencing them and sanctifying them by His Spirit. We may believe that Christ has authorized us to do his work ; we may feel that we can have no power to do anything for the saving of souls but by an authentic commission derived from Him. But it is possible at the same time, with all this reverence for his authority, with all this ascription of our power to his grace, to form an erroneous view of our ministerial importance. We may, as I have said, still detach ourselves from Christ Himself; we may come to suppose that though it is a *derivative* power only that we possess, still it is a power given to us to possess *in ourselves,* and to communicate *of our-selves,* without a constant immediate agency of the Author Himself of the power.

1 may illustrate what I mean by the analogy of God's agency in the natural world. There may be great piety in that philosophy which ascribes all physical agency to powers originally impressed on matter and sustained in operation by the wise and good Author of Nature. Still this piety will not reach the truth of the case, if we suppose that these secondary powers, when once established, are endued with an inherent efficacy to perpetuate themselves and their operation, without the constant presence with them of the Almighty Author Himself. Far more pious and more sound is that philosophy which withholds its assent from any theory of inherent powers in the natural world, and which refers every event in nature to a superintending, ever present, ever active, Providence. So it is in the work of grace which God is carrying on by his Church. He is ever present Himself to all the acts of grace which are done in his Church. The ministrations of those who preach his Word and administer his Sacraments, in themselves and apart from Him, have no vital influence. So

far as they have power to do good to the soul, they have it through his immediate operation who appoints and blesses them. Man must not assume to himself the power,—no, not even in the sentiments and phrase of piety ;—but he must ever remember in his holiest acts that he has nothing whereof to glory, but that it is Christ strengthening him, Christ working in him both to will and to do of his good pleasure,—that when he is truly serving God in the ordinances of the Church, it is Christ that prays,—it is Christ that sanctifies the water of Baptism to the mystical washing away of sin,—Christ that feeds his members by the bread and wine of his Holy Supper,—Christ that speaks to the heart the word of Salvation preached,—Christ that persuades, and entreats, and wins men to Himself,—Christ that labours in all the labours of love,—Christ that is afflicted in all the afflictions of his servants. Such, then, is the view which the text would have us take of the importance of our holy office—of the ministrations and ordinances of the Church ; such is the Scriptural notion of their spiritual dignity and value. It is essentially self-denying,—a ministry of *the Cross*, —a bearing about continually the dying of the

Lord Jesus,—a " filling up what is behind of the afflictions of Christ in our flesh for his body's sake, which is the Church."

To those, again, of this congregation who are now in course of preparation for the ministry, the subject before us presents a salutary Christian instruction. It warns them against attaching an unchristian importance to man in their views of the sacred office; bidding them look forward to it with a single eye and single heart as the work of Christ Himself, to which they are about to give themselves. Whilst it teaches them to hold fast their bond of membership with the Church, it checks the tendency which this just principle may take in some minds to degenerate into a spirit of partizanship,—the having " respect of persons " in matters pertaining to God, or what St. Jude calls, " having men's persons in admiration ;" the being zealous for men, or bodies of men, rather than giving themselves in simplicity to the body of Christ, of which they are members, and to Christ Himself, to whom their allegiance is primarily due. The spirit of Christ is the true Catholic spirit, which holds together the Church wheresoever dispersed over the face of the earth ; and he who cleaves to that

is the true Catholic, the true adversary of sectarianism and party-zeal; whilst he who has not
the spirit of Christ is no Catholic Christian,
however sound his external profession.

This, therefore, is the spirit for which the candidate for the ministry must pray and strive.
Jesus Christ, he must remember, is the Head of
the Church, not as the Church denotes the
Clergy, but as it stands for the whole congregation of faithful people throughout the world.
The call to the duties of the ministry only draws
more closely the original bond subsisting between
Christ, and the member of his body who receives
the call; giving grace to that member for special
sacred duties towards the body, which he is already bound to serve as a simple member of it.
His obligation to serve God is the same *in principle*, whether he be regarded in his capacity of a
private Christian, or of a minister of the Church.
It is the call *of Christ* that he is obeying; it is
the love *of Christ* that he is diffusing; it is the
sufferings *of Christ* which he is exemplifying in
each capacity. As a minister he is only more
intensely employed in going along with the Spirit
of Christ, and more expressly sent forth to bear
the cross of Christ. " For other Foundation can

no man lay than that is laid, which is Jesus Christ*." To impute the efficacy of his ministrations to the circumstance of his belonging to the particular body of the ministry, is to invert the foundation; it is to hope for strength and grace from the body, and not from the Head; it is to build on the Church, and not on Christ; it is to " preach ourselves," and not " Christ Jesus the Lord†."

We have an example of the danger which may be incurred by ascribing to ourselves in any degree the power and holiness of our ministrations before God, in the rebuke of Moses and Aaron at the water of Meribah‡. They were commissioned by God to speak to the rock, and God had promised that it should give forth its water; so that the act itself was no presumption on their part. They did it by a real divine authority. Yet, because they gave not God *alone* the glory of the miracle, but spoke unadvisedly, calling the attention of the people to themselves, and making a display of their authority as if it had been their own, God pronounced on them the grievous sentence of exclusion from the promised land. Here, then, is a warning to all who handle

* 1 Cor. iii. 11. † 2 Cor. iv. 5. ‡ Numbers xx. 1–13.

the things of God, to take heed to themselves, lest the spirit of self-confidence should intrude into their sacred ministration. They may learn, that it is possible to be betrayed into rebellion against God, even whilst they are exercising an authority with which He has duly invested them, —magnifying themselves, like Moses and Aaron, and not " sanctifying the Lord God" alone " in the eyes of the people."

Let, then, the future candidate for the ministry contemplate the proper responsibility which he will take on himself by being *Christ's minister*, in the highest sense of the term,—let him take up the elevating thought that he will become " the servant of the Church for Jesus' sake,"—that his business will be to go about with Christ doing the work of an Evangelist. Let him take to himself the comfort that Christ will sympathize with all his faithful exertions, accepting what is done for the least of his little ones as done unto Himself, and blessing with his present influence what is done by his faithful servant as if done by Himself.

But it is not to the ministers and stewards of Christ *exclusively* that the doctrine of the text ap- plies ; it comes home to all faithful followers of their Lord,—to the body at large of which He is Head.

All certainly are not called to suffer for their Lord according to the ordinary estimate of suffering. The fiery trials of faith—persecution, and peril, and famine, and the sword,—happen but to few; yet every man's work, we are told, is to be tried " by fire,"—every Christian, humble as his sphere of duty may be, is to pass through that ordeal which shall strictly put to the test *his* faith,—which shall be *his* " fire." There is no following of Christ without taking up the cross; there is no partaking of his glory without partaking also of his sufferings. Thus has the Gospel of Christ been well described, as a " covenant of sufferings; his very promises, as sufferings; his beatitudes, sufferings; his rewards and his arguments to invite men to follow him, as taken from sufferings in this life, and the reward of sufferings hereafter*." Indeed the very expression, θλίψις, which Scripture so often employs to denote the struggles of the Christian in the world, drawn as it is from the constraint and pressure of wrestling, shews that the Christian's conformity with his Lord is not only in

* Bishop Taylor's Sermons. Works, vol. vi. p. 529.

bearing adversity, but in all the difficulties of his condition in life,—in wrestling with temptations under every form, no less than with outward circumstances of trouble and affliction. A Christian, accordingly, may fill up the remainder of the sufferings of Christ, whilst he is striving to enter at the strait gate, passing on through the narrow pass which closes upon him and obstructs him in his way to eternal life; and may derive strength and comfort from the assurance that his Lord is with him; and that, whilst he is sore let and hindered in his course, his pressure is the Lord's pressure, as much as his who is conformed to his Lord also in distresses and persecutions from without.

The task of self-denial and mortification—the sorrow of the broken and contrite heart—is that affliction of Christ which is common to all men. And I address myself, therefore, to this general condition of human nature, that all may receive edification, through the grace of God, from the subject of this day's discourse; and that none may evade its force from the idea, that they are not called eminently to suffer for Christ, or to exemplify the patience of the martyr. Happy, indeed, are they who are so called to suffer, if they possess their souls in patience, and do resist, stedfast to the end. Happy are they to be so conformed to their Lord and Saviour. But blessed also are all whom He enables to keep the faith, under whatever circumstances they may be placed. And let us not despise or make light of the trials which earthly prosperity, and the charms and smiles of the world, may raise up in our path. " How hardly shall they that are rich," said our Lord, " enter into the kingdom of heaven ! " Happy shall it be for them, too, if they can be led, out of their abundance of worldly goods—out of the very things which tend to draw them away from Christ—to abound in sufferings for Christ's sake—to do their part in filling up the measure of his afflictions for his Church's sake.

Do we then, Brethren, find ourselves dull and cold, and wanting in spirituality, in our Christian exertions ? How can this be in those who are truly living in communion with the Head of the Church,— who are drawing out sustenance and strength from the everlasting Fountain of life,— who know that the Lord is with them in all their conflict with the world ? It must be, Brethren, that we quench the Spirit which has been given to us; we think not, amidst our interest in things present and visible, how very nigh the Lord our God is unto us, how intently He is watching over us. Engrossed with the blessings of His providence, we regard not the secret inspirations of His grace. We bow before the miracles of His *power*, but we own not in our hearts the far greater miracles of His *mercy*.

Consider then, Brethren, the greatness of your Christian privilege as members of the body of Christ. Put to yourselves the question of Moses to the Israelites, and which still more strikingly applies to the children of Abraham's faith than to his children according to the flesh; " What nation is there so great, who hath God so nigh unto them, as the Lord our God is in all things that we call upon him for*?" If God's nearness to the ancient Israel was so forcible an argument to obedience on the part of that people, what must we think of the endearments of holy living which are presented to the *Israel of this day* from God's nearness *to them*? Israel of old could only approach God by a subordinate priesthood—a priesthood of men, and by sacrifices requiring ever to be renewed. But Israel now approaches

* Deut. iv. 7.

God by Him who is a Priest for ever,—who was
" consecrated for evermore,"—who " by his own
blood entered in once into the holy place, having
obtained eternal redemption for us *," making us
henceforth "children of God by faith" in Him†.
Having, then, access through One so unutterably
holy,—through " him who, though He is the
" 'fellow of Jehovah‡,' became man for our
sakes,"—how nigh, indeed, must we not say, is
God now brought to the Christian! Surely we
are holy, and we know it not— we feel it not—as
we ought ; surely the temple of the Lord are we,
—our souls and bodies are God's—and yet we
render Him not his own as we ought.

This it is to take a truly *Christian* view of our
religion. Thus may we preach and exemplify
Christ Crucified through all our life and conversation. For when we think of God present with
us in all our warfare with the world, what other
grounds of such a persuasion have we, or can we
have, but the all-prevailing Sacrifice and Intercession of the Saviour? It is through Him, and
Him only, that we have the Father, the Son, and
the Holy Spirit now dwelling with us,—pardoning, justifying, sanctifying us. With Him, and

* Heb. vii. 28 ; ix. 12.   † Gal. iii. 26.   ‡ Zech. xiii. 7.

the grace through Him, Scripture emphatically connects all our knowledge and perception of the things of God. He is in every respect *our mediator* between God and ourselves—in Himself, at once enabling us to rise up to God, and bringing down God to us.

He, therefore, who through grace walks with God in the world,—believing himself a real member of the mystical body of Christ, and humbly guarding himself as made holy to the Lord,—is one who, like the Apostle Paul, always bears about in his body the dying of the Lord Jesus, ever striving to " fill up in his body what is behind of the afflictions of Christ." Can such an one ever think, that his own sufferings as a member of Christ's body have any remedial virtue in them,—that, even as the fruits and evidences of the Holy Spirit working in him, they can contribute in any way to propitiate the favour of God ? So far from entertaining such a fond imagination, the humble believer in the presence of Christ with the Church, will feel his own unworthiness and inability to do anything to save his soul, the more, as he the more closely cleaves to, and depends on, his union with Christ as the principle of his spiritual life. The more firmly he is attached to the Church as the body of Christ, the more will he renounce all superstitious devotion to the Church *apart from Christ**. Asceticism and formalism will never grow up in such a person in the place of the self-denying lowliness,—the true Gospel self-forgetfulness before the Cross of the Redeemer. Like the penitent who bathed the feet of our Lord with her tears, he will look for forgiveness,—not to any acts of contrition which he may perform,—not to the inherent sanctity of his confession of the true faith and incorporation with the company of faithful people,—but to the love of God poured forth in a Saviour's atoning blood, and "shed abroad in his heart by the Holy Ghost which has been given unto him†." He will not undervalue the privilege of belonging to the Communion of Saints ; but he will not *rest* on that privilege ; lest haply he be found to be exchanging the spirituality of the Gospel for the carnality of Judaism,—making Christ of none effect whilst he is seeking to be justified by holy ordinances,

* How aptly does Ignatius touch in a few words the nature of the Church, where he says, ὅπου ἂν ᾖ Χριστὸς Ἰησοῦς, ἐκεὶ ἡ καθολικὴ ἐκκλησία.—Ep. ad Smyrn. c. 8.

† Rom. v. 5.

—and to have fallen from grace in his undue reverence for the holiness of man. He will never lose sight of the fact that man is naturally corrupt and sinful,—that this fault and corruption of nature remain even in them that are regenerate, —that assemblies and bodies of men, though possessing peculiar privileges in their union in Christ, must still retain in them that corruption which exists in the hearts of the individuals of which they are composed,—that, as a man cannot make his peace with God, *of himself*, though he be *the best* of the sons of men, so neither can any body of men effect the same, though it be the best, the purest, the holiest society on earth. He loves the Church as the body of Christ. He rejoices with the Apostle in all his sufferings for those that are Christ's. He is willing in his place, as a member of the body, to fill up what remains of the afflictions of Christ. But with the Apostle he also confesses, in the simplicity of his faith,—" I am crucified with Christ: nevertheless I live; yet not I, but Christ liveth in me: and the life which I now live in the flesh I live by the faith of the Son of God, who loved me, and gave Himself for me*."

* Gal. ii. 20.

SERMON III.

CHRISTIAN DISCIPLINE.

PREACHED IN THE CATHEDRAL OF CHRIST CHURCH,

On SUNDAY, November 13, 1839.

SERMON III.

CHRISTIAN DISCIPLINE.

———

1 Cor. ix. 24–27.

Know ye not that they which run in a race run all, but one
receiveth the prize? So run, that ye may obtain. And every
man that striveth for the mastery is temperate in all things.
Now they do it to obtain a corruptible crown; but we an in-
corruptible. I therefore so run, not as uncertainly; so fight
I, not as one that beateth the air : But I keep under my body,
and bring it into subjection ; lest that by any means, when I
have preached to others, I myself should be a castaway.

St. Paul is here, after the manner of our Lord,
drawing a lesson of Gospel truth and duty from
a scene familiar to the observation of those whom
he immediately addresses. It is Corinthians that
he is instructing by a reference to the Isthmian
games ;—it is persons accustomed to witness the
intense exertions of those who entered on the
lists, and the long course of hardy training which
they underwent in order to qualify themselves for

the contest, and the eager spirit of emulation which the crown of leaves bestowed in the presence of assembled Greece called forth ;—it is persons, we find, familiar with such things that he is animating to a sense of the necessity of the like exertion, the like course of preparation, the like zeal, in order to obtaining the crown that fadeth not away. "Know ye not," he says to them, appealing to associations and feelings dear to every Grecian heart, and connected with religious observances, "know ye not that they which run in a race run all, but one receiveth the prize?" And so he proceeds to inculcate on them the parallel Christian truth on which he is engaged. He had just before been speaking to them of his own various and unremitted endeavours in preaching the Gospel,—how he had "made himself" servant unto all, "that he might gain the more," and was "made all things to all men, that he might by all means save some." Thus had he set an example of one, who, like the combatants in the games of Greece, had inured himself to every species of exertion, had practised every mode of contest, had tried every expedient, regarding no trouble as too great, no sacrifice of self too mean and unworthy, so that he might

win his way in preaching the Gospel to the
various classes of men—that, by this previous
course of service under every form, he might
successfully compete with every antagonist in
the world for the prize of diffusing the Gospel.
By a natural transition, therefore, he is led to
illustrate the account of his own labours by the
case of the competitors in the games of Greece;
and further, by that illustration, to present a
general truth bearing on the disciple no less than
on the preacher of the Gospel—the truth, that
the life of a Christian is a life of various and
continued struggle,—a striving for the mastery,
—an anxious pains-taking effort on the part of
each individual as if he were contending for a
prize. "So run," he says, "that ye may obtain."
Exert yourselves, that is, not as those who think
they have no chance of success, and accordingly
slacken their efforts as they proceed, but keep up
your vigour in the course to the last, not doubting
that you will at length grasp the crown. "Every
man that" thus "striveth for the mastery," he
immediately adds, "is temperate in all things,"
—exercises, that is, a perfect self-command,—
keeps himself under constant discipline,—not
indulging himself in one respect whilst he restrains

himself in another, but extending this discipline to all his conduct; as the person in training for the games placed himself under an entire restraint during that period. Then he enforces the argument from this instance, by urging the far higher inducement to Christian exertion in contrast with the motive which impelled the competitors in the games. "They do it," he observes, "to obtain a corruptible crown, but we an incorruptible." If an earthly, short-lived honour, a crown of perishable leaves, has power to call forth such energy, how shall the unfading crown of glory, the everlasting crown laid up in heaven by the hands of Him who won it for him, fail to stimulate and sustain the Christian runner in his course?

Having thus far made the application of the instance general, the Apostle recurs to his own case in particular, and points out how he was humbly setting a pattern to the Christian Church, in his own station, of that unceasing labour and self-command which he is sending them to learn from the Isthmian games. " I therefore so run," he continues, "not as uncertainly; so fight I, not as one that beateth the air: But I keep under my body, and bring it into subjection; lest that by any means, when I have preached to

others, I myself should be a castaway." He tells
them that he did not, for his part, flag in the
course on which he had entered,—he did not
stop or waver in it, as if he were not sure of the
prize, as if he did not clearly see his way before
him ; he did not merely make a prelude of fight,
and idly beat the air without giving effect to his
blows ; but he boldly presented himself to the
contest, endured the buffets and every severity
of the discipline without shrinking ; fearing nothing, but only, lest he who in preaching the
Gospel was acting as a herald in the games, calling others to the lists,—ἄλλοις κηρύξας—should
be found on trial unfit to enter the lists himself,
—ἀδόκιμος γένωμαι—should be rejected altogether
as one not duly qualified for competing for the
prize.

This, then, is the simple instruction resulting
from the beautiful passage of Scripture now before
us. We are taught that, whilst an incorruptible
crown has been secured for the Christian by
labours and sufferings not his own,—even by Him
who wrestled with the powers of darkness and
overcame them,—yet labours and sufferings are
the probation through which the Christian must
pass to his crown of glory ; that whilst his

Saviour has offered for him that one only Sacrifice which gives him the final victory in all his conflicts with the world, yet sacrifices on his part are also required ; he must also suffer with Christ, if he would in the end conquer and reign with Christ.

The illustration conveyed in the text brings the whole Christian life before us as a *Discipline*, —as a training of the character at once by a course of strenuous exertion and of rigorous self-command,—as a constant series of efforts, stimulated by the greatness and certainty of the reward set before us, and controlled and chastened by a humble anxious fear, lest we should in the end, on the day of our trial, be found unworthy of the prize to which we have aspired.

Obviously as this instruction results from the passage, the error of extending an illustration beyond its broad and direct outlines to the points of detail contained in it,—from the leading principles of which it is an instance, to the circumstances and particulars which are its accessories,—has found a place here, and has perverted this text, among others of the like import, to teach a very different doctrine from that of the Apostle.

St. Paul, it has been argued from the passage, is here inculcating on the Christian the necessity of bruising and subduing the body by a course of hardships, and privations, and labours, analogous to those which the competitor in the games was obliged to go through ; at least, if he would be a candidate for the crown of immortality ;—that, by an austere course of exercise, he must macerate and chasten his bodily nature, that so at length he may become complete master of its antagonist principles, and disencumbered of its weight, may freely run the race set before him with the pure naked powers of the soul. In support of this construction of the passage, that portion of our text has been particularly insisted on, in which the Apostle speaks of his " *keeping under his body, and bringing it into subjection.*" We are referred here to the Greek text* as properly expressing, not simply the general command over the body, but the act itself of *bruising* the body, and of bringing it, like the slave among the Greeks, whose spirit had been broken by the lash and the torture, to a state of absolute degradation and submission to the master-soul. Thus both the exhortation and the example of the Apostle have been most erro-

* Ὑπωπιάζω μου τὸ σῶμα καὶ δουλαγωγῶ.

neously, yet plausibly, brought forward as giving
a Christian sanction to all the rigours of Asceticism.   And accordingly the victorious combatant
in struggles and dangers of his own seeking, has
usurped the place of the humble-minded Gospel-
penitent,—if not even the place of Him, the One
mighty Conqueror of Death and Sin, who " was
wounded for our transgressions and bruised for
our iniquities, upon whom was the chastisement
of our peace, and with whose stripes we are
healed*."   The true Christian indeed dies daily ;
yet not because *the bodily nature* is becoming
weaker and weaker in him ; but because *in spirit*
he is " crucified with Christ," and because " the
life which he is living in the flesh " is a spiritual
life, which he " lives by the faith of the Son of
God, who loved him and gave Himself for him†."

I have said that to interpret the passage before
us in such a sense is the error of transferring to
the truth illustrated the mere *circumstantials* of
the illustration, instead of looking simply to the
great principles for the purpose of which it is
adduced.   The candidate for the Isthmian crown
did indeed afflict and punish his body,—he did
enforce on himself a rigorous abstemiousness,—

* Isaiah liii. 5.   † Gal. ii. 20.

he did make a sacrifice of himself, of every feeling of his nature, to the one engrossing thought of the prize of honour which he had in view. But these are not the points of imitation to which the Apostle's instruction, as arising out of his own example of devoted zeal for the Gospel, refers. The competitor for an earthly crown, for the reward of deeds of the body, would naturally train and discipline the body, would nerve and brace it by temperance and hardy exercises, to the utmost perfection of its powers of endurance and daring. But the aspirant to a heavenly crown is disciplining, in fact, not the *body*, but the *soul*. His body may be bent with infirmity and disease,—may be utterly incapable of enduring abstinences and hardships which others submit to with comparative ease: but his soul at the same time may be in far more vigorous training for the prize of its own high calling. And the analogy further completely fails, if it be carried to this extent; since the mortification of the body which the athlete proposed to himself was not a contumelious degradation of it, but the perfection of its vigour and dignity and grace: whereas that subduing of the body which the ascetic Christian aims to accomplish, heaps every indignity on the body, and seeks to wear it away as intrinsically evil, and by its nature obnoxious to punishment. Such is the injury done to the force of the Apostle's animated exhortation to perseverance in true Christian discipline, by straining the just and beautiful analogy which he employs beyond its general import.

It is not, however, the main burthen of the Ascetic system, that it strains the application of this or that particular text. To be seen in its proper deformity, it ought to be viewed as a departure into another Gospel,—as an estimate of the nature and effects and remedies of sin, totally different from that which the true Gospel propounds. If any truth stands forth in the Bible, it is this;—that man is by nature utterly lost and condemned, and that nothing he can do is of avail to repair the ruin of his nature; that, merciful and gracious as God is, no tears, no prayers, no works of lost man, can turn aside the words of truth denouncing the dread consequence of sin: "In the day thou eatest thereof, *thou shalt surely die.*" But what does the Ascetic system teach? It teaches not indeed that man has effected the restoration of fallen man. The Bible speaks here again too plainly of Him, who came down from heaven for us men, and for our Salvation, and was made man, and suffered *for* us and *instead* of us, obtaining for us a free pardon, and justifying us through His holy Sacrifice and Intercession, for any system which recognizes, as this does, man's degradation and misery in the world, to overlook the counterpart truth of man's free redemption through Christ. But while the Ascetic system in its scheme of doctrine holds the truth both of man's Corruption and Salvation by the blood of Christ, it practically tells its followers (for it is such that it wins upon and cheats with its fond illusions,) that the tears and the prayers and the works of man *can avail* to undo the evil of his corrupt nature. Ask of it from books, descriptive of it and recommending it to your adoption, what it is; and you will find it shadowed out to you, as the offering of a heart, full of the sense of human guilt, and of the merit of the Redeemer's blood—the tribute of a daily sacrifice to God rising up with the sweet savour of the one great sacrifice of Christ. But contemplate it as it has practically exemplified itself. See it in its mature development in the lives of those who have been at once the saints and martyrs of the system. How have they been led to think that Christian religion consisted in abstraction from the world,—in denying themselves the ordinary and innocent gratifications of life,—in searing the domestic affections,—in penances,—in abstaining from food, or taking coarser or less nutritious food,—in neglect and torturings of the body? Unlike indeed has been their training to that of those saints of whom the Apostle writes to the Hebrews*, as through faith enduring trials by "mockings and scourgings" and "bonds" and "imprisonment" at the hands of *others*; who "were stoned, were sawn asunder, were tempted, were slain with the sword;" who "wandered about in sheepskins and goatskins; being destitute, afflicted, tormented (of whom the world was not worthy), who wandered in deserts and in mountains, and in dens and caves of the earth." These have been taught to inflict severities on themselves; not to labour to make their faith their strength and support under necessary unavoidable trials, as the Scripture-worthies did, but to court such trials as athletic exercises of their faith, in order to effect the independence of their souls on their bodies, and to attain a high-wrought spirituality.

* Heb. xi. 36.

You know that the name of *Religion* became, in process of time, attached to the profession of the monastic life in contradistinction to the popular Christianity which mingled in society. And this fact sufficiently marks the tendency of Asceticism to appropriate to itself all that is holy,—to substitute, in fact, a sanctity of man's device and man's working for the righteousness of God in Christ. Let a person indeed once resolutely set foot on the thorny and intricate path of the ascetic, and the flattery of the world and of his own heart will soon smooth it to him, if not strew it with roses. The difficulty is at the outset, when the ground is as yet untrodden,—when the heart is yet to be steeled to a stern enthusiasm from which it instinctively recoils. But as he proceeds, the praises of men encourage him on ; his heart begins to see its own holiness—*its imaginary holiness*—reflected in the admiration of others : and experience has shewn that an inward self-righteousness may creep over and benumb the inmost soul, while the outward man is covered with sackcloth and ashes,—while the flesh is wasted with macerations and bruises and tortures.

The sorrow of sin is indeed far too awful a

thing to be dealt with by formal methods of man's invention. God has consigned it to the secret chambers of the soul,—there to be duly awakened only by the touch of His grace,—not to be artificially excited by the importunity of penances and the exercises of a laborious spiritual discipline. A sense of guiltiness is doubtless felt at times by every human heart, however hardened. But a godly sorrow,—a sorrow which has respect to the exceeding sinfulness of sin,—which hates sin as the object of Divine wrath, as that which demanded the love of the Son of God in order to its expiation,—does not enter so readily into the heart of every man. It must be called down by faith in the Atonement made for Sin, and by Communion with the Holy Spirit, its Author and Giver, in prayer. He that would attempt to obtain this grace by laborious painful methods of human contrivance,—that would humble himself with a humiliation which is not of God's appointing,—does but tempt God, and feed his own soul with vanity. Like the priests of Baal, he piles the wood for the sacrifice, and calls upon his Lord to hear him and kindle it with the fire of heaven; but no fire descends: whereas the simple believer, like the true Prophet of the Lord, relying simply on the promised blessing, lifts up his heart in faith, and through faith obtains at once that fire of heavenly love— the gracious influence of the Holy Spirit,—which enlightens and purifies the soul, creating in it living holiness, and stimulating it to active obedience.

But that artificial discipline which a perverted piety would substitute for the proper discipline of the Gospel, not only checks and tends to destroy Gospel convictions of sin, but it presents sin before the mind as something quite different in its nature and effects from what we learn of it in the Bible. We are taught by the Bible that sin is a disorder of the Soul,—that the Soul is its proper seat,—that it is strictly a *moral* and not a *physical* evil. It is called indeed "the law of the flesh," "the law in the members," "the lust of the flesh," and the like ;—expressions which closely connect sin with the frailty of the body, but at the same time by no means imply that sin is the same thing as a sinfulness of the bodily nature. It is by the flesh that sin works ; the body is its instrument. The bodily perceptions are the occasions and exciting causes of sin ; and therefore sin is naturally described as " the law

of the flesh" or of "the members." But though
the body were entirely inert, though its avenues
of pleasure and pain were stopped, still would
sin, as an inward disorder of the soul, as a corruption of the moral powers, remain in the nature
of man. For as the Apostle well describes the
case,—it is the being " carnally-*minded*" that is
" death," and the being " spiritually-*minded*"
that is " life and peace ;" and the " carnal *mind*,"
not the mere flesh itself, that is " enmity against
God*."

But is this the view which the ascetic life presents of the *nature* of sin ? Does it not lead men
to think that, if they could shake off the burthen
and obstruction of the flesh, they would stand
pure before God ? Does it not assume that the
body is intrinsically evil ?—that it is, not merely
the occasion and outlet as it were of sin, but the
very seat and ground of the malady ; and that
the soul, on the other hand, is spotless and pure,
the unhappy captive immured in the darkness of
the body, and polluted only by the accident of its
connexion with the body ? For what else do the
severities which the ascetic discipline imposes on

* Rom. viii. 6, 7. φρόνημα τῆς σαρκὸς—φρόνημα τοῦ πνεύ-
ματος.

the body mean, but that the bodily sensations are in themselves noxious and evil? If it were with *excesses* in the bodily enjoyments that the system were concerned,—if it inculcated moderation and temperance, and not *entire abstinence*, or at least the utmost attainable approach to an entire abstinence,—then it might be said to be regarding sin as, partly at any rate, a disorder of the *moral* constitution of man. But when this discipline prescribes an absolute and literal mortification of the body,—when it would cut off and dry up every channel of communication between the soul and the body,—what is it but to declare that the fault of man's nature is in the flesh? What is vice, then, but the pollutions of the bodily nature cleaving to the soul? What is virtue but the cleansing of the soul from the bodily pollutions adhering to it? What is religion under such a system but a process of dishonouring of the body and detaching of the soul from it,—the continual endeavour to spiritualize it entirely,—to extricate it from its earthly and physical conditions of existence, and present it to the eye of God in its own simple spirituality? Or, lastly, what is life itself but, according to Plato's description,

G

μελέτη θανάτου,—" a meditation (or discipline) of death*?

But how different is such a view of sin, and man's recovery from sin, from the teaching of the Bible! There we are told, that both our bodies and souls are God's own; that our fall has corrupted our faculties both of body and soul; that we shall stand before the Judgement-seat of Christ, not in the simple nature of our souls only, but with *our bodies also*, to receive according to the things *in the body*, whether *they be good* or whether *they be evil*†; and that we are bound to "glorify God" in our "body" as well as in our "spirit," "which are God's‡." We are commanded again to cleanse ourselves from

---

* Such are Plato's views of human perfection:—Οὐκοῦν καὶ ἐνταῦθα ἡ τοῦ φιλοσόφου ψυχὴ μάλιστα ἀτιμάζει τὸ σῶμα, καὶ φεύγει ἀπ' αὐτοῦ, ζητεῖ δὲ αὐτὴ καθ' αὑτὴν γίγνεσθαι;—Phædo, p. 148. ed. Bip. ἐὰν μὲν καθαρὰ ἀπαλλάττηται, μηδὲν τοῦ σώματος συνεφέλκουσα, ἅτε οὐδὲν κοινωνοῦσα αὐτῷ ἐν τῷ βίῳ ἑκοῦσα εἶναι, ἀλλὰ φεύγουσα αὐτὸ, καὶ συνηθροισμένη αὐτὴ εἰς αὑτὴν, ἅτε μελετῶσα ἀεὶ τοῦτο. κ. τ. λ.—Ibid. p. 183. The "dishonouring of the body," spoken of by St. Paul, Rom. i. 24, is very different from this. According to the Apostle, this "dishonouring" is effected by criminal indulgences, not by privations, and abstinences, and sufferings.

† 2 Cor. v. 10.   ‡ 1 Cor. vi. 20.

all filthiness *of spirit* as well as *of flesh* ; and the
Apostle prays for the Thessalonians, that they
may be " *sanctified wholly,*"—that their " whole
spirit and soul and body" (thus denoting the con-
crete nature of man) may " be preserved blame-
less*." Again, when St. Paul says, in writing
to the Colossians, " Mortify your members which
are upon the earth,"—does he mean the bodily
members, or the mere appetites and desires of the
body ? Certainly not ; for he goes on to enume-
rate vices of the soul ; for besides vices of uncleanness, he speaks of " evil concupiscence, and
covetousness, which is idolatry," " anger, wrath,
malice, blasphemy, filthy communication out of
the mouth, lying†." And when St. Peter speaks
of Christian purification, is it at all to the mortifying of the flesh that he directs our attention ?
Far from it. "Gird up the loins of your mind,
be sober, and hope to the end for the grace that
is to be brought unto you at the revelation of
Jesus Christ ; as obedient children, not fashion-
ing yourselves according to the former lusts in
your ignorance ; but as He which has called you
is Holy, so be ye holy in all manner of conversation." Christians are further enjoined to make

* 1 Thess. v. 23.   † Col. iii. 5–9.

their bodies " a *living* sacrifice," not like the dead
animals in the sacrifices of the law, mortified, or
deadened, with severities, and thus made to re-
semble a real sacrifice ; but, on the contrary, to
present their bodies quickened with a spiritual
life,—fit for the active service of God throughout,—and so, analogously to a real sacrifice, such
as He will accept in his service and to his glory
for Christ's sake.   Such is that evangelical discipline which this Apostle enjoins,—a discipline
exclusively of the soul as the *source* of uncleanness ; as he more distinctly shows, when he adds,
" Seeing ye have purified *your souls in obeying
the truth through the Spirit* unto unfeigned love of
the brethren, see that ye love one another with
a pure heart fervently*."

Or it may be enough to advert only to the
manner in which our Lord Himself speaks of the
relation of body and soul, when he says, " Fear
not them which kill the body, and are not able
to kill the soul: but rather fear Him which is
able to destroy both soul and body in hell†."
Thus, according to the statement of our Lord,
the body may be killed, while the soul has not
been reached. So may it be tortured and brought

* 1 Pet. i. 13–22.   † Matt. x. 28.

to the brink of the grave by a man's own hands, as by the hands of a persecutor, and yet the source of life and death in the man—the soul itself—not touched. Do we not further learn here, in opposition to the ascetic doctrine, that it is not on account of the *body* that the soul suffers, but the *body on account of the soul*; for that the destruction of the soul will involve that of the body? Still more pointedly is the same truth taught in what our Lord says of the defilements of a man. "Not that which goeth into the mouth defileth a man; but that which cometh out of the mouth, this defileth a man." "For out of the heart proceed evil thoughts, murders, adulteries, fornications, thefts, false witness, blasphemies; these are the things which defile a man*."

Then, too, consider our Lord's own example of Christian perfection in its contrast with the example of John the Baptist. "John came neither eating nor drinking, and they say, He hath a devil. The Son of man came eating and drinking, and they say, Behold a man gluttonous, and a wine-bibber, a friend of publicans and sinners†." The world regarded John as wild and strange;

* Matt. xv. 11. 19, 20.   † Matt. xi. 18, 19.

but he did not appear to them irreligious and immoral; whereas our Lord was condemned by the world, as given to its luxuries, and the associate of sinners, because he joined in social intercourse, and practised no austerities. Has He not shown us in this contrast, on the one hand, what the world naturally approves as the mark of the religious character, though little disposed to adopt such austerity in its own practice; and what, on the other hand, He Himself proposes as the true pattern of the Christian life to his followers, though it be less specious and attractive to the outward eye? The privations which He underwent were not self-sought. "The Son of man," indeed, "had not where to lay his head *;" but it was the necessary labours of his ministry that placed Him in these circumstances. He fasted forty days and nights; but it was when He was led out of the Spirit into the wilderness to be tempted of the Devil. It was part of that mysterious conflict with the powers of darkness which He came into the world to accomplish.

As the Ascetic discipline misapprehends the nature and effects of sin, so does it further misapprehend the *remedies* of sin.

* Matt. viii. 20.

It will be said, perhaps, by some of its advocates, that they fully admit that man's corruption lies at his heart's core,—that the body, as it is material, is incapable of sin, and cannot be, intrinsically and apart from the soul, evil by nature. But they will appeal to the intimate connexion of body and soul, —the mutual influence which they exercise on one another,—and that eternal union in which they will hereafter subsist for happiness or for misery; and as we can evidently exercise a considerable power over the actions of the body here, they will contend that we may, and ought to apply that power to the benefit of the soul. By a series of bodily abstinences, by penances, and mortifications of the body, it will be urged, we may induce habits of sobriety, of purity, of tenderness of conscience, of humility, of resignation, of devotedness, of holiness. Thus a course of conduct, which, it may be granted, has no merit or Christian import in itself or in the several actions of which it consists, may yet conduce, it is asserted, in the result, to that which *is precious* in the sight of God,—the *holy and humble heart.* This seems the fairest apology that can be made for the Ascetic discipline. But let us consider how far it avails to recommend the Ascetic discipline *generally* as a discipline of *holiness*.

First, I would observe that the discipline itself, supposing it could accomplish this result generally, is essentially defective. It affects only half of man's nature—that which is the seat of the desires or the softer passions—or what ancient moralists called the "concupiscible" part of the soul,—whilst it leaves undisciplined the rougher principles, or those which belong, according to the ancient classification, to the "irascible" part of the soul. May we not, indeed, rather say, that the system tends to encourage the growth of this latter class of principles,—to foster the severe temper,—to turn the hatred of sin into a hatred of sinful man himself,—to produce a confidence in one's own strength and superiority, which is not the patient waiting of a faith reposing on a strength *not its own*,—to engender a rashness in encountering spiritual dangers, which is not a courage of the Lord? Evil, indeed, can scarcely but result from an *exclusive* attention to any one part of our moral nature. He who is taught to consider himself as becoming like the angels of God for practising the virtues of abstinence exclusively, will soon, it is to be feared, fall below the standard of ordinary humanity in the *general* tone of his moral principles. For our moral nature is essentially a constitution, or system, made up of several parts adjusted to a common end. Its adjustments or proportions cannot, therefore, be disturbed without serious injury. The habit of exercising one class of principles only, must leave one part of the constitution neglected and undisciplined. The work of that part of the system is then either not done at all, or badly done. In some cases this effect will probably be to reduce the neglected principles to feebleness and almost extinction; and thus much will be lost that the Creator designed to be cultivated for the good of the individual and of society. In other cases, the undisciplined passions will run into wild and fierce excess, and produce disorder in the system*.

It will be found, however, that the actions of the Ascetic life do not of themselves, except so far as they are directed by a religious principle antecedent to them, conspire to form those moral and religious habits to which they are thought to contribute. If a man improves in holiness under

* See Bishop Butler's Sermons on Human Nature, with the Preface.

them, it is not by means of them, but from the cultivation of the principle itself of devotion manifested by them. We must not construe the eccentricities of a devout heart, or the weaknesses which it may betray,—whilst, through Divine grace, it is kept essentially right and alive with God,—as attributes and characteristics of its real piety. Who can doubt, but that, amongst those whom the world has celebrated for their ascetic sanctity, there has existed, in some instances at least, a real sanctity, which the world has not seen or commended,—a sanctity of the hidden man,—the gift of the Holy Spirit,—a faith working by love, preserved as a sacred fire in the midst of alien elements, and never extinguished, though obscured? But let us not incur the error, when we would imitate the pious character, of copying its aberrations, and defects, and peculiarities which lie on the surface, instead of seeking faithfully to represent the principles which constitute its life and expression. Let us look at Asceticism as it is in itself,—not as it is the foible of a higher principle,—and judge, how far it can produce or sustain that religious temper to which it is said to be instrumental.

In order to produce or cherish any habit, we

must clearly have a series of actions performed of the same nature as the habit itself which we would induce. For it is not (as the great master of the ancient school of Ethics has justly observed) from doing particular actions merely that the habit follows, but from the *spirit* in which those actions are done; they must be done as the person who has already attained the habit sought would do them; they must belong, that is, to the *principle* which they are intended to produce in the result. To be religious, we must exercise the *religious temper*; to work humility into *the soul*, as an *habitual Christian feeling*, the *soul itself* must be humbled.

Now where is the tendency of bodily mortification,—of endurance of the pains of hunger and thirst, of cold and heat, or other arbitrary and violent restraints on the natural desires,—to produce a Christian lowliness of mind? It is not mere dejection and humiliation of the spirit that we ask for, but *Christian* dejection, *Christian* humiliation. And may not these austerities be practised without any exertion of Christian lowliness of mind? Have they not been practised under *every* religion, under every form of *false* religion, as well as under the *one true* religion?

It is not as with Prayer, which we also find under every form of religion. For Prayer is essentially an act of the religious instinct in the soul,
and the exercise of Prayer must therefore tend
to cultivate the principle from which it flows;
unless indeed it be merely formal, ceremonial,
outward Prayer, in which case it belongs rather
to the body than to the soul. But those self-
inflictions and self-denials which the ascetic discipline prescribes, are not necessarily exercises
of the soul, still less of the mortified Christian
soul, over itself. They may be nothing more
than exercises of the soul over the body,—forming a habit of abstinence indeed,—rendering abstinence more easy to be performed, and thus
subduing the *body*,—but not at the same time
necessarily subduing the soul,—not subduing
that *which must be subdued*, if the doctrine of the
Cross is to be duly received there.

Doubtless there is a very great advantage to
the Christian wrestler, as to the competitor in
the games, to have his body under perfect command,—to be patient of the greatest extremes,
—to know with the Apostle how to want as well
as how to abound,—to be thus fully provided for
the possible exigencies of his situation as one

who has an arduous contest before him in the world. A discipline of endurance may in this way be an effectual preparation for the trials that a Christian may have to encounter. Rightly, therefore, do we pray that God would give us " grace to use such abstinence, that, our flesh being subdued to the spirit, we may obey His motions in all things * ;" that is, that we may through His aid acquire such command over the body, that we may be fitly disposed, not for endurance as an end, but for active obedience to the will of God,— not hindered from obeying his call,—to whatever trials He may summon us. Such was the Christian hardihood which St. Paul had acquired when he " gloried after the flesh," describing how, among his other apostolical labours, he had been " in weariness and painfulness, in watchings often, in hunger and thirst, in fastings often, in cold and nakedness†." Such was that discipline to which our Lord called his first disciples, when He foretold their impending trials in reply to the inquiry of the disciples of John ;—" Can the children of the bridechamber mourn, as long as the bridegroom is with them ?

* Collect for 1st Sunday in Lent.
† 2 Cor. xi. 27.

but the days will come when the bridegroom shall be taken from them, and then shall they fast*." If the labours of Asceticism were simply directed to this end, who could object anything against those, who, being able to bear them, practised them for this great end,—*active*, zealous obedience to the will of God under every extremity of trial? But such is not the view which the advocates of the Ascetic discipline propose. According to them, it must be pursued for its *perfection in itself*,—for the accomplishment of that passive power of endurance,—that angelic exemption from the trammels of the body,— which to them is an *end* to be attained by the perfect Christian. They urge it on the Christian as something holy in itself,—as a discipline of Gospel-purity,—as a state of nearer approach to the Divine perfections. It appears, on the contrary, to be a mere instrument in order to better things. It may, or may not, be beneficially applied for the advancement of the Christian soul in holiness. It has no *direct* tendency to form the Christian temper in us, terminating, as it does, in a habit only of command over the body —a command which has been possessed to a very

* Matt. ix. 15.

great degree by some of the worst of mankind*.
Sin may remain in all its malignity in the soul,
and yet the ascetic may have reduced his body
to a phantom. Whilst he is vainly relying on
his factitious remedies, the cancer at his heart
may be rankling and threatening to destroy both
body and soul in hell.

"Bodily exercise," therefore, we say with the
Apostle, "profiteth little†." Vain is the endeavour of man to devise remedial methods for the
wounds of his soul, when the Gospel tells us
there is but *one way* of salvation, *one method only*,
by which he may obtain health and strength.
"Believe in the Lord Jesus Christ, and thou
shalt be saved." What does man want more
than this assurance?—"God will give the Holy

---

* "Caloris ac frigoris patientia par: cibi potionisque desi-
derio naturali, non voluptate, modus finitus. Vigiliarum som-
nique, nec die, nec nocte, discriminata tempora. Id quod ge-
rendis rebus superesset, quieti datum: ea neque molli strato,
neque silentio arcessita . . . . Has tantas viri virtutes ingentia
vitia æquabant: inhumana crudelitas, perfidia plus quam Pu-
nica, nihil veri, nihil sancti, nullus Deûm metus, nullum jus-
jurandum, nulla religio."—Liv. lib. xxi. 4.

† 1 Tim. iv. 8. Ἡ γὰρ σωματικὴ γυμνασία πρὸς ὀλίγον ἐστὶν
ὠφέλιμος· κ. τ. λ. The Apostle expressly contrasts this kind
of exercise with the exercise of εὐσέβεια, godliness, or true
Christian piety.

Spirit to them that ask him." What more present help does man yet look for?—Only let him bring home to his daily struggles with the temptations of the Devil, the world, and his own heart, his faith in these all-powerful remedies,—let him constantly call them down to him by prayer and the Sacraments, and other ordinances of religion and by Christian watchfulness,—and he will experience in himself a real discipline of righteousness,—a sure advancement towards that perfection which is the end of his calling.

Such an one indeed will not despise any relief that may present itself to enable him to bear up against the burthen and heat of his day. He will neither court temptation nor rush into it, nor expose himself to it where the way lies open for his escape. Should he find that to mix in the busy society of the world acts injuriously on his character as a Christian, he will, so far as his various complex duties will permit him (and this point should well be considered *first*,—for it may be his peculiar trial,—it may be most important to himself and to others that he should continue under it), withdraw himself from such intercourse. If even the innocent gratifications attached to the present life engage him too strictly, he will restrain himself in regard to these. If the cares for the body, for what he shall eat or drink or what he shall put on, take up too much of his time and thoughts, he will moderate them; he will avoid a luxury that tempts him to forget, that his labour should be for the meat that perisheth not, and for the garment that waxeth not old. In short, so far as he may, he will remove from him whatever offends—whatever is a stumbling-block in the path of his Christian profession. He will "lay aside every weight, and the sin that doth most easily beset him, that he may run with patience the race that is set before him." Thus did our Lord advise the rich man, whose heart, he knew, was fixed on his possessions, to sell all that he had and follow Him. The rich man could not submit to the sacrifice; but our Lord saw that it was needful in *his* case; for that his riches would make it hard for *him* to enter into the kingdom of heaven. Thus again did He resolve the difficulty proposed by the disciples on the subject of marriage*. By his answer on that occasion, he showed that the question, whether it was good for a man to marry or not, was a

* Matt. xix. 10.

H

strictly practical one,—that it was to be decided in each case by the peculiar circumstances of the individual; and according as it might be found, that either to marry, or not to marry, might remove a temptation and facilitate the Christian's progress to the kingdom of heaven, or as it might encumber and perplex him on his course. Such, too, is the tenour of St. Paul's admirable counsel to the Corinthians throughout the seventh chapter of his first Epistle to that Church. The Apostle, with a Christian tenderness for his sons in the faith, is only anxious in all that he says there that they might be " *without carefulness*;" that " using this world as not abusing it," they might escape the snares of the Devil, and be at liberty to serve God without distraction of thought.

But the system of the Ascetic is the reverse of all this. It *multiplies* temptations, whilst it professedly removes them; for it calls upon all who would be *perfect Christians*, to place themselves in situations which it is given only to some to hold with advantage to their souls. If we require a weak brother to practise an austerity to which he is not equal, surely we lay a stumbling-block before him; we excite in him an artificial scrupulousness of conscience,—we alarm him with fears which the Gospel knows not, making sad the heart which the Lord has not made sad,—we tempt him, on the one hand, to a superstitious deference to the circumstantials of religion rather than to its substance; on the other hand, to an insincere profession of religion, when he finds himself called by it to particular observances, which he is not disposed, or perhaps not able, to practise. And even those who with the best resolutions have set themselves to work out the Ascetic system in their own conduct,—how must they at times feel the perplexity and difficulty of the situation in which they *have placed themselves*! They may have grace to support the trial, though it be of their own seeking; but they may *fail in it*: and how will they then have tempted God, and wilfully hurt their own souls! Temptations, we know, which God himself sends, he will also " give us a way to escape from, that we may be able to bear them." But as for those which men bring down on themselves, what ground have they for believing that they shall have strength to bear them?

Let us beware therefore, Brethren, how we

pervert the notion of Religious Discipline, and increase our dangers in the world by false refinements of religious practice. Let us guard our simplicity in Christ with a jealous watchfulness, in Christian practice no less than in Christian doctrine. Especially, indeed, let us guard against those errors in practice which seem only a laudable excess of what is right,—which seduce our affection and veneration by the piety with which they may be associated,—which powerfully interest our imagination, as appearing only the faults, if they be faults, of the high and devoted soul, and such as inferior spirits would not incur. It is not that such errors are worse than many other more palpable corruptions of Christian conduct. But they demand a more active vigilance against them on account of their seductiveness,—on account of the absence in them of that external grossness which at once offends the eye and the heart in some other practical errors. Still they are errors, however lovely and venerable they may seem to our superficial view. For, as I have endeavoured to shew, they offend against Christian simplicity ; they withdraw our attention from the One only Atonement made for sin, and attempt to apply remedies to the soul which cannot heal its wounds, but rather aggravate its danger.

The effectual security against the morbid discipline of Aceticism is to work out that living strenuous discipline of the Christian soul, which St. Paul sets before us in the words of our text, simply understood, and heartily applied to our actual unavoidable difficulties and temptations in the world. A race is before us,—let us run it with all our energy : a conflict is proposed to us,—let us strive for the mastery : an incorruptible crown is the prize for which we are to contend,—let us so run, and so strive, that we may obtain it. We are not *naturally* qualified for this exertion. God has, however, given us capacities and powers, and placed us in a condition, for acquiring by our efforts under his grace the necessary qualifications for the conflict. Let us therefore be temperate in all things—exercising a strict command over ourselves—exemplifying in all our conduct that true Christian self-denial, which faithfully does all that the Lord commands and forbears all that he forbids, and yet feels its own unprofitableness, and its entire need of the Saviour's righteousness and the sanctification of the Spirit, to commend it to the favour of God.

God forbid that we should deny to those thus earnestly contending for the crown of glory the edification and strength and comfort which the pious ordinances of the Church provide for them, or their own experience of what is good for them prescribes, in setting apart seasons and occasions for especial penitential prayer, and stricter meditation on the guilt and misery of sin, and God's infinite love and mercy in Christ. These are no essential parts of the Ascetic system, though that system would claim them as its own. They are wise and benevolent adaptations to the infirmity of our nature; reminding us by solemn warnings of the danger of our condition in the world; calling on us to stop and reflect, what we are— what we have done and are doing—what God has done and is doing for us—how He will finally deal with the impenitent sinner—and how we shall render our account to Him of our stewardship. And, though Repentance is the daily and hourly business of our lives, yet such is the dulness of the heart—such is its proneness to the world, even in its regenerate state,—that our very repentance needs to be repented of,—our very tears (as has been said) need washing. And it is well, therefore, for us that days and seasons and solemn services of Repentance are appointed in the ritual of our Church. Eagerly, then, will the devout Christian avail himself of these ministrations to his soul's health,—eagerly will he follow them out in his own private devotion,— not indeed as acts of penance or as propitiations of the Divine wrath,—but as knowing that the sacrifices of God are a broken spirit, and that the broken and contrite heart is what He will not despise. Thus will the devout Christian walk humbly with his God, confessing his sins and mortifying the deeds of the body; yet *actively* striving for the mastery, as one called by his Lord to work out his own salvation.

Nor let it be thought that a caution against the delusions of Asceticism is needless in these times; for that there is far too much sound evangelical feeling in our Church for the establishment of such a system among us. I trust indeed in that superintendence of its Divine Head, which has hitherto so wonderfully preserved our Church as a beacon on the hill to Christendom, that it will be still preserved. I pray that we may have strength, according to our day, to withstand the evil. But it can never, at the same time, be needless to guard against errors, to which the human heart, in spite of its better convictions, naturally leans. For the natural heart will not receive the mystery of the Cross in simplicity; it is ever interposing its own means and resources between the Saviour and the saved,—ever delighting in hewing out a way for itself, rather than willing to go *at once* to the Rock and the Fountain of Salvation. Our Church, however, has in it the seeds of resistance to all anti-Christian error; and if *we*, its members, are not wanting to it, the Church will not be wanting, through Him who is its Life and Strength, to its duty to the Christian world. We must only take care that, by keeping to the Foundation,—by maintaining the fervour of its first love,—it may now, as ever, protest against every delusion of doctrine or of practice, that may ask admission into its sanctuary,—however importunate, however recommended by pious eloquence or pious example, however endeared by sentimental or imaginative associations, and however guarded by specious distinctions from some kindred more obvious delusion or grosser corruption.

We indeed, who, as a Church, have been signally called in God's Providence and Grace to preach, like the Apostle of the Gentiles, the Gospel of the Lord Jesus Christ, free from all admixture of human inventions, to God's people both within and without the Church,—we indeed shall have just cause to fear for ourselves—*if we* "*preach not the Gospel,*"—if we at all shrink from and desert our principles, or relax our first labours,—lest, after having preached to others,—having acted as heralds to the spiritual combat,—we should ourselves be put aside and rejected as unworthy even of being admitted among the competitors for the crown that fadeth not away.

SERMON IV.

THE LORD OUR RIGHTEOUSNESS.

PREACHED IN THE CATHEDRAL OF CHRIST CHURCH,

On SUNDAY, November 24, 1839.

SERMON IV.

THE LORD OUR RIGHTEOUSNESS.

JER. XXIII. 5, 6.

*Behold, the days come, saith the Lord, that I will raise unto
David a righteous Branch, and a King shall reign and prosper, and shall execute judgement and justice in the earth. In
his days Judah shall be saved, and Israel shall dwell safely;
and this is his name whereby He shall be called, The Lord our
Righteousness.*

ON this particular Sunday, we hear the voice of
the Church calling us to turn our faces towards
the city of David, and to look with the eye of
expectant faith to the coming of the Lord in the
flesh. That event, indeed, is already past to us.
We have seen that day, which prophets and
saints of old desired to see, and for which they
patiently waited. Year after year, we have listened to the message of the angel of the Lord
bringing the good tidings of great joy to all
people; " Unto you is born this day in the city

of David, a Saviour, which is Christ the Lord."
With the shepherds,—with holy Simeon and
Anna,—with the wise men from the East,—with
the faithful company that " waited for the consolation of Israel," and that " looked for redemption in Jerusalem,"—we have, again and
again, blessed God, that our eyes have seen His
salvation. " Blessed" indeed, then, may we say,
are our " eyes ; for they see." But the Church,
acting in the spirit of the Gospel, is not content
to let us look at the things of Christ, as objects
fully realized to us, as matters simply of historical truth and certainty. The Church would have
us rather know and remember and feel that " we
walk *by faith*, and not by sight." It would inculcate on us, that, though we know, of a surety,
that unto us a Saviour has been given,—that the
word of prophecy, once a light shining in a dark
place, as it spoke of the Redeemer to come, has
brightened into clear day by its actual accomplishment in the Word made flesh,—yet we are
not to rest on the past ;—we are not to think, that
the labours, and anxieties, and patient waitings
of faith, are over ;—that they were the burden of
God's servants of old only, and not ours too.
The Church, accordingly, by the course of its

services, commenced from this day, and carried through the season of Advent, leads us back to the faith of God's saints under the old dispensation, and bids us learn of them, how the Christian should bow his heart before the Lord his Saviour.

Awful indeed is the thought, Christian Brethren, that, in point of spiritual privileges, the " least in the kingdom of God," the humblest member of the Church of Christ, is " greater " than the greatest of the saints of the old dispensation,—enjoys an illumination of divine knowledge and grace, from which holy patriarchs and prophets were excluded,—sees, as it were, near at hand, what the ancient Fathers saw only far off! Awful I say is the thought! And how should it stimulate our feeling of responsibility! How should it kindle in us a fervent aspiration after the like patience of hope and faith to that with which they held on in their calling! Earnestly therefore let us listen to the voice of evangelical exhortation, which is this day sounded in our ears. Let us sit at the feet of the Prophet of the Lord, whose words the Church reads and interprets to us this day, and learn of that Spirit, who consigned them to the perpetual instruction

of the heirs of the promises given to the Fathers,
what manner of persons we should be, as the sons
of their faith,—as the successors and followers
of men who *believed God*, and whose faith was
counted to them for righteousness.

" Behold, the days come, saith the Lord, that
I will raise unto David a righteous Branch, and
a King shall reign and prosper, and shall execute
justice and judgement in the earth. In his days
Judah shall be saved, and Israel shall dwell
safely ; and this is his name whereby He shall
be called, The Lord our Righteousness."

We only follow the general consent of interpreters, when we understand this passage in the
sense in which it is evidently received by our
Church, from its introduction in the Epistle of
this day, as speaking of the Shepherd of shepherds, the King of kings, and Lord of lords, the
blessed and only Potentate, the Lord Jesus Christ.
It characterizes the future Restorer of Israel, in
terms which refuse any other interpretation short
of that which applies them to the person and
office of the Redeemer. For who else could be
the righteous Branch of the house of David, but
he who was at once the Son of David, and David's
Lord,—" the Holy One and the Just" alone of

that chosen line? And who else could be the king who should reign and prosper, and should execute justice and judgement in the earth, but He to whom all power is given in heaven and in earth,—who triumphed over principalities and powers,—a King, as He owned Himself, and as the glad hosannas of his people hailed Him on his triumphant entry into Jerusalem, though his kingdom was not of this world? In whose days, again, could Judah be said to be saved, and Israel to dwell safely, but in his, who "assembled the outcasts of Israel, and gathered together the dispersed of Judah from the four corners of the earth,"—by whom the wall of partition between Jew and Gentile was broken down, and all the families of the earth were called to dwell together in peace, as the true Israel of God, the children of Abraham's faith, without respect of persons? And lastly, who could be the Lord our Righteousness, but the Word made flesh, and dwelling among us, the only-begotten of the Father, full of grace and truth,—He who knew no sin made sin for us, that we might be made the righteousness of God in Him?

And yet, manifest as the bearing of the passage is on the person and office of the Saviour, there has been an endeavour, as you will know, to pervert it to another sense.   It has been represented as nothing more than a prediction of the restoration of Israel ; and in support of this construction of the passage, it is urged, that the designation of " The Lord our Righteousness " must be taken as merely descriptive of the blessedness of that time ; in like manner as, in other passages of Scripture, significant names, including the name of the Lord, or Jehovah, are given to places and persons, to commemorate some special providence or mercy of God connected with them.

The context, however, whether in this passage, or in the parallel one of the 33rd chapter, in which the words recur with some variation, clearly shows that this explanation of the phrase, " The Lord our Righteousness," will not apply here.   The prophet is contrasting the good Shepherd of Israel with the profane and unfaithful pastors, who were destroying and scattering the sheep of the Lord's pasture.   These he describes as claiming to have been sent when the Lord had not sent them,—as prophesying of their own heart, " causing the people to err by their lies and by their lightness."   Against these he denounces the anger of the Lord. But he declares, at the same time, the promise of mercy to the sinful people. The Lord will "set up other shepherds over them, which shall feed them." Nor is this all. He will further give them one who shall guide them in peace,—a righteous Branch of the house of David, —one in whom they may trust,—who will not fail to lead them in safety. And what is the ground of this confidence? He is one truly sent by God, in a sense in which no other person ever was. He to whom they are to look is " God, and not man:" He is the Lord our Righteousness. Naturally, therefore, are we led, by the tenour of the passage, to contrast person with person,— personal character and office with personal cha- racter and office,—and thus to understand the words of the text as simply and strictly denoting the one good Shepherd of the sheep, the Blessed One who came in the name of the Lord, even the Lord Jesus Christ.

Were there, however, any doubt, from the con- text, of the right interpretation of the passage, this doubt would be removed by a reference to the language of the New Testament. Read over the chapter of Jeremiah now before us; and compare with it our Lord's express application to Himself of the office of "the good Shepherd." " I am the good Shepherd, and know my sheep, and am known of mine. As the Father knoweth me, even so know I the Father: and I lay down my life for the sheep. And other sheep I have, which are not of this fold: them also I must bring; and they shall hear my voice; and there shall be one fold and one Shepherd."—Observe too, how, " when he saw the multitudes," He is said to have been " moved with compassion on them, because they fainted, and were scattered abroad, as sheep having no shepherd."—Observe again, how, in the Gospel of this day, we may find a living commentary on the words of Jeremiah; when we read there of our Lord acting the part of the kind shepherd of his flock, preparing for them a pasture in the wildernesss, sustaining their bodies with the food needful for this life, and their souls with that spiritual meat which nourishes to the life everlasting. Compare further St. Peter's description of the salvation obtained for us by the perfect righteousness of Christ, as a return to the fold. " For ye were as sheep," he says, " going astray; but are now returned unto the Shepherd and Bishop of your souls."—Refer also to St. Paul's emphatic setting

forth of *the Righteousness of God*, as that which
is brought down to man by the Incarnation and
death of Christ ; and more particularly to that
passage of his first Epistle to the Corinthians,
where he speaks of Christ, as " of God made
unto us wisdom and righteousness and sanctification and redemption ;" and where the Apostle
seems almost to lay his finger on the text of
Jeremiah now before us. With these divine com-
mentaries to illustrate the meaning of the prophet, (not to cite others bearing on the point,)
we may well disclaim those minute criticisms,
which would pervert this text from its high evangelical import ; and may without doubt read in
it the mind of the Spirit revealing to us, in one
short mysterious phrase, the perfect Divinity of
our Lord and the effectual grace of his Atonement. Well indeed may we hold, with the multitudes whom he fed, that He who thus cares for
the sheep, is, " of a truth that prophet that
should come into the world,"—the Emmanuel
of Isaiah,—the Lord our Righteousness, of Jeremiah,—" gathering the remnant of his flock out
of all countries," and " bringing them again to
their folds," and " feeding them," that they

should " fear no more, neither be dismayed, neither be lacking."

But perhaps I am dwelling too long on the interpretation of our text; I would pass on to draw out of it that instruction in the faith of Christ which it involves, and apply it to our own spiritual benefit.

The words of the prophet are but a summary of the great truth which the Gospel expands to us in its full proportions ;—that the work of man's salvation is wholly divine ; divine in its first cause ; divine in the means by which it is wrought ; divine in its end. What the prophet intimates is, that Salvation is of the Lord, from first to last. The righteousness by which man stands before God, as a sinful being saved by God's mercy in Christ, the righteousness of the Gospel, is not the righteousness of *man*, but of *the Lord Himself*, who has mercy on us. The stupendous miracle of the Divine Goodness displayed in the redemption of a fallen world, is not, that man can now obtain the utmost perfection, and utmost felicity, of *his own nature*. The Gospel scheme of mercy is infinitely more than this. The ground of our pardon, the title of our acceptance, is in the nature of God Himself. As sin has abounded unto the condemnation of man, so grace has much more abounded unto his justification; inasmuch as *now*, in the merits of Christ, we are blessed with a blessedness belonging to *Him*; for the Lord Himself, Jehovah Himself, is become *our* Righteousness.

It is then to lower the character of the Gospel scheme of mercy, to regard the attainment of Gospel righteousness as consisting in any thing of ourselves. We must never forget in all that we think and do as Christians, that we are " accepted" only " in the Beloved." We must stand fast in the grace in which we have been called. We must constantly look unto Jesus, as, at once, both " the Author and Finisher of our salvation." The moment that we abandon this ground,— in whatever way we suffer any thing less holy to enter into the sanctuary of that Divine Righteousness, which, by the charter of the Gospel, is made over to us,—we impair the perfection of our standard of Gospel religion and Gospel virtue; we substitute a righteousness of another kind for the one perfect righteousness of the Lord the Saviour.

The history of man has shewn how little he is

disposed sincerely to cast all his care upon God, and to rest in simple unwavering confidence on the righteousness of God for acceptance. Nothing seems easier to us at the first view, than thus to go to God, renouncing ourselves, and wanting no other assurance but that of His goodness. Practically, however, this is not the case. We hear indeed sometimes Christians professing to hope, that God will be merciful to them in spite of their continuance in sin, and so far taking comfort to themselves from a confidence in the infinite goodness of God. But is this profession and this comfort, anything more than a flattering of their own souls,—a treacherous dealing with their own hearts,—a palliation of the pain of sin,—an encouragement to themselves in a course of sin to which they are committed? Surely if such persons truly relied on the *goodness* of God, they would see His goodness, not in that false light in which it appears *indulgent* to sin, but in its real awfulness as it recoils from everything unholy, and in its proper endearment, as it engages and leads men to repentance. Let not such persons, then, be brought forward as instances of the disposition of the corrupt heart to rely on the righteousness and mercy of God.

They are instances, rather, of,—what the doctrine of Gospel righteousness implies,—the hope-
lessness of sin,—the necessary distrust of the
sinner in any efforts of his own to emancipate
himself from the tyranny and misery of sin,—
and of the recklessness of one who feels that the
ground is sinking under his feet, and catches at
any apparent stay which offers itself, though he
knows it cannot support him. On the contrary,
that there is a tendency in the heart of man to
seek out a mode by which he shall come before
God not empty-handed, or as the Apostle expresses it, to " go about to establish his own righteousness," is abundantly evident, in various ways;
—from the rites of superstition,—from the voluntary humility and will-worship which some have
practised,—from the punctiliousness of formal
observances which some have been found to prescribe for themselves,—from instances again of
persons claiming a merit for their exemption
from particular errors and sins, thanking God,
like the Pharisee in the parable, that they are
not as other men are, or compensating, in their
own view, their demerits in one way by their
supposed merits in another. These and many
other forms of the same indisposition to rely on

the alone righteousness of God, sufficiently indicate, that the Gospel method of salvation, whilst it is an open and free one, stretching out the hand of God to all, is yet not an easy one in that way in which the world reckons easiness.

External indeed is the principle of that righteousness. It arises not from anything in ourselves. We have only to lay hold of it and cling to it, and thus make it our own. For though it is the Lord Jesus Christ who is made unto us Righteousness, we must for our part own him as *our* Righteousness. We must have, that is, no thought of ourselves apart from Him, in seeking to justify ourselves before God. We must come for acquittal, and ask for mercy, as being dead unto sin with Christ and raised again with Him, —as vitally incorporated with Him, and made one with Him, in the mystical body of His Church.

It is not that we must plead His righteousness as a *supplement* to our imperfect endeavours. In such a plea lies the very leaven of human self-righteousness. It is not, that we must *substitute* His righteousness for *our own unrighteousness,* so as to think that we are justified through Him, *in the midst of our sins,*—whilst we continue in our sins,—and without repenting of them, and for-saking of them. Were these the modes of pre-ferring the righteousness of Christ in our behalf before the throne of God, then indeed might the free Salvation of the Gospel be regarded as an easy method. Neither of these modes present us before God as claiming an entire inseparable in-terest in the merits of the Saviour. We must be *His throughout*,—conformed to His holy life and death to the utmost,—living in communion with Him ; and so have confidence before God to speak of Him as the Lord our Righteousness.

And here is the task of difficulty. The task is no other than that of a true and lively evan-gelical faith. To do all that we can do in working out our own salvation, through the grace of God giving us the will and working with us ; forsaking known sins,— resisting and avoiding temptations,—adorning the doctrine of God our Saviour in all things, by prayer, by religious observances, by faithfulness and diligence and contentedness in our daily callings, and thus continually perfecting holiness in the fear of the Lord ;—and yet to remember, that all this is *nothing in order to our justification in the sight of God*,—to feel an unspeakable comfort in the revelation of the *Lord as our Righteousness* ; this is the high prerogative of a Gospel faith. He that is satisfied with being partially holy, or who adopts a standard of holiness after the measure of man, or who wilfully continues in sin with the Righteousness of Christ set before him as the means of Salvation, may indeed take up the words, and profess to own the Lord as his Righteousness. But he cannot have a right appreciation of that Righteousness. Its value is felt only by him, who loves and cherishes every element of holiness which the Spirit has implanted in him,—who deeply feels and grieves over his fall from original righteousness, and longs to be restored to the Divine Image, and yet finds in himself impediments to holiness which he cannot overcome,—a principle of inertness and resistance to good, which holds him back in his course. Such an one, as St. Paul describes him in that striking passage of his Epistle to the Romans, is almost ready to faint under his burthen. " O wretched man that I am !" he confesses, under his struggles, " who shall deliver me from the body of this death ?" And yet he it is in whose mouth the evangelical thanksgiving is put ; " I thank my God through Jesus Christ our Lord."

True it is, that Jesus Christ came not to call the *righteous*, but *sinners*, to repentance. True it is, that the virtue of his Sacrifice is effectual to the quickening of the dead in trespasses and sins; and that there is no unrighteousness of man which it cannot put away. Some of the earliest saints of the Gospel had, in their unconverted state, been grievous sinners, but had obtained the grace of repentance and remission of sins through Christ, and were become faithful disciples of the Lord their Righteousness. "Such were some of you," says St. Paul, after enumerating several classes of grievous sinners, in writing to the Corinthians; " but ye are washed, but ye are sanctified, but ye are justified in the name of the Lord Jesus, and by the Spirit of our God." These instances shew indeed that *none are excluded* from the grace of the Gospel. In every particular case of a sinner brought to a Gospel repentance, as in the general gift of a Saviour to our fallen race, it is, we know, God's first motion which brings about the happy change. He takes away the heart of stone, and gives the heart of flesh to the sinner of every degree and complexion of sin, who is brought to bow himself before the cross of Christ.

Let us not be thought, then, presumptuously to limit his mercy, in saying that the saving truth of the righteousness of Christ is only duly *there* received, where there is the earnest desire, and the longing after holiness. The holiest of men are still among those sinners for whom Christ died. Nor in them can we dare to analyze all the motions of their hearts, or attempt to account for that faith which first leads them to the cross, and lays hold for them of the Lord their Righteousness, otherwise than by the free grace of God calling them, and holding them in the way of Salvation. Only we contend, that the doctrine of man's Salvation through the Lord his Righteousness,—by a righteousness, that is, essentially *divine* and *external* to man,—is not a doctrine of licentiousness, or of indolence and ease. It is a truth for *every sinner*—every fallen son of Adam, (for all are by nature dead in trespasses and sins;) but it is a truth, which comes home *only* to the quickening of those, who, having received it, love it in their hearts, and cherish it as their own.

And the trial, it should be observed, is greatest to those who thus receive it. They know best the labour of self-denial in its true Christian

sense, as a denial of all intrinsic worth in human
works,—as an entire renunciation of *self* in their
plea before God,—who are most actively and intensely purifying themselves from the pollutions
of the flesh and the world. They, I say, best
know the preciousness of a *gifted* righteousness ;
for they have sought after a *personal* righteousness, and have not attained to it : they are especially tempted to trust in their own strength,—
to " count " themselves " to have apprehended,"
—to rest with satisfaction in what they have accomplished, (for Satan is busy still in persuading
man that he " shall not surely die;") but through
grace, they still feel themselves *sinners*, and cry
out each from the bottom of his heart, " God be
merciful"—God be propitiated—'Ο Θεὸς ἱλάσθητι
—" to me a sinner ! "

The greatest difficulty, however, which attends
the Christian in his reception of the Lord as his
Righteousness, appears to lie in this point ; that
he is tempted to join with this one simple ground
of his justification, other principles of his religion ;—principles, equally true, equally necessary
in their way, equally good in their kind, and yet
all *infinitely below* the one meritorious cause of
justification, the Righteousness of the Lord the

Saviour, in spiritual efficacy and dignity. The sincere and humble Christian is comparatively secure against those dangers to the simplicity of his faith in Christ which arise from *wrong* principles. He will not regard himself as exempt from the obligations of the Divine commandments,—because the righteousness which saves his soul is derived from a source without himself. Nor will he debase and corrupt his faith with superstitious additions. But he will not be so much on his guard against the intrusion of what is good, as he will be against that which is positively evil. I will proceed to give some instances of this.

The Church, for example, is holy. It is the body of Christ. Who then shall despise the Church,—who shall think lightly of its teaching, its discipline, its ordinances, its ministers? Undoubtedly then the Christian has an indispensable religious duty towards the Church. But, *for that very reason*, he must watch, lest, in his excess of reverence towards the Church, he should remove from its place the great Corner-stone of his faith, and build *in fact* on the *Church*, and not on Christ.

The Sacraments again are holy. They are

means of grace, especially instituted by our Lord
Himself for our regeneration and strengthening
in the life of righteousness which we live in Him.
They form, therefore, essential constituents of
the religion of the Gospel. They cannot be dispensed with by any, who are within the reach of
them, and are able to obtain them. The wanton
or careless neglect of them, we must believe, will
incur the forfeiture of our Christian privilege of
having the Lord for our Righteousness. But,
for that very reason,—*because* the sacraments are
appointed means of grace,—because we cannot
expect that, without them, the seed of the spiritual life will be implanted and grow in us,—
the Christian must watch against the notion of
justification *by the sacraments*. In their place he
cannot estimate them too highly. As means of
grace he cannot cherish them too much. But
he must remember, at the same time, that they
cannot *justify* him,—that, though they are channels of the spiritual life and strength obtained
for us by the merits of Christ, they are not in
themselves communications of *His merits*, (as the
Church of Rome speaks,) to the soul,—that Christ
is *the Lord our Righteousness*, independently of
anything that we do, however religious and holy,

K

—that we are accordingly justified "*freely,*" as the Apostle says, and by no other instrument, therefore, than that faith, which simply owns the freedom of the gift, and reserves the exclusive glory of our Salvation to Christ.

Again, Repentance is indispensable to every one that would come to Christ truly. It is joined in the Gospel with remission of sins. We may conclude, therefore, that Repentance is no less required of the Christian, than forgiveness on God's part, in order to Salvation. And we should conclude truly. Where, then, is the point of difference in regard to the religious importance of the two principles? It is clearly this. Repentance is absolutely necessary as a religious duty; but, however necessary, it has no *efficacy* to repair the ruin of sin, and reinstate man in that righteousness in which he once stood. It is most true, therefore, that except we repent we shall undoubtedly perish everlastingly. And it is also most true that, however humbly contrite we may be, our sinful nature calls for some external remedy of its disease. Such a remedy is provided for us in the righteousness of Christ. To this remedy, then, we must look *exclusively* in all our own humiliations before God, lest our very

acts of humiliation become a snare to us,—lest
we be tempted to think, that our sorrow for sin
is accepted with God for *righteousness*; because
God, we are assured, will forgive the penitent,
and despises not the humble and contrite heart.

Take another instance of the class of good
principles, which the Christian may, unless he
keeps a strict watch over himself, unsuspectingly
apply to the corruption of his faith in the alone
merits of his Saviour. " If thou wilt enter into
life, keep the commandments ;"—" this do, and
thou shalt live ;"—" without holiness no man
shall see the Lord." What can be plainer than
these and the like precepts of holy living scattered through the Scriptures ? And not only do
we read such injunctions, but we are further told
expressly, that the Lord will " give every man
according as his work shall be." So strongly
are the necessity and the value of good works
impressed on the Christian. Nay, we even read
in one place, that " by works a man is justified,
and not by faith only." Who can doubt then,
that God strictly requires of us obedience to the
moral law, and that He will account none as
righteous in his sight, who are not careful to
maintain good works ? The faithful Christian,

then, will feel himself imperatively called to shew
forth his faith by his works. He will regard acts
of obedience to God as indispensable in order to
his personal salvation,—that, though justified, he
may be justified still. And the danger accordingly will be to him, lest he should come to think
that his justification is the *result* of his obedience,
—the *aggregate*, as it were, of the several acts of
holiness which, notwithstanding his manifold infirmities and sins, he has performed through life,
—a justification, graciously granted indeed by
God rewarding his own gifts in his servant for
Christ's sake, but still as the merited recompense
of service done. Whereas, on the contrary, he
that would hold fast to the *foundation*, must feel
that after he has done all, he is an *unprofitable*
servant; and that the crown of righteousness,
which the Lord, the righteous Judge, has laid up
for him, (if happily he shall attain to it when his
wrestlings and his race are done,) is not *his own*,
but the Saviour's who won it for him.

Lastly, consider another form still in which the
Christian may, unawares, through his very piety
—through his earnest desire to work out his salvation—slide into an erroneous notion of his justification. What is more needful to the Christian

than the *Divine Grace*, the continued and increasing influence of the Holy Spirit, that he may think and do anything in order to his salvation? For this he prays unceasingly; on this he lives as the daily food of his soul; on this he depends for help and comfort in all trials; by it he trusts that he shall finally be perfected,—desiring that he may grow in grace, until he "come unto a perfect man, unto the measure of the stature of the fulness of Christ." But shall he therefore derogate from the work of Christ? Shall he think, that anything is wanting to complete that righteousness which justifies him before God? Not so indeed. He will remember that that work is *accomplished*,—that that righteousness is *perfect*, that our Lord himself declared the work "*finished*," when He hung on the cross; and that He afterwards, on His ascension to the Father, sent down the Holy Ghost, not to fulfil anything wanting in it, but to strengthen and enlighten and comfort those for whose sake it had been wrought. The humble Christian will therefore devoutly lean on the promised aid of the Spirit. He will not dare to hope for the grace of justification, without the indispensable grace of sanctification. He must, however, watch himself, lest he confound the grace of sanctification with the grace of justification ;—the grace which is implanted in him, and given him " to profit withal," that he may increase and bring forth fruits of righteousness,—with the grace which is external to himself, and which admits no increase or diminution. Whilst he prays daily, " Lord, increase my faith!" he prays for that which is most needful for himself ; for if he believes not with his whole heart that Christ has died to save him from his sins, he cannot hope to be saved. But, as I have said before, with regard to other matters of indispensable Christian obligation, he must, *for this very reason*, guard against a practical substitution of the principle of faith, as it exists in his own soul, for the principle which is its object,—the principle of faith, for that of the righteousness of Christ the Lord.

That the dangers to which I have been adverting, are not merely theoretical,—that they are such as beset the path of a conscientious profession of the Gospel,—may be abundantly illustrated from the history of the doctrine of justification as held by the Church of Rome. That church does not deny the *foundation* of the Christian hope. It asserts, as strongly as our own,

that " the meritorious cause of our justification
is the well-beloved, only-begotten Son of God,
our Lord Jesus Christ, who, when we were enemies, through the exceeding love with which he
loved us, merited for us, by his most holy passion
on the cross, justification, and made satisfaction
for us to God the Father."   Nor in building up
its system of doctrine and discipline, does it attribute a vitality or saving efficacy to anything
in it, apart from the life-giving virtue of the
Saviour's Passion.   So far it teaches well.   So
far we honour it for the love of our Lord Jesus
Christ.   When, for example, the Church of Rome
teaches that the sacraments confer grace by their
own intrinsic efficacy, it does not state this in
such a way as to exclude the primary agency of
the merits of Christ.   When, again, it asserts an
inherent righteousness in man, and a power of
satisfying the divine law, and meriting eternal
life, it refers the effect ultimately to grace received through Christ.   For, according to that
Church, it is by the influx of the virtue of Christ
into his members, that the righteousness of God
becomes the righteousness of man.   So studiously
does the Church of Rome maintain in theory its
devotedness to the cross of the Saviour.   Well

had it been for the cause of Christian truth and holiness, had it consistently held this principle of its life; had it never forsaken this its first love, this, its *once* simple gospel profession, in those years of its uncorrupted youth, when an Apostle could rejoice over it, and thank God that its " faith was spoken of throughout the whole world." But what has it done in fact? How fatally has it obscured the doctrine of the Cross, in effect, by the system which it has built on it! Still, indeed, you may see the depth and breadth of the foundation when you search to the bottom of the fabric. But when we ask of the system as a whole, whether it simply preaches and sets before us *the Lord our Righteousness*, how does it disappoint us by the answer! It presents us only a shadow of His righteousness, instead of the substance itself; turning our thoughts from him *practically* to ourselves,—to trace the work of justification as a process carried on in each individual soul, and not (what the Scripture tells us it is) an Atonement made *once for all*,—one common act of mercy and oblivion, covering the sins of the whole world. For what else is the Roman doctrine of Sacramental Justification, but an *internal process* in the soul of man, by

which the sinner is gradually turned from a state
of ungodliness to one of righteousness,—from a
state of demerit, to one of positive merit in the
sight of God? The first cause, indeed, of the
efficacy of that process, as I have observed, is
admitted by Rome to be external to man.   Still,
justification, in the sense of that Church, is essentially an inherent righteousness, varying with
the spiritual condition of him who receives it;
growing with his growth, decaying with his decay,
in grace. The true scriptural view, on the other
hand, appears to be, (as has already been stated)
that the grace of justification is wholly external
to man;—the miracle of mercy in God's kingdom
of grace, analogous to his miracle of creation in
the world of nature. We must indeed *apply* the
grace of our justification, if we, to whom it is
revealed, would benefit by it;—that is, we must,
by faith, take it along with us, in all our warfare
with the world, as the shield wherewith we shall
quench all the fiery darts of the wicked. The
truth of our free justification by the righteousness of God is indeed *our own*, if we only know
how to apply it to our souls' comfort. There is
no duty of the Christian life which it cannot be
brought to stimulate,—no circumstance of Chris-

tian trial which it does not descend to sanctify.
But it is a mystery which angels desire to look
into: how then shall man attempt to deal with
it beyond the simple direction of God's word?
The sure result of such an attempt will be, as
the case of the Church of Rome has shewn, that
the truth will be overlaid by the mass of human
additions.   Men will continue to speak, indeed,
(as the Council of Trent has done in the very
decrees which bind on the Church of Rome its
antichristian corruptions,) of the righteousness
of Christ as the sole meritorious cause of salvation; but the spirit of the doctrine will have
evaporated from their profession; and the righteousness of man, though protested against in
theory, will, to every practical purpose, become
all in all under the ascendency of such a system.

But though we may have cast from us the
grossness of the corruptions of the Church of
Rome, we must not flatter ourselves, that we are
altogether secure from the same dangers which
induced those corruptions. Disclaiming spiritual
pride in ourselves individually, (and may God
keep it from us!) let us not subject our Church
to an imputation of spiritual pride in its collective capacity, by imagining it incapable of falling

from that purity of faith by which it stands,—or
that its holy jealousy of the honour of the Saviour,
and the fervour of its love of Him, impressed on
all its words and conduct, can never be impaired.
" Let him that thinketh he standeth, take heed
lest he fall." The observations to which I have
directed your attention throughout this discourse,
have all tended to this point,—to shew the dangers, to which a pure and conscientious profession
of the faith in Christ is exposed,—dangers arising
from the very earnestness and zeal of the Christian in his holy calling,—from his anxiety to fulfil
all righteousness, to believe and to do all that
God has required of him in the Gospel. Such
observations, therefore, peculiarly apply to the
members of a Church such as ours,—a Church,
so careful to maintain good works in those whom
it brings to Christ ; so scrupulous in exacting a
due estimation and observance of the ordinances
of religion, whilst it inculcates also the secret
religion of the heart ; so true to apostolic order
and discipline, whilst it owns no master but Christ.
The members of such a Church, I say, are peculiarly required to be on their watch against seductions on the side of piety,—against excesses
which admit of being defended on the ground of

some religious principle involved in them, but which at the same time destroy the adjustment of the system of faith by a disproportionate attention to particular parts of it.

There is, for example, little danger to us, comparatively, from the error of Antinomianism, as from that of an extravagant estimate of Good Works : because, while the error itself shocks the feelings, there is no just pretence for saying that the articles and formularies of our Church give any countenance to Antinomianism. Neither indeed do they give any countenance to the error of ascribing an *undue* importance to good works. But they do attribute, and rightly, a *very great importance* to good works. And hence, occasion may be easily taken, to overrate that importance—on the part of *teachers*, to speak of it almost exclusively in their ministrations,—on the part of *private Christians*, to dwell *principally* on the requirements of the moral law —to disquiet themselves with fears not belonging to the Gospel, and lose sight of the counterpart principle—the consolation of the Lord their Righteousness. And the state of our Church, about a century ago, was an illustration of this ; when the preaching of its ministers had, for the most part, degenerated into mere exhortation to the duties of morality and piety, without distinct reference to the great truth of the Righteousness of God in Christ.

The same may be observed with regard to the doctrine of the Sacraments, and the Authority of the Church. We have *comparatively* no temptation (trained as we are by the sober wisdom of our Church) to adopt the *extreme* views set forth by the Church of Rome on these heads, as we have to take intermediate ground—to lay, that is, an undue stress on these particular points of our system,— to give them an undue prominence in our teaching and practice,—to interpret and apply everything else in our religion by a reference to them. This is a line of error into which we may be tempted to deviate; because it recommends itself, by counteracting a laxity of opinion in the opposite direction; and it appears to be only a revival of attention to a portion of the teaching of our Church, which has been at times too much cast into the shade. In this way, men's minds may be drawn into a disproportionate regard for the Sacraments and the Authority of the Church, and to acquiesce in high-wrought statements of the truth respecting them, whilst they would at once reject the full doctrines of Sacramental Justification, and of the Infallibility of the Church, as taught by the Church of Rome. Thus does error in doctrine, as in morality, *seem* to lose its evil, by losing its grossness. And we have need to guard against seductions which address themselves to our right feelings, and which may be in some respect corrective of error, even more jealously than against those, which present themselves in a more repulsive form, and carry a warning against themselves on their very front.

Be it our anxious endeavour, then, brethren, to " keep the good deposit committed to our trust by the Holy Ghost which dwelleth in us." What is it that the Apostles themselves, the first receivers of the truth as it is in Jesus, are found ever labouring to teach and enforce ? It is the doctrine of the Cross—the Righteousness of God in Christ. Looking ever unto Jesus as the Author and Finisher of Salvation, they proclaim His exceeding love to the world in dying for us to save us from our sins, as the burden of their preaching and their comfort under their trials. Hear especially St. Paul putting aside all other ground of confidence but this, and exclaiming,

"But what things were gain to me, those I counted loss for Christ. Yea, doubtless, and I count all things but loss for the excellency of the knowledge of Christ Jesus my Lord, for whom I have suffered the loss of all things, and do count them but dung, that I may win Christ, and be found in him, not having mine own righteousness, which is of the law, but that which is through the faith of Christ, the righteousness which is of God by faith."—Following in their steps, the reformers of our Church only revived the preaching of the Apostles, when they disentangled the doctrine of the Cross from the intricate mazes in which it had been involved, and called upon men to renounce all other claims to justification before God, but the self-denying one of faith in the merits of their Saviour. Shall we then be "ashamed of the testimony of Christ?" Shall we dread the reproach of fanaticism, or of a rash and irreverent zeal, in boldly, and loudly, and unceasingly publishing to the world, in its original simplicity, a truth, which has filled the hearts of Apostles and Saints with joy,—which Apostles and Saints have ever had on their tongue,—in the scandal of which Apostles and Saints have ever gloried, —which, though regarded by the world as a

stumbling-block, and as foolishness,—Apostles
and Saints have ever held forth as the power and
the wisdom of God unto salvation ? Or shall we,
under the name of preaching the cross of Christ,
and the righteousness of Christ, preach *our own*
cross, *our own* righteousness, turning our glad-
tidings into a message of despondency to frail
sinful man,—giving ashes for the bread of life,—
the sackcloth of human holiness, for the white
garment of the righteousness of God?—Woe is
unto us who are ministers of the Lord, the in-
heritors of the Apostolic commission to preach
the Gospel, if we *thus* preach the Gospel, unsaying
the word which the Lord has put into our mouths
to speak ! Woe is unto us, rather, if, so preaching it, we *preach not* the Gospel ! Woe is unto
us, if we preach any other righteousness but that
of the Lord our God and Saviour,—any other
holiness but His, who "*only is Holy*,"—any other
life but that which is hid with Christ in God.
Woe is unto us, if, whether as pastors, or as
sheep of the Lord's flock, we follow any other
shepherd but Him, the good Shepherd, who laid
down his life for the sheep.

Him, indeed, we must follow, wheresoever he
leads us. If we be truly His, we shall know Him,

and hear his voice. The faithful dependence on his merits alone,—the patient waiting of hope for the righteousness of God in Him,—is not without his Spirit guiding us in all his counsel. He is our King, therefore we obey His law ; He is our Prophet, therefore we receive His teaching ; He is our great High Priest, the Lord our Righteousness, needing no purification for Himself, mighty to make intercession for others, and therefore coming to Him, and casting ourselves on Him, we obtain, through Him, the grace which sanctifies us—which makes us righteous even amidst our unrighteousness. Having Him for the Lord our Righteousness, we are assured, that we have One who knows our infirmities, and will accept us, according to what we have, not according to what we have not ;—that, as " Hezekiah prayed to the Lord, saying, The good Lord pardon every one that prepareth his heart to seek God, the Lord God of his fathers, though he be not cleansed according to the purification of the sanctuary: and the Lord hearkened to Hezekiah, and healed the people ; "—so, of those who have not fulfilled the requirements of the moral law,— who are not cleansed according to the purifica-

L

tion of the Gospel,—the Lord God will accept
the preparation of the heart, and heal them ;—
not weighing their merits, but pardoning their
offences, through Jesus Christ our Lord.

SERMON V.

THE TRIAL BY FIRE.

PREACHED IN THE CATHEDRAL OF CHRIST CHURCH,

On SUNDAY, January 31, 1841.

L 2

SERMON V.

THE TRIAL BY FIRE.

---

1 Cor. iii. 13–15.

Every man's work shall be made manifest: for the day shall de-
clare it, because it shall be revealed by fire; and the fire shall
try every man's work of what sort it is. If any man's work
abide which he hath built thereupon, he shall receive a reward.
If any man's work shall be burned, he shall suffer loss: but he
himself shall be saved; yet so as by fire.

THERE are two leading interpretations of this
passage. According to the first of these, it is
to be understood of the ministers of the Divine
word. They are conceived to be the persons
whose work, it is here said, shall be tested at
some future day, and tested by fire. The ground
of this application of the passage is, that St. Paul,
in the earlier part of the chapter, is speaking of
himself and Apollos as ministers by whom the
Corinthians had believed, and of the Corinthian
Church, as " God's husbandry, God's building,"

by *their* labour. From describing himself, accordingly, as a wise master-builder, who had laid the one only foundation which is Jesus Christ, and others who had built thereon; the transition is natural to the case of all other ministers and other Churches,—to the one regarded as builders, to the other as the work built up. Then the passages would be construed thus;—that those who are employed in teaching the faith of Christ, must not think it enough that they hold to the foundation, and that they may raise up the spiritual building of the members of Christ, as they please, or may happen to think right; but that the preaching and teaching of the faith, the edifying of the body of Christ, must be in accordance with the foundation; it must be God's work throughout, holy and imperishable the structure, as the foundation is holy and imperishable. For a "day" will come which will try the stability of the workmanship—which will shew who have been the faithful builders—which will act as a refiner's fire, separating the gold and silver and precious stones from the worthless materials associated with them; when he who has laboured faithfully shall see the fruit of his labour, in the standing living members of the church in which he has laboured; he, on the other hand, who has trained up men in principles alien from the Gospel, will suffer disappointment, in seeing his work come to nought, and himself hardly escape with his life from the surrounding conflagration.

The second interpretation of the passage applies it to the case of false doctrine and corrupt practice built on the foundation of Gospel-truth and Gospel-piety. And the passage is then brought home to the *hearer* of the word, rather than to the teacher. St. Paul is in this view considered to be warning his Corinthian converts against the seductions of the false teachers who had followed in his track, and who professed to be carrying them on to greater heights of religious knowledge and perfection. He tells them, therefore, to take heed how they heard; not to be respecters of the persons of men in hearing the word of God; for that neither Apollos nor himself were anything but instruments in God's hand for their edification; that there is but *one* foundation, to which nothing could be added. As this foundation then had been already laid among them, in the preaching of the Cross of Christ; nothing remained but for them to raise the proper superstructure upon it—those true doctrines, and those sound religious and moral practices, which belong to, and accord with, their fundamental right profession. If Christians thus adhered to the simplicity of their faith—if their work were faithfully wrought on the one only Foundation, which they had not laid for themselves; it would stand the fiery trial at a future day, and obtain for them a reward. But if their work were ill-assorted to the foundation—if, unlike the gold and silver and precious stones of God's workmanship, it were mere wood and hay and stubble; it would be all lost labour—it would perish in the burning. The builder with these worthless materials, would have bitterly to repent his unprofitable pains, and should at last only barely escape with his life, as one out of a burning house, through the imperishableness of the foundation itself on which he has built.

Both these interpretations agree sufficiently with the context, and the general subject of the Epistle itself, to be regarded with attention : and both have the authority of good critics in their favour. I am inclined, however, to adopt the latter interpretation ; that which applies the passage to the hearer of the Gospel, rather than to the teacher. For it appears to me, that the Apostle is here opposing a check in the minds themselves of his converts, (his Epistle is addressed to the Church at large ; " to the Church of God at Corinth, with all that in every place call upon the name of Jesus Christ ;") to the corrupt teaching by which they were assailed. He could not expect that his admonitions would act immediately and directly on the minds of these false teachers. As they despised his person and address, so would they be little disposed to listen to any cautions he might give them against adulterating the faith of the Gospel. Nor could he be present on every occasion of their seductive teaching, so as to protect his flock against their attacks. But by preparing the minds of his people to discern between a true and false profession of the Gospel,—by inculcating strongly on them the perfect simplicity of a Gospel faith,—he was effectually neutralizing the poison of the false teachers, securing the converts in his absence, as well as when present, and discouraging the false teachers from attempts to win them over by refinements of worldly wisdom.

Before I pass on, however, I should not omit

to notice a third construction, which has been put on the passage before us, according to which it is supposed to give evidence to the doctrine of Purgatory. According to this view, St. Paul is referring to the distinction between mortal and venial sins, and affirming that a day will come, before the day of final judgement, when the sinner, who has not committed such sins as exclude from salvation, shall be submitted to the action of remedial fire—shall endure pains and afflictions, by which his dross shall be purged away; "the wood, hay, and stubble," which he has piled up on the Foundation of Christ, shall be burnt, and himself rescued through this process of sufferings —this remedial fire—and so pass to the life eternal. It is hardly necessary to refute such an exposition of the text. It is evidently nothing more than a mere accommodation of the passage to a doctrine not derived from Scripture,—one of those very refinements of the wisdom of this world, against which the real meaning of the passage is directed. It is plain, that the effect here attributed to the fire, is not to purify and amend, but to "declare" and to "reveal." It is simply spoken of as a test to discriminate the true doctrine and practice,—the faithful profes-

sion of the Gospel,—from all false, adulterated
profession; according to the analogy of Scripture
in other places; as in Zechariah xiii. 9; "And
I will bring the third part through the fire, and
will refine them as silver is refined, and will try
them as gold is tried:" and in Malachi iii. 2, 3;
"But who may abide the day of his coming? and
who shall stand when he appeareth? for he is
like a refiner's fire, and like fuller's soap; and
he shall sit as a refiner and purifier of silver, and
he shall purify the sons of Levi, and purge them
as gold and silver, that they may offer unto the
Lord an offering in righteousness:" and again,
in the Revelation, iii. 18; "I counsel thee to buy
of me gold tried in the fire, that thou mayest be
rich:" and in other places. Then as to the day
here spoken of; there is no ground to suppose that
it refers to any such period as that asserted in the
doctrine of Purgatory. For here also the analogy
of Scripture leads us to apply the expression either
to some great visitation of God in this world;
such as the destruction of Jerusalem, or some
expected outbreak of persecution on the Church;
or else to the great day of final Judgement; and
probably to both; to the former, as types of the
latter; the great Day of Judgement being the

ultimate test of the Lord's faithful servants,—
the crown and completion of those former tests,
which every passing trial in the world has in some
measure furnished. For thus our Lord says, "I
am come to send fire on the earth ; and what will
I, if it be already kindled * ?" referring, in language like our text, to the severe trials which
his disciples would have to undergo in the present
world. And Isaiah, in like manner, " Behold, I
have refined thee, but not with silver; I have
chosen thee in the furnace of affliction †." And
St. Peter, " Beloved, think it not strange concerning the fiery trial which is to try you, as
though some strange thing happened unto you :
but rejoice, inasmuch as ye are partakers of
Christ's sufferings ; that when his glory shall be
revealed, ye may be glad also with exceeding
joy."—" For the time is come that judgement
must begin at the house of God : and if it first
begin at us, what shall the end be of them that
obey not the Gospel of God ? And if the righteous
scarcely be saved, where shall the ungodly and
the sinner appear ‡ ?" Here, indeed, St. Peter
almost expresses the same truth that St. Paul
does in the latter part of our text. For this

* Luke xii. 49.   † Isaiah xlviii. 10.   ‡ 1 Pet. iv. 12, 13. 17, 18.

expression, that " the righteous shall scarcely be saved," appears to be only another mode of stating what St. Paul, as we have already interpreted him, says, that there will be difficulty and suffering in the way of their salvation to those who, professing the true faith, have not held it consistently; that the work of salvation, as far as it rests with man, is a work of hazard—a struggle against temptation—an escape from danger.

We may conclude, then, that the general view of our text, as given in the two leading interpretations of it before stated, is correct.

Now, in whichever of these senses the text be taken, the spiritual lesson conveyed in it is in effect the same. For whether it be addressed primarily to minister or people, it no less warns both minister and people against departing, in any degree, from the simplicity of the Faith as it is in Jesus—against every sort of compromise between the Faith which saves the soul, and the opinions of a specious but carnal wisdom. It tells all of the increased hazard which they run of losing their salvation, by either teaching or listening to the enticing words of man's wisdom; that the foundation may be held, and may happily be the means of saving those who hold it, amidst grievous errors of doctrine and practice which they have built upon it ; but that, though the Christian may in such a case eventually be saved, it will be with great personal sacrifice and fearful hazard, through a course of bitter repentance and extreme suffering. And as this is true of the individual Christian, so is it true also of Christians in their collective capacity—of whole Churches. We may infer from the text before us, that a particular Church may, by God's blessing, preserve the truth which is the charter of its existence,—the doctrine of Justification by Faith only in the atoning blood of the Saviour,—and thus be kept alive among the great families of Christendom ; but that it must pass through the ordeal of severe suffering, and may be brought to the verge of destruction, if it suffer the truth on which it stands to be covered over with corruptions of doctrine or of practice. It will be saved, we may hope ; it will escape from utter extermination, by the firmness of the basis on which its errors are built. Its sound members will survive the surrounding desolation, which will one day visit it. But the fire will separate the gold from the dross—the hard and precious material from the vile and combustible ; and the trial will be a severe one even to those who ultimately survive the test.

The history of the Church has illustrated the practical evil resulting from such refinements. The Gnostic heresiarchs, against whom the Apostle appears to be warning the Corinthians, presumed to carry on their hearers to a perfection of knowledge beyond the elements of the simple saving faith inculcated by St. Paul and his brother Apostles. They were not content, like the true Apostles of our Lord, to preach " Christ crucified,"—a doctrine for the poor, and the weak, and the humble, rather than for the great and wise of the world. But they sought to remove that which was a stumbling-block to the Jew, and foolishness to the Greek. They left the holy truth to be embraced by those grosser natures, as they judged them, which were capable of simply acquiescing in it. But for the higher and more spiritual natures,—for those, that is, whom they found susceptible of intellectual excitement,—such as were anxious rather to satisfy the cravings of a morbid curiosity, than to obtain support to their moral infirmities and needs by the informations of religion,—for these, they had built up a fabric of knowledge, having, indeed, for its foundation the truth declared by the Apostles, but in fact annulling and debasing that truth,— if it could be annulled and debased,—by their mystic expositions. For what did all their teaching, whilst it professed to carry its votaries into the regions of inaccessible light, really amount to, but an attempt to reconcile the doctrine of Christ Crucified to the proud understanding and unholy heart? They taught either that the Christ was distinct from the suffering Jesus; or that there was no reality in the sufferings of Jesus Christ on earth as they were presented to the eyes of men, but that there was merely a phantom-representation of sufferings, from which the Lord of Glory Himself was exempt. Thus did they virtually, by either supposition, deny the proper personality of our Lord, His taking the manhood into God, and His atoning by real sufferings and a real death on the Cross, for the sins of the world. Thus they removed a great part of the difficulty in accepting the doctrine of Christ Crucified to the understanding of their hearers, and the whole of the difficulty to the corrupt heart. To the understanding, instead of the simple mystery of God made man, and coming down from heaven, for us men and our salvation,—a mystery for

angels no less than for men,—was substituted a
dreamy mystery of man's invention, such as the
imagination of man might prompt and readily
follow. And to the corrupt heart, naturally in-
disposed to yield itself to the purifying doctrine
of the Cross, was held forth an excuse for retaining its impurity under its profession of the very
holiest of truths. For he that could blind his
eyes so as to see no *reality* in the awful Sacrifice
made for Sin, would no longer see Sin in that
deadly form in which the simple truth of the
Atonement presents it. The false mysticism
which he had spread over the doctrines of his
faith would extend itself soon to his moral perceptions. Nor were there instances wanting,
accordingly, of persons indulging themselves in
the defilements of sin, and asserting all the while
that sin had no real contact with them ; for that
their perfection could not be sullied even by the
grossest impurities.

That the effect indeed of such teaching was
deeply to corrupt the morals of the Christian
communities, among which it found its way, may
be seen from the earnest reproofs addressed by
St. Paul, in this very Epistle, to a portion of the
Corinthian Church ; from his complaint of their

M

schismatical spirit; their slighting of his authority; their jealousy of each other's gifts and want
of charity; the denial of the Resurrection of the
dead by some of them ; their profanation of the
Lord's Supper; their sensuality.   Hence the
anxiety which he evinces to make them "sorry
with a letter," as he says.   He saw the spirit of
Antichrist working among them with all deceiva-
bleness of unrighteousness ; and he had no rest
in his soul, until he could bring them back to the
simplicity of their faith in Christ.

What, again, has been that great corruption
of the Gospel, which grew up under the teaching
of the Church of Rome, but the result of an
endeavour to carry the doctrine of the Cross to
an imaginary perfection of man's devising,—a
building on the Gospel-foundation with materials
having no solidity or strength in them,—a raising,
as it were, of a city and a tower with men's hands,
whose top might reach unto heaven, but destined,
like the real Babel, only to prove the folly and
wickedness of the design ! For when we listen to
the teaching of that Church, whether expressed
in its formal acts, or in the expositions of its
ministers, what do we learn but an elaborate
scheme for working out the salvation of the

Gospel—a scheme, assuming as its basis, indeed, the foundation laid in the Gospel, but soon losing sight of that foundation, in the counsels which it gives of another kind of holiness—the holiness of the ministrations of its priesthood, and of the discipline prescribed by itself? The principle of its teaching, like that of Gnosticism, is the elevation of the Christian to a knowledge and perfection beyond the simplicity of the Gospel. It professes to develop the truth for him, and to lead him to the method by which he is to apply it to the salvation of his soul. The consequence has been, like that of Gnosticism, that, whilst a theory of transcendental perfection has been taught, and a discipline of extraordinary sanctity professed, by the Church of Rome, a lax casuistry has been introduced into its very bosom; and men, under its training, have practically forgotten that they were the disciples of a faith which crucifies the flesh with the affections and lusts. The Reformation has, happily for that Church, as well as for Christendom at large, proved a fire by which it has been practically, at least in some measure, purified of its corruptions. Theoretically, indeed, those corruptions remain, and much of their practical evil also still remains. But though the Council of Trent formally built up again and cemented together the errors which that fire threatened utterly to consume, it has been powerless to reinstate them in their original form of delusion. It has been shewn that they are but wood, and hay, and stubble, destined for the burning; and that a day will come which shall utterly destroy them, though many, it may be hoped, who have professed them, shall for the Foundation's sake escape with their life.

To come then to the more immediate application of the text to ourselves.

It leads us to inquire of ourselves, whether we are sufficiently alive to the danger here set forth by the Apostle—the danger of being drawn from the simplicity of our Faith by ingenious and seductive words of man's wisdom. The danger, we see, is to persons who have received the pure Faith;—such were the Corinthians, whom St. Paul is here warning;—to persons studious of the gifts of the Spirit. For the Apostle returns thanks to God in their behalf, "for the grace of God which was given them by Jesus Christ, that in everything they were enriched by Him in all utterance and all knowledge, even as the testimony of Christ was confirmed in them, so that they came behind in no gift; waiting for the coming of their Lord Jesus Christ." Because, therefore, we belong to a Church richly blessed in spiritual things, and feel ourselves, as faithful members of it, animated with a sincere love of the Truth as it is in Jesus, we must not think that we are secure against the wiles of false teaching. Rather we ought to be more on our guard on that very account. For it is to win over the seriously disposed,—those whose sensibilities are awakened to religious impressions,—that the language of religious instruction is studiously framed. To such it addresses itself. By the careless and irreligious it passes unnoticed: whilst to the man of earnest devout feeling, whatever presents itself in the form of piety is attractive. And thus has it not unfrequently been found, that in particular places, where the minds of men have been awakened by the faithful ministry of the word, the sectarian teacher has also obtained the greatest influence, and most successfully propagated his tenets, from the very circumstance that men were there alive to the subject. Hence it was, probably, that the false teachers, at the outset of the Gospel, always appear to have followed on the steps of the Apostle,

and to have succeeded in seducing to their heresies some whom he had reason to regard as among
his dearest sons in the Gospel,—the Galatians,
for example, who in the warmth of their zeal
" received him as an angel of God," and the
Corinthians, whom in the Epistle now before us,
he characterizes as " the seal of his apostleship,"
and to whose affectionate feelings towards him he
so touchingly appeals in the midst of his reproofs,
in saying to them, " I write not these things to
shame you, but as my beloved sons I warn you:
for though ye have ten thousand instructors in
Christ, yet have ye not many fathers; for in
Christ Jesus I have begotten you through the
Gospel."

Nor is it such teaching as is in *direct* opposition
to sound doctrine, that always carries with it the
most danger. All are, in great measure, on their
guard against what palpably and ostensibly mili-
tates with their right convictions. But it is false
teaching, which is an approximation to the truth,
—which departs apparently but slightly from it,
—teaching, which professes rather to draw forth,
and explain, and illustrate the truth already possessed,—that may be most effectually applied to
undermine the truth itself. For, as it has been

remarked by writers on politics, that little changes in the government of a state are to be most carefully watched, since such changes are often the beginnings of revolutions ; so in religious teaching, even little variations are to be especially noted as the serious indications of greater intended changes. And though the liability to be abused is no argument against what is undoubtedly good and true, yet in questionable matters we ought to look to such liability, and take our precautions against the probable evil at its rise.

Take, for example, the doctrine of the Sufficiency of Holy Scripture unto Salvation. No teacher would stand any chance of being heard among Protestant Christians, were he to take the direct contradictory of this truth as his thesis. If he desires therefore to gain a hearing, he must commence with the admission of this truth. Then, if he only possess some sophistical talent, it is easy for him to suggest doubts as to the *extent* of the principle,—as to what it includes or excludes,—as to whom, and to what purposes, it is to be applied. Thus may he, by introducing subtile differences and modifications of the principle itself, bewilder the hearer, and lead him to a conclusion—not indeed absolutely contradictory to it in terms, for this would expose the delusion, —but inconsistent with it, and indirectly subverting it by destroying its practical intention and force.

Great, doubtless, have been the errors into which persons have fallen from an improper use of the Scriptures,—from reading them, that is, without preparation of mind and heart, without humility, without prayer, or only to support their preconceived views. But great as these errors may have been, greater, and more widely spread, and more inveterate, are those which have been disseminated by the personal activity of false teachers: and it may seem strange, that whilst the errors into which the private exposition of Scripture has often deviated have been so much noticed and exposed, it has been comparatively overlooked that false teaching has also been a manifold source of heresy and schism. Such was the mode in which those fearful heresies of the early ages took their rise. The heresiarchs of those times would appeal to the Scriptures, and challenge the orthodox to a vexatious warfare on the ground of Scripture. But the strength of their cause lay, not in the Scripture which they perverted, but in their personal talent and address, and their importunate zeal in pressing their opinions on the attention of men.

It is not for us, then, to repose on our advantages, or on our right convictions and feelings, as if these were a perfect security to us against the seductions of error in religious doctrine and practice. Whether as ministers of the Church, or as private individuals in its communion, we are to take heed to ourselves, lest that good thing, which by God's grace is in us, our love of Gospel-truth, and desire to uphold it, should be turned by the adversary of our souls into a snare, and become the very means of our corruption.

Let us accordingly, Christian Brethren, not only know that we have the right foundation, but let us take special heed how we build thereupon,—what principles and views we join with the ground of our salvation. In the day of our ease and prosperity, and amidst the shades of literary leisure, we may be able to assert and defend, with the arms of controversy, by subtile distinctions and guarded statements, many an erroneous principle, which, under the test of that fiery trial of which the Apostle speaks, would not abide for an instant. The many specious attempts which have been made to approximate the true and the false in religion, and adjust and confound them in one scheme, shew, what the dexterity of the acute intellect can accomplish in softening and recommending error, so long as the question of its truth is debated only in the field of controversy. But let the trial of affliction be applied. Let that day come when the work of our hand shall pass through the furnace of the refiner: and then will surely appear the pure gold, and silver, and precious stones of our building, whilst the wood, and hay, and stubble shall be utterly consumed. Let us build then, Brethren, against that day. Let us prepare for that trial. Let it be a small thing to us to be "judged of any man's judgement;" remembering, that "He who judgeth" us "is the Lord:" it is *His* trial, *His* judgement, that we are to abide,—*His* praise that we are to look to, when He shall come to "bring to light the hidden things of darkness," and to "make manifest the counsels of the hearts." Our errors, as the text instructs us, may, by God's mercy in Christ, not be fatal to our salvation. But the text at the same time warns us, that they *may* be fatal. If we escape on the day of trial, it will be at imminent hazard of our lives, we shall be as "brands snatched

out of the fire." And we should misconstrue its
charitable warning, if we did not learn from it,
that he who thus ventures on the brink of ruin,
may haply venture too far, and be himself involved in the destruction of the building of his
hands.

The only safeguard presented to us is constantly
to have an eye to the foundation on which we
stand. As consistent Christians, we must determine with the Apostle, not to know anything
save Jesus Christ, and Him Crucified. This is
our real spiritual knowledge. For in Christ are
hidden all the treasures of Divine wisdom. To
know Him truly, and the power of His death
and resurrection, is the sum of the knowledge of
the Christian man. For he who knows the Son
knows the Father also, and the Holy Spirit by
whom he is enabled to confess that Jesus is the
Christ. He who knows what Christ has done
for his soul, knows how corrupt he is by nature,
and what the strength of sin is, and how unable
he is to stand before God, without the continual
presence of Divine grace in his heart, both to
give him the first motions towards holiness, and
to keep him in the path of life. Ever looking
to Christ, he holds in vital union all those holy

truths, whether respecting the Divine Being or
his own condition in the world, which the Holy
Spirit has written for his instruction and edification in the volume of the Bible.   Looking to
Christ as the only Fountain of Salvation, he keeps
himself sober and watching unto prayer, that he
may obtain the continual " supply of the Spirit
of Christ."   Rejoicing that he has already been
made a partaker of the Spirit in Baptism, he
clings with affectionate devoutness to every other
means of grace ; seeking counsel from the study
of God's word ; communicating with his brethren
in the public services of the Faith ; and nourish-
ing his soul with the spiritual food of the Body
and Blood of his Lord.   And so throughout, in
all his conversation with the world as in all his
belief, he, who with the Apostle determines to
know nothing else but Jesus Christ and Him
Crucified, will prove himself to be the most fully
instructed Christian, and the most devoted follower of his Lord, and thus be the most effectually
prepared for that day, when the fire shall try every
man's work of what sort it is.

Oh that we would indeed, Brethren, make the
Cross of Christ our Life and our Glory ; that we
would bow our imaginations before it ; that we

would hush our perverse disputings in humble
reverence at the awful mystery of the Divine
Love revealed in it; that we would calm our
mutual distrusts and jealousies by the heartfelt
acknowledgment of that unutterably holy tie of
brotherhood in which it unites us all! Do we,
I ask, think of it sufficiently? I mean, not merely
as men of the world, but as men of religion who
desire to serve God faithfully, to work out our
salvation, and enforce His truth by our teaching
and example. I ask, whether in this character
we sufficiently think of Christ as the Lord who
has redeemed us by His Cross and precious Blood?
Or are we not too apt to keep back this holy truth,
—to put forward other truths, rather, in the front
of our profession,—and thus to appear as if we
were ashamed of the Cross of Christ? Far too
sacred, indeed, is the mystery of the Cross to be
spoken of, or thought of, but with the lowliest
reverence,—but with the most thankful, pious
remembrance of the infinite mercy declared in it.
But at the same time, far too sacred is it, ever to
be lost sight of by the believer on any occasion,
or in its connexion with the other truths of his
Faith. For this mystery it is, which holds together the whole Christian faith and life. Our sins,

though repented of, are still imputed to us, unless we nail them with our own hands to the Cross. Our righteousness is but dross and filth fit for the burning, unless it be washed in the blood there poured out. Our belief of each article of our religion is no Christian belief, unless it be held in communion with this one only foundation of Christian life and hope. Shall we dread the reproach of using a profane familiarity with the sacred mystery, in thus giving it prominence in all our religious profession? The Apostles were not afraid of this reproach. "We preach," they say, "Christ Crucified:" "I am not ashamed of the Gospel of Christ." " I determined to know nothing among you save Jesus Christ, and Him Crucified," says that Apostle, who also most abounds in the exposition of Christian doctrine. That reserve, which a mistaken sense of Christian sacredness would suggest, was not St. Paul's mode of shewing his reverence for the mystery. He is ever recurring to it, ever shewing his familiarity with it, and, together with that familiarity, his unabated—nay his increasing—reverence and devotion at the contemplation of it. Like him, then, if our hearts are full, as his was, of the love of Christ, we shall ever be putting forward the

same blessed theme of our Christian thanksgiving
and joy ; like him, acquiring a reverent familiarity
with it, and making it the daily meat and drink
of our souls.

There is indeed an appearance of great reverence in that silence of the devout heart, which
owns the mystery of the Cross, but shrinks from
speaking of it. But let us remember, that it was
under the prevalence of such a notion, that man
was taught to look to the mediation of his fellow-
man and the ritual of the Church for obtaining
the pardon of his sins, so that the Apostolic
doctrine of Justification by Faith only had well
nigh disappeared from the world. We have witnessed, in the history of Romish corruptions, what
the effect is of putting a veil over the mystery of
the Cross ; how men soon learn to acquiesce in
the symbol and external representation, instead
of going for life and strength to the great realities
themselves, and give to secondary objects the
glory which is due to the Cross itself of the
Redeemer. Let us beware, by the light of this
example, how we substitute an imaginative sentiment of awe, for the practical habitual lowliness
of mind which is the true characteristic of Christian devotion. It is our blessed privilege to have

God brought nigh to us. It is in Christ that we
have access to Him. Let nothing then separate
us from Christ. Let us draw near to Him with
faith, believing on Him in the heart, and confessing Him with the mouth unto Salvation;
whatsoever we do in word or deed, " doing all
in the name of the Lord Jesus, giving thanks to
God and the Father by Him." " Rooted and
built up in Him," we shall stand fast on that day
when every man's work shall be made manifest.
Walking with Him in all our trials in the world,
we shall escape unharmed through the fire. For
though we have done much that cannot abide the
test, His help is at hand to those that call upon
Him, and He will surely pluck us out as brands
from the burning.

SERMON VI.

THE ONE SACRIFICE FOR SIN.

PREACHED IN THE CATHEDRAL OF CHRIST CHURCH,

On SUNDAY, February 14, 1841.

SERMON VI.

THE ONE SACRIFICE FOR SIN.

HEB. IX. 27, 28.

And as it is appointed unto men once to die, but after this the
judgement : so Christ was once offered to bear the sin of many ;
and unto them that look for him shall he appear the second time
without sin unto salvation.

I WAS speaking, in my last Sermon from this
place, of the delusion and danger accompanying false teaching in general. My observations
applied to such false teaching as builds its superstructure on *the truth*,—which assumes the
foundation as already laid, and raises upon it
the wood, hay, and stubble of its own inventions,
—such as shews a respect for that which is received among Christians, and adopts it into its
own system, but vitiates and perverts the truth
by its explanations and refinements. I purpose,
on the present occasion, to illustrate this general

N 2

observation in one striking particular,—the perversion of the great doctrine of the Real Sacrifice
made *once for all* on the altar of the Cross, by
the refinements introduced into the subject by
the Church of Rome; and to point out how the
notions which that Church has incorporated with
the true scriptural doctrine of Sacrifice, whilst
they affect studiously to maintain the truth, in
fact lead men widely astray from the truth.

The text is a summing up of the argument of
the Chapter, and indeed of the whole preceding
part of the Epistle, which states the oneness and
perfection of the Sacrifice of the Death of Christ.
The Apostle had been demonstrating the imperfection of the sacrifices under the Law; how they
needed constant repetition and a succession of
priests to carry them on.   Hence it was evident,
he argues, they had no efficacy in themselves to do
away sin, or to render the comers thereto perfect:
whereas the offering of Christ, the Mediator of a
better covenant established upon better promises,
had an intrinsic efficacy to put away sin, and
therefore sufficed, being once made for all.   The
priests under the Law, each in his generation,
were but types of Him who " abideth a Priest
for ever."   The things under the Law, as passing

shadows of the great abiding realities of the
Gospel which they prefigured, must need be
purified again and again with that typical blood
which represented the blood of the Lamb slain
from the foundation of the world. Year after year,
the High Priest must enter that Holy of Holies
in the Temple, which was only the symbol of
the Heaven of Heavens, into which the Eternal
High Priest should pass once for all, never again
to appear before men until He should come to
Judgment. Nothing can bring before us, in a
more forcible and lively manner, the reality, and
the extensive and permanent efficacy, of the One
Sacrifice of the Cross, than the contrast, and
illustration of it, at the same time, here presented
by the Apostle, in his reference to the sacrifices
of the Law. He exhibits it as *first* in the order
of the Divine counsels—as that to which the
whole Mosaic dispensation had reference, and
was subordinate—as perfecting in one mysterious
offering, all that had been shadowed out by the
countless offerings of the ancient Covenant. And
in the text, more particularly, he illustrates the
oneness and efficacy of this the great and emphatically true Sacrifice, by the image of the
congregation waiting without, for the coming

forth of the High Priest from the Holy of
Holies, into which he had gone with the blood
of atonement. The congregation of Israel might
indeed look for *their* high priest; for he would
come forth again, to offer the still needful sacrifice of atonement for his own sins and those of
the people. But the spiritual Israel, the sanctified in Christ, the holy congregation of the Christian Church, must not expect their High Priest
again until He shall come to Judgment. For
His offering is perfect; it is accepted in heaven
as a full and sufficient Atonement for the sins of
the whole world; and there remaineth no more
offering for sin. In that He has died, He has
died unto sin once, and in that He liveth, He
liveth unto God. So that, as the Apostle elsewhere says, Christians must likewise " reckon
themselves as now dead unto sin, but living unto
God." They have nothing now to do but to die
with Christ unto sin; to look unto Him as at
once both the Author and Finisher of their Salvation; and be prepared to meet Him when He
shall appear again, not to bear sin, but to dispense judgment.

The earnestness with which St. Paul throughout this Epistle to the Hebrews dwells on the

absolute oneness and perfection of the Sacrifice
of the Cross, is very remarkable. We find him
recurring to the thought, as what he is most
anxious to impress on the minds of his readers.
It is but a cold commentary on his argument
here, to say that it utterly refuses a Socinian interpretation. This, indeed, it does. For how can
the Sacrifice of the Cross be regarded as spoken
of in accommodation to the Jewish ritual, when,
as the Apostle here instructs us, that Sacrifice is
the *primary truth*,—the *substance*, of which the
sacrifices of the law were but the *shadow*,—the
antitype, of which they were the *type* and imperfect representation? Certainly, those whose
eyes unhappily are blinded that they cannot discern their Lord's glory under the veil of His humiliation, must ever find in the Epistle now before
us a living protest against their error. Nor can
they evade its distinct evidence to the reality of
what they would resolve into metaphor and accommodation, without detracting from the importance of this whole portion of Holy Scripture,
and refusing to accept, what must be felt by
every one as a most satisfactory and elevating
account of the ritual of the Law. But to say

merely that the argument of the Apostle refuses
to be bound down in the trammels of the Socinian
construction, is, as I have said, but a cold view
of his doctrine on the Sacrifice of the Cross. He
draws forth the truth on the subject from the
fountain of Truth itself. He shews how the
reality and perfection of the Atonement made
once for all on the Cross, derive themselves
from the real and perfect Divinity of Him who
offered it ; how all other sacrifices failed of their
object, as expiatory offerings for sins, by reason
of the imperfection both of the offerer and the
victim offered. He leads us at once, at the very
outset of his argument, to the contemplation of
the Eternal Generation of the Son distinguishing
Him from the highest created Intelligences, as
the God whose throne is for ever and ever, and
the sceptre of whose kingdom is a sceptre of
righteousness. He then shews how the Eternal
Son took not on Him the nature of angels, but
of man ; how the Father, in fulfilment of the
ancient types, " prepared for Him a body," that
He might bear the sins of his brethren, and atone
for them in that nature, and taking the manhood
into God exalt it to perfection. Thus does St.

Paul anchor the great doctrine of the One atoning Sacrifice of Christ on the Cross on an immovable rock. After the example of St. Peter, he confesses Jesus to be " the Christ, the Son of the living God," grounding that good confession on the union of the Divine and human natures in the one Person of our Lord.

But strange as is the Socinian denial of the reality of the Sacrifice of the Cross, no less strange, perhaps, is the perversion of the same truth by what the Church of Rome terms the " Sacrifice of the Mass." I say no less strange, not with reference to the comparative enormity of the errors, but on account of that departure which the doctrine of the Mass involves from the admitted truth. The Council of Trent, indeed, refers to this very Epistle in proof of the *one* offering of Christ to the Father " on the Cross," and the " eternal redemption wrought by it." But immediately afterwards it introduces another atoning priesthood, and another atoning offering of Christ, through the ministers of the Church. For the Council asserts, that " it is one and the same victim, the same now offering by the ministry of the Priests, who offered Himself then on the Cross, *the method* alone of the offer-

ing being different*." And it interprets the
Apostle, as if he had said in his account of the
sacrifice, that Christ only shed *his blood once* on
the Cross, instead of simply saying that the *offering* itself there made was but *one*, and could never
be *repeated*. For that Church distinguishes between the Sacrifice of the Mass, as the " unbloody offering," and the Sacrifice of the Cross
as the " bloody offering." Thus, in fact, by its
refinements does it contradict the plain language
of the Apostle, when, speaking of Sacrifice, he

* Concil. Trident. Sess. 22, held Sep. 17th, 1562. "Nam
celebrato veteri pascha, quod in memoriam exitus de Ægypto
multitudo filiorum Israel immolabat, novum instituit pascha
*seipsum ab ecclesia per sacerdotes sub signis visibilibus immo-
landum* in memoriam transitus sui ex hoc mundo ad Patrem,
quando per sui sanguinis effusionem nos redemit, eripuitque de
potestate tenebrarum, et in regnum suum transtulit," cap. 1.

" Et quoniam in divino hoc sacrificio, quod in missa peragi-
tur, *idem ille Christus continetur, et incruente immolatur*, qui in
ara crucis *semel seipsum cruente obtulit*, docet sancta synodus,
sacrificium istud vere propitiatorium esse, per ipsumque fieri, ut,
si cum vero corde et recta fide, cum metu et reverentia, contriti
ac pœnitentes, ad Deum accedamus, misericordiam consequa-
mur, et gratiam inveniamus in auxilio opportuno. *Hujus quippe
oblatione placatus Dominus*, gratiam et donum pœnitentiæ con-
cedens, *crimina et peccata, etiam ingentia, dimittit : una enim
eademque est hostia, idem nunc offerens sacerdotum ministerio*,
qui seipsum tunc in cruce obtulit, *sola offerendi ratione diversa*,"
cap. 2.

says, that "*without shedding of blood* is no remission*;" according to which, evidently, an *unbloody* sacrifice would in truth be *no expiation*. Hence in regular sequence has followed the whole peculiar sacerdotal system of Rome. Hence her sacrificing priests, her many altars, her oblations for the dead and the living, her tampering with the consciences of men in her doctrine of pardon and indulgences, her domination over the Lord's heritage, and other manifold delinquencies of doctrine and practice.

Our Church, with true Christian zeal for the honour of its Lord, has lifted up its voice of remonstrance against this head of corruption; asserting the exclusive and undivided Sacrifice of the Cross in its 31st Article, in those strong words—" The Offering of Christ once made is that perfect redemption, propitiation, and satisfaction for all the sins of the whole world, both original and actual; and there is none other satisfaction for sin but that alone. Wherefore the sacrifices of Masses, in the which it was commonly said, that the Priest did offer Christ for the quick and the dead, to have remission of

---

* Heb. ix. 22. By the tenour of St. Paul's argument, this text applies *à fortiori* to Sacrifice under the Gospel.

pain or guilt, were blasphemous fables and dangerous deceits."

Accordingly whilst, no less than the Church of Rome, we hold the doctrine of the Everlasting Priesthood of our Lord, and believe that He is ever interceding for us with the Father in Heaven, pleading the merits of his death and passion in our behalf, and sending down the gracious gifts of the Holy Spirit to strengthen and assist us; first uniting us to Himself in Baptism, then continually binding us to Him, by the grace vouchsafed to faithful prayer and the spiritual food of his body and blood in the other Sacrament: we are taught by the training of our Church to look for no other expiatory Sacrifice than that of the Cross itself. We do indeed apply the word Sacrifice to the Lord's Supper; but it is in the sense of an eucharistic, not an expiatory or propitiatory sacrifice,—a " sacrifice of praise and thanksgiving;" a symbol and representation, not a repetition, or " unbloody " offering anew, of the once bloody offering of the Cross. We do not degrade that Holy Sacrament which brings before us the lively emblems of the Saviour's Passion, and the preciousness of it to our souls, into a mere commemorative rite. We remember that our Lord has spoken of it, and of its special benefits to his Church, in terms far too holy to admit that construction of it, which would sacrilegiously empty it of its divine mystery and grace. But our Church, at the same time, religiously avoids that notion of it which makes it a propitiatory offering, and which confounds it with the Sacrifice of the Mass.

The more, indeed, we study the language and tone of our Church on the subject of the Eucharist, the more shall we find throughout it a protest against the unscriptural doctrine of the Mass. Is the oblation of Christ spoken of in our ritual of the Eucharist? it is the " full, perfect, and sufficient Sacrifice, Oblation, and Satisfaction, made on the Cross by His one oblation of Himself once offered." Are the oblations and offerings of men spoken of? we ask God to accept our alms and oblations, meaning the fruits of our benevolence towards his Church for Christ's sake ; and we are said to " offer ourselves, our souls and bodies, to be a reasonable, holy, and lively sacrifice unto God." Nor does it allow a *solitary* service of the Eucharist. It inculcates upon us that that service is essentially a *communion*—a communion of Christians in the living body of Christ their life and

head. What again mean those words of our
Catechism, that "the Body and Blood of Christ
are verily and indeed taken and received by the
faithful" in that sacrament—(words which the
Romanist sometimes adduces against us, as an
evidence that we hold in effect his notion of
transubstantiation)—but a marked intimation
that we are not to rest in the emblems of the
body and blood, or in any representative rite,
as if this were a real Sacrifice ; but to lift up our
hearts to the Lord Himself, and fix our thoughts
solely on the One only Atonement of the Cross,
—to feast, in truth, not on bread and wine alone,
—not on mere shadows and types,—but on realities,—*by faith*, spiritually, on that "flesh which
is meat indeed," and that "blood which is drink
indeed." So simply does our Church cleave to
the truth of the *One* oblation of the Cross, and
teach its members to hope for redemption, and
pardon, and sanctification, by *immediate* deriva-
tion from the Everlasting Priesthood of the Saviour Himself.

But this the Church of Rome does not. It
asserts, as our Church does, the One oblation
of the Cross, and the Everlasting Priesthood of
the Lord, as the source of grace and all spiritual

blessing to his people. But this, in fact, is
the very danger of its teaching. If it departed
altogether from the truth, there might be little
fear comparatively of its corruptions. It could
not in fact have survived to this day among the
families of Christ, had it altogether renounced
the saving confession of Christ Crucified. I observed, in my former Sermon, that the Council
of Trent had in vain attempted to re-establish
the errors of doctrine which the Reformation
had fully shewn to be destined for the burning.
It has so far succeeded, however, that it has invested those errors with a plausibility which they
did not before possess*. It has interwoven them
in a specious polemic with the substantive truths
of the Gospel. It has given the world a pretext
for professing those errors and yet maintaining
the very truths which they undermine. It has
given them, therefore, a temporary currency and
a prolonged existence. The same thing has come
to pass in that Church, which was found in the

---

* Speaking of the sacrifice of the mass, the Council throws
in the specious caution, which experience has shewn to be
utterly unavailing except for the purpose of controversy : " Cu-
jus quidem oblationis, cruentæ inquam, fructus per hanc uber-
rime percipiuntur : tantum abest, ut illi per hanc quovis modo
derogetur. Quare non solum," &c.—Sess. xxii. cap. 2.

corrupt Judaism reproved by our Lord. They have kept the word of God and its truth; but they have made it of *none effect* by their traditions. We must beware lest the truth associated with the error, incline us to indulgence to that error, and especially in so capital an article of our faith as the doctrine of the One oblation of Christ on the Cross.

I lay the more stress on this, because there seems a disposition in these times to dwell on the fact that the Church of Rome is a *true* church, —true in its profession of the fundamental truths of the Gospel, and its inheritance of an Apostolic commission,—and to speak with indulgence and extenuation of its gross corruptions. God forbid that we should speak of any individual members of that Church but with the charity of brethren, and with that respect which is due to many of them for their conscientious profession of its system, and whose exemplary devotion and faithful Christian walk may be a shame to many who profess a purer faith. It is the theory or system of the Church to which I refer, and that system, not so much as it is actually professed by its own members, but as it may be indulgently regarded by others not of their communion. Admitting, as we do, that the Church of Rome is, in its origin, a true Church, it is the more necessary, to keep us in allegiance to our own particular Church, that we should protest at the same time most strenuously against those corruptions, which might otherwise too fatally recommend themselves, as parts of the profession of a Church confessedly Apostolic in its origin.

There is a disposition, too, to regard superstition as comparatively harmless ; a notion which, if generally prevalent, would soon prepare the way for a return to the errors of Rome. Persons compare superstition with the evil of positive unbelief. From such comparison they would lead us to infer that, as superstition may be better than unbelief, superstition itself may be tolerated in the practice of the Christian. This is as if, because of two evils one is less than the other, the former may therefore be regarded as good, or at least not very evil. The fallacy is that of the Pharisee in the Parable comparing himself with other men and with the Publican in particular, and complacently inferring his own worth from the comparison. The truth is, neither superstition nor unbelief is to be admitted into Christian practice. Both are to be guarded against, and

O

both at the same time. For they appear each to
bring the other after it in its train. Superstition
is commonly found attended with unbelief even
in the same mind. And unbelief is just that state
of mind, which, if alarmed into some low sense of
religion, takes the form of wild and trembling
superstition. We must not think, then, that we
are at least on the safe side, when we add to the
Gospel errors, of which the excuse is, that the
utmost to be said in their condemnation is, that
they are superstitious. It is no slight condemnation of them that they are superstitious. It
is no insignificant intimation that they do not
belong to the Gospel of Christ.

I pass on to point out another head of corruption which the Church of Rome has brought
in to detract from the simple doctrine of the One
oblation of Christ on the Cross. It is summed
up in one word—its theory of Mortification. It
leads its members, under this theory, to seek to
approach God with other atonements besides that
of the Cross. They are taught that God will
accept their tears, and penances, and self-priva-
tions, and works of charity, as Sacrifices in the
proper sense of the term. Neither in this respect
does that Church inculcate the value of such

sacrifices apart from the Oblation of Christ. To that it attributes their virtue. But in the importance with which it invests them in working out the salvation of the Gospel, it draws off the Christian from a simple reliance on the real Sacrifice of the Cross. He is induced to look at himself, and the process going on within himself, instead of adoring the free mercy and grace of God external to himself and independent of anything he can do. He is taught to aim at an *inward perfection* as his *title of acceptance* with God,—a perfection wrought by his own sacrifices; and not that perfection of which the Gospel speaks, when it tells us of the offering once made on the Cross as that which *perfects* the Christian in the sight of God*.

It is true that the Scriptures do speak of the crucifying of the flesh,—that our Lord does call upon us to make sacrifices,—to take up our cross and follow Him,—to give up our dearest ties of kindred,—to forsake all,—for the kingdom of God's sake;—that, in a particular case, he tells one who sought to be his disciple, that if he would be perfect he must go and sell all that he had and then come. These passages, how-

* Heb. x. 14.

ever, only describe what the spirit of the Christian
is in his warfare with the world, and the devil,
and his own corrupt nature; how he should
resist temptations; how he should be willing to
undergo the severest losses and afflictions, rather
than lose his faith, or act unworthily of it; how
he should be ever in a contrite, lowly state of
mind; feeling his own intrinsic unworthiness, the
dangers with which he is surrounded in the world,
and the awful responsibility laid on him of working out a salvation purchased for him at the cost
of the precious blood of the Son of God; how he
should anxiously and unceasingly strive, through
grace, to attain a conformity to his blessed Saviour.

And in the instance in which our Lord puts
that searching test to the conscience of the rich
man,—" If thou wilt be perfect, sell that thou
hast and give to the poor,"—we ought to consider
the circumstances of the case more closely before
we construe it into a general rule of Christian
perfection. When we thus consider it, instead of
inculcating such a method of *perfection*, it pointedly shews the impracticability of it, and the necessity of seeking perfection in some other " more
excellent way." For here was a person well-

satisfied with himself,—one who flattered himself
that he had kept all the commandments ; and that
by his own works he could attain eternal life.
" What good thing shall I do," was his inquiry,
" that I may have eternal life ? " Our Lord saw
his misapprehension of the goodness by which
man is justified, and by his answer exposed the
weakness of such a reliance as his. He could
not abide the test. " He went away sorrowful,"
we are told, " for he had great possessions*."
How unavailing it was to labour after such a perfection, is more distinctly shewn by what follows ;
when the case is applied by our Lord as a general
instruction concerning the way of Salvation. The
disciples, struck with the difficulty here presented to him that would be saved, put the question among themselves,—" Who, then, can be
saved ? "—when they obtained from our Lord that
pregnant answer,—" With men this is impossible,
but with God all things are possible." The answer very clearly signified that the righteousness
which saves the soul is not of man's own working, but the gift and power of God. Then the
sacrifice to which this person was called, was not,
it should be observed, a self-imposed one. It was

* Matt. xix. 22.

not a self-mortification in the Romanist sense;
but it was one laid on him by our Lord Himself.
It corresponds therefore with those trials and
afflictions, which, not being of our own seeking,
but brought on us by the Divine dispensation,
we must be ready to bear, if we would "have
eternal life," through the Gospel. These it is,
—trials sent by the Divine hand, and adapted
by Him who knows our hearts to our peculiar
deficiencies and needs,—which both form and
exemplify the Christian spirit. In these there is
humble endurance, and submission, and resignation, conformable to the patience of our Lord
Himself, who prayed that the cup of sorrow might
pass from Him, but yet drank it to the dregs,
saying, "Not my will, but thine be done."

Trials of this kind too, it may be observed, are
far more difficult to be borne, and are more real
mortifications, than self-inflicted sufferings. In
self-inflicted sufferings there is the consciousness
of power over ourselves, of superiority over others,
— often a knowledge of relief at hand, and of the
means of extricating oneself: there is also the
approbation of the world, ever disposed to admire
the heroism of self-devotion, besides other considerations of the like kind, to enable the sufferer to

bear them.   Sometimes, too, they are in accordance with a person's natural complexion of mind.
For instance, the man of austere and melancholy
temperament will relish an austere and melancholy course of life.   Those in whom the irascible
feelings predominate, may, without much struggle,
prefer a rigid exclusion from even innocent pleasure, and thus deny one part of their moral nature
while they indulge the other.   There are cases,
doubtless, of this kind.   On the other hand,
we may believe, that there are some, to whom
their self-inflicted mortifications are real privations ; by whom they are undertaken with the
simple intention of subduing selfishness and all
evil passions, and to dispose themselves to serious-
ness of thought.   I am not, however, speaking of
individuals but of principles.   Let such mortifications be undertaken with the purest and highest
motives : still they are not properly Christian
mortifications ; they are the marks of one seeking
perfection by his own ways, and not duly remembering that he is already *dead* with Christ to the
world ; that by his very vocation as a Christian,
not by his own choosing, or by any voluntary
act of his own, he is " a debtor, not to the
flesh to live after the flesh," but " through the

Spirit to mortify the deeds of the body," forsaking " all those things for which the wrath of God cometh upon the children of disobedience."

Admirably has our Church guarded us, if we be only faithful to its teaching, from joining any notion of our own mortifications with our faith in the perfection of the Sacrifice of the Cross. The Church of Rome has ingeniously blended the two together,—maintaining *in terms* the perfection of our Lord's Sacrifice, by deriving from it the merit of all human acts of mortification, yet really destroying its perfection, by allowing anything else to be regarded as a sacrifice. But our Church far more spiritually and effectually, as well as more simply, exhorts us to acts of holiness, and a life conformable throughout to the example of our Crucified Lord, by insisting on the necessity of good works as the fruits of our faith in the One perfect Sacrifice of the Cross. It suffers us not to look upon even our best works as in any sense either expiatory of past sins, or *propitiatory* of the Divine favour for the future; but requires them of us as strictly, for Christ's sake, as if our Salvation entirely depended on them.

To this simplicity, then, of our own Church,

let us, I would add on this point, as in regard to
the Sacrament of the Eucharist, firmly adhere.
Let us not seek plausible arguments, by which
we may reconcile error, or approximations to
error, with the holding of the fundamental truths
of the Gospel. Full as those truths are of high
and incomprehensible mystery, they are very
plain and very simple in the utterance. They
can be suffered to stand forth without diminution or apology. Elaborate attempts, therefore,
to erect an artificial scheme of doctrine, though
they may contain much of the substantial truth
of the Gospel, may with reason be suspected
to be only dangerous recommendations of error.
Some may think that the truth existing in the
system will render the error harmless. But the
fact will be found otherwise. The human heart
readily embraces the error congenial to its own
corruption, and eschews or foregoes the truth
which cuts at the root of that corruption. A
doctrine of penance and human merit, and human
satisfaction for sins, and the mediation of man for
man, approves itself to the carnal mind. It naturally finds its place there ; and soon takes the
form of a transcendental piety. The altars are
set up at Dan and Bethel ; and the Lord's people

are kept away from the one holy altar of His own Temple, where alone His glory and His blessing rest.

Emphatically, indeed, does the Apostle appear to warn us throughout this Epistle, against all encroachment on the doctrine of the One Christian Sacrifice of Atonement. " Be not carried about," he says, " with divers and strange doctrines. For it is a good thing that the heart be established with grace; not with meats, which have not profited them that have been occupied therein. We have an altar, whereof they have no right to eat which serve the tabernacle*." He would have our hearts firmly established on " Jesus Christ, the same yesterday, and to-day, and for ever:" and he inculcates on us, that they who make the vain oblations of sacrifices,—whether sacrifices of God's appointment under the old Covenant, and now abolished under the better promises of the new Covenant,—or sacrifices of their own device,—deprive themselves of their privilege of partaking of the one subsisting Sacrifice of the Cross ; or, as he elsewhere says, they " make Christ of none effect to them." Nor should it pass unobserved, that when he speaks of *our* sa-

* Heb. xiii. 9.

crifices, he speaks of them in a sense of thankful cheerful offerings to God, not as expiatory; and even then as acceptable only through Christ. " By Him, therefore," he adds, " let us offer the *sacrifice of praise* to God continually; that is, *the fruit of our lips* giving thanks in His name. But to do good and to communicate, forget not: for with *such sacrifices God is well pleased* *."

The holy truth, to which I have been directing your solemn attention throughout this discourse, is full of great comfort, as well as of great awe to every Christian soul. The text brings forward the One great and only Atonement for Sin, in connexion with death and Judgment. All have but one appointed time for preparation for the great day of Judgment. Every man dies but once, to receive after that an eternal reward, or eternal punishment, according to what his life has been. Let him cast away the One Atonement made for him by the Sacrifice of his Saviour, during the probation-time of his present life; and there remains for him then only a fearful looking-for of Judgment. Infinite is the mercy of God poured out in the One Oblation of Christ. But its very infiniteness precludes every other ground of hope

* Heb. xiii. 15.

but that. In that there is pardon and purification for the worst of sinners. All sins may be washed away by it; but none can be washed away without it. "There remaineth," as the Apostle declares, "no more sacrifice for sins." He then who, by unrepented sins,—by wilful commission of sin,—by a course of sin against his convictions, against his warnings of providence and grace, his opportunities, his chastisements, his blessings,— undervalues the blood of the Covenant,—he who passes from this world unsanctified by that blood, —must for ever be shut out as unclean from the congregation of the Lord. The Lord will appear again,—no longer, however, "bearing sin,"—but glorious in His majesty as the Conqueror of death and sin, and as the righteous Judge dispensing justice and judgment, and establishing the kingdom of his saints in peace. How shall he, whose sins have crucified the Son of God afresh, look on Him whom he has pierced? Oh, the unutterable anguish of not being able to bear *His* presence, who is the very Life and Joy of the soul; of being doomed to everlasting separation from *Him*, *without whom* there is nothing but death and misery! May He grant us all grace to see, in this our day, that we are not merely the disciples

of One who has taught us the evil of sin and
shewn us how to avoid it by His Example, but
who has made Sin an *accursed thing*, by " *bearing
it*," by himself becoming " a curse," and under-
going its extreme penalties in His own Most Holy
Person! The penitential season to which we are
now approaching, has been wisely set apart for
the more special meditation on this awful view
of the nature of Sin. May we all so apply it,
that, by God's grace, we may be brought to deep
and abiding convictions of the " exceeding sinfulness of sin," and to an unreserved simplicity
of faith in the One only Atonement by which its
curse has been, or ever can be, removed!

Nor, while we dwell on the awfulness of the
subject, let us lose sight of its surpassing, inestimable, comfort. What a joyous thought it
is, that Atonement *has been made* for sin, once
for all! that the Great High Priest has entered
into the Holy of Holies with His own blood, and
by His One Offering perfected for ever them that
are sanctified! It is a joy with which no stranger
can intermeddle,—of which no hand of man can
deprive us,—of which nothing but our own apostasy and unfaithfulness can incur the forfeiture.
Are we then weighed down by the weight of our

unworthiness and guilt? Let us not, indeed, cease to sorrow over our sins. Let us not cease to watch and to pray against them. But, amidst our sorrows of repentance, let us take comfort, looking unto Jesus, the Author and Finisher of our salvation. There is nothing to keep back the truly penitent sinner from the benefits of that Atonement, which we are assured is an effectual Sacrifice for sins, or from the merciful and pre-vailing intercession of Him, who came not "to call the righteous but sinners to repentance." It is enough, that with truly penitent hearts and lively faith, we suppliantly look to Him as our merciful High Priest, now seated at the right hand of God. For our condition here is not one of full assurance. It is one of hope, and patient endu-rance. Like the congregation of Israel waiting without for the coming forth of the Priest from the sanctuary, we are to *wait for* the appearing of the Lord. And "to them that *look for Him*," it is said, "He will appear the second time with-out sin unto Salvation."

Let us not then, Brethren, presume to cast away fear, knowing the infirmities and dangers with which we are beset in the world, and how holy the Lord our Saviour is. But let us, at the

same time, come boldly to the Throne of grace;
not doubting that we shall " obtain mercy," and
find " grace" to help us " in our time of need."
This at any rate is clear; that there is none other
Name given under Heaven whereby we can be
saved; there is no other way of Salvation but
that of Faith in His Blood.   For though the Holy
Spirit is pleased to say, that " the sacrifices of
God are a troubled spirit," and that God " will
not despise the broken and contrite heart," He
has not told us that God will accept these *in
remission of sin.*   They are but " vain oblations"
and the " sacrifices of fools," if they are offered to
God with such presumption of their efficacy.   God
has provided for us a better way.   " Let us therefore," I would conclude in the words of our
Church*, " return unto Him who is the merciful
receiver of all true penitent sinners; assuring
ourselves that He is ready to receive us, and
most willing to pardon us, if we come unto Him
with faithful repentance; if we submit ourselves
unto Him, and from henceforth walk in His
ways; if we will take His easy yoke and light
burden upon us, to follow Him in lowliness,

* Commination Service.

patience, and charity, and be ordered by the
governance of His Holy Spirit; seeking always
His glory, and serving Him duly in our vocation
with thanksgiving."

SERMON VII.

THE WAY, THE TRUTH, AND THE LIFE.

PREACHED IN THE CATHEDRAL OF CHRIST CHURCH,

On SUNDAY, October 30, 1842.

SERMON VII.

THE WAY, THE TRUTH, AND THE LIFE.

JOHN XIV. 6.

*Jesus saith unto him, I am the Way, the Truth, and the Life:
no man cometh unto the Father but by Me.*

How natural was the anxiety here evinced by
the disciples to follow the steps of their departing
Lord! He was going from them, they knew not
whither. The very mode in which He had spoken
of his departure filled them with fearful mysterious apprehensions about the future. With
minds as yet only partially opened to the understanding of the nature of his mission into the
world, they were sorrowing over the departure
of a master and friend whom they revered and
loved,—one for whom they had forsaken all,—
whom they were prepared, as they fully thought,
to follow even to death. But they were now told
that they were to be left alone,—that He was

P 2

going where they could not go along with Him,
—that they would remain a little flock without
their shepherd,—left to endure persecution and
danger, apart from Him whose presence had been
a strength and encouragement—everything indeed—to them, in their new course of life. In
this extremity how natural was their anxiety, as
I said, to learn how they might follow Him still!
Well may we suppose the zealous Peter to have
expressed a feeling common to them all, when
he asked Jesus, "Lord, whither goest thou?"
and to the Lord's answer, "Whither I go thou
canst not follow me now, but thou shalt follow
me afterwards," he replied, "Lord, why cannot
I follow thee now? I will lay down my life for
thy sake." They knew not indeed the weakness
of their own strength. They knew not the depth
of the afflictions of Christ at this time, when, in
the warmth of their hearts, they pledged themselves so entirely to Him. But now doubtless
they were desirous of continuing with Him at
any rate in his persecutions; if they could only
have Him still for their companion and guide,
they were content to bear any hardships through
which He might lead them.

If we inquire why their zeal for their Master,

warm and sincere as it was, should have failed them in the hour of trial,—why those who so feelingly disclaimed the thought of deserting Him, having resolved to follow Him even unto death, should have all forsaken Him and fled, when they were put to the actual test,—we shall find that their zeal as then professed was not a Gospel-zeal in the high sense of that term. This is plain, I think, from the turn which their anxiety took, —from their importunity to know whither He was going, and how they still might follow Him as they had hitherto done. We perceive this more particularly from the words immediately preceding the text, in which our Lord appears to be correcting this erroneous impression on the mind of his disciples respecting the nature of his departure. " Whither I go," he says, " ye know, and the way ye know ;"—an information which greatly surprized them : for it assumed as known the very point about which they were most soli-citous. This surprize was naturally expressed by that disciple who afterwards shewed the like reluctance and slowness in admitting a spiritual conviction. " Thomas saith unto him, Lord, we know not whither Thou goest ; and how can we know the way ? " And then our Lord, in his

answer on this occasion, as on the subsequent
one, when after his Resurrection He vouchsafed
to the hesitating Thomas a conviction of his truth
and Divinity, more explicitly removes the mistaken ground of the apprehension of his disciples,
by the declaration, " I am the way, the truth, and
the life; no man cometh unto the Father but by
me." It was as if he had said; "You are inquiring about the place to which I am going and
the way to it; thinking that I am still proceeding
on the course of my ministry, and that you may
still follow me with the eye of flesh and witness
my labours with your bodily presence. But the
things concerning me in the flesh have an end.
The way which I go is an invisible one. Henceforth you can only follow me by the eye *of faith*.
You will be my disciples and followers as you
walk *by faith*,—as ye look up *to me* and walk after
my example; regarding me as *all in all* to you,—
as the way, the truth, and the life,—the only
WAY by which your Father in heaven is to be
approached." Then proceeding to open to them
the mystery of his union with the Father in the
Godhead,—of the indwelling of Himself in the
Father and of the Father in Him,—He tells them
that in seeing Him they had seen the Father;

intimating, as before, that the knowledge of God and enjoyment of his presence were henceforth to be sought through Him alone,—and that, not by an earthly fellowship and converse with Him such as they had hitherto had during the days of his ministry,—but *by faith* in Him,—by believing in Him as they believed in God ; going to Him as *the way* ; knowing Him as *the truth* ; living in Him as *their life.* " Lord, shew us the Father," said Philip, " and it sufficeth us." They thought of some other way of seeing God than in Him. What then was his answer? " Jesus saith unto him, Have I been so long time with you, and yet hast thou not known me, Philip ? He that hath seen me hath seen the Father ; and how sayest thou then, Shew us the Father ? Believe me that I am in the Father, and the Father in Me ; the words that I speak unto you I speak not of myself; but the Father that dwelleth in Me, He doeth the works."

This very emphatic manner in which our Lord points to Himself as the Way, the Truth, and the Life,—while it corrected the mistaken zeal of these his first chosen disciples, and prepared their minds for the fuller revelation of the mysteries of the kingdom of God, first by Himself during the forty days of his sojournment among them after his Resurrection, and afterwards by the effusion and inspiration of the Holy Spirit,— cannot but be regarded as a strong admonition to his disciples of all ages against the like error. None must think that there is any way of knowing God, worshiping and obeying God, and of having the life of God formed in them, but through Christ; or that there is any other way open to the Christian but that which leads *directly* to Him at once, as the means and the end of the Christian's walk through the world. Are the disciples of Christ ever disposed now to ask, " Lord, whither goest thou?" Christ has given them an answer, " Whither I go ye know, and the way ye know." It is enough that you look to Me. It is enough that you believe in Me. " I am the Way, the Truth, and the Life : no man cometh to the Father but by Me."

We cannot read anything said or written by the Apostles, without observing how scrupulously they bear out our Lord's instruction on this head. It is Jesus Christ whom they ever preach directly and immediately. It is no other way that they teach,—no secondary, indirect, additional way of coming to God,—but only Jesus Christ. It is in

the name of Christ that they go forth to publish
the Salvation of the Gospel. It is into Christ that
their converts are baptized. It is Christ that is
proclaimed by them, as " the end of the law for
righteousness to every one that believeth*." The
case is not, as has been hastily concluded by
some, that they require nothing more of the believer than a simple acknowledgment that Jesus
is the Christ. The fulness of their teaching on
all the great articles of faith is a sufficient refu-
tation of such a statement. But what I would
point out as so evident in their preaching is, that
Jesus Christ is ever put forward by them as first
and midst and last in all the approaches of the
Christian to God, whether in order to Christian
knowledge or Christian holiness ; and that they
thus strictly exemplify the great Christian principle taught by our Lord Himself, that no man
cometh to the Father but by Him.

In like manner, when we come to the writings
of those who immediately follow them, as the
Apostolic Fathers, Clement and Ignatius, we find
them full of the savour of Jesus Christ. Having
received the truth fresh from the hands of the
Apostles, they shew from whom they had learned

* Rom. x. 4.

it by reproducing the Apostolic character in their own instructions to the Church. It is Christ accordingly, and the faith in Him, that they also preach throughout. Without reference to any other, any subordinate, or indirect, way by which the disciple may be brought to God, they inculcate the simple doctrine proclaimed in our text, that Christ is the Way, the Truth, and the Life.

But yet, whilst the pure doctrine of Christ was thus preserved by the Apostles and their immediate successors, there began that very corruption on this head which has been a fruitful source of other corruptions of the faith, and has subsisted down to these days,—the introduction into the Church of *another way* besides Christ Himself,— another way *in addition to* Christ, not absolutely superseding Christ, but bringing in other agents into the scheme of the Gospel.

It would seem hardly credible to us, did not history report the fact, that in the face of these strong declarations of our Lord, teachers under the Christian name,—teachers too professing superior knowledge of the truth,—and at a time when the voice of the Apostles had not long ceased to sound in men's ears,—should have

studiously inculcated the notion of a Truth and a
Life distinct from the Saviour Himself. Among
the mystic beings introduced by the Gnostics into
their system, we find the personifications of Truth
and Life. Such personifications may seem to us
absurdly fanciful, because in the present state of
knowledge, and with our habits of thought, we
feel no temptation to reveries of so wild a character. But they are worthy of our attention, as
instances of the working of the human mind on
that Gospel-truth, which has been given to discipline and to prove it. They are only peculiar
illustrations of the principle, which is even now
exemplified, of the natural tendency of man to
refuse the simplicity of the Gospel, and to receive
its truths, not as what they really are, the direct
and ultimate objects of our belief in themselves,
but as mere elements in a complex system,—the
bases of a fabric of theological speculation.

Do we imagine that the presumption and the
folly of these early attempts to facilitate the advance of the soul towards God, by multiplying
the number of subordinate agents, and thus refusing the one great and simple principle of faith
in Christ only, have ceased with the breaking
of its tissue of speculation? Let us look to the

Church of Rome, and inquire whether this Church has not, though in a less palpable form, equally contradicted the words of Christ declaring Himself the Way, the Truth, and the Life.

What then must we say of the peculiar importance attributed by the Church of Rome to the notion itself of *the Church*? What in its origin means that very personification of the Church (which occurs also in the Gnostic system) which is now so prevalent, and so established indeed in ordinary use, that many employ it familiarly in speaking and writing, without thinking any more than in other phrases of speech of the first intention of the expression? I do not, of course, mean to say, that the expression may not be used, as it often is, to give dignity or animation to style, and to express a lively feeling in speaking of the Church, without derogating from the supremacy of Christ; nor that we may not take up the language of the beautiful analogy of Scripture, under which the Church is described as the bride or spouse of Christ. But the principle of the Gnostic corruption of the faith in Christ lurks under the personification of the Church, when that personification is applied to the matter of doctrine, as it is by the Church of

Rome. When the Romanist, for example, speaks of the Church, as that " out of which there is no salvation," and as " the holy mother" of Christians, or as dictating by an infallible authority the rule of faith and the particular doctrines to be believed, it is here plainly applying to the Church what belongs exclusively to Christ Himself. For it is *without Christ* that there is no salvation—it is in Christ that we are born again and adopted into the family of God—it is in Christ alone that all the treasures of divine wisdom are contained. In Him alone is the Truth without the possibility of falsehood or error. It is His word alone that possesses in itself authority to declare the truth. The Romanist may say that he does not intend to exclude the Saviour from this supremacy in the Christian scheme— that he regards the Church as holy, only as it is founded on Christ, and as it is instinctive with His Spirit. But if, in speaking of acts proper to the Saviour Himself, the Romanist drops the mention of Christ and substitutes that of the Church, the Church is then presented to the believer as the immediate and principal agent in the work, and *practically* becomes to each member in itself the *way*.

Again, though persons may not go the whole length of the Romanist representation of the Church, it is possible so to put forward the importance of the. ministerial office, and of the Church in general, under the name of *Church-Principles*, as to lead men to think more of the Church than of Christ—of the body than of the Head of the body. Who, indeed, would deny that Church-principles are right, or that we ought to uphold them and be actuated by them? But where is the foundation and the soundness of Church-principles, unless they are the same as Gospel principles—unless they are rooted and grounded in Christ,—unless they point to Him exclusively as the Way, the Truth, and the Life? The term indeed may be limited to denote the true principles of Church government, and order and authority. Nor can there be any objection to such a limitation of it. But the wrong application of it, on account of its tendency in such case to mislead, is, where Church-principles are constantly or chiefly represented to the believer as the great object of his pursuit in following out his religion. Let it be granted that the teacher who adopts this language, has no design of keeping the doctrine of Christ out of sight, or of undervaluing its importance. But he does practically keep it out of sight; he does in effect undervalue it, when he forbears to exhibit the most promi- nent point of the Christian scheme as the *most* prominent, and is constantly insisting on another point, which, though highly important, is not the *most* important. Let it be granted, too, that the needs of particular times may call for a more frequent reference on the part of the Christian teacher to certain truths comparatively not so important as others. Still it requires great dis- cretion so to treat these comparatively less im- portant subjects,—as those, for example, popu- larly understood under the name of Church- principles—that we may not divert attention altogether from the one paramount doctrine of Christ alone as the *Way*. Our own Church pro- poses to us a wise and safe example in this respect; when in the 19th Article it describes "the visible Church as a Congregation of faithful men, in which the pure Word of God is preached, and the Sa- craments be duly ministered according to Christ's ordinance, in all those things that of necessity are requisite to the same." Here we have the faith- fulness of the members put in the front, and the object of their faith, the pure Word of God, and

the great instruments of grace, the Sacraments;
particulars, all having direct reference to Christ
Himself. The order and authority of the ministrations exercised in the Church are doubtless
implied in this description. But we may observe,
that they are not brought prominently into notice
in the description of the Church. Our view is
directed, where Scripture directs it, to Christ as
the Way. We are not told, as the Romanist
is, that the Church makes Christians, but, on
the contrary, that Christians make the Church.
Wherever Christ is—wherever two or three are
gathered *in his name*—wherever He is believed in
and followed as the Way, the Truth, and the
Life; there we shall find the necessary elements
of a congregation of faithful men. And though
in some cases, through untoward circumstances,
there may be wanting some portion of the right
constitution and order of a Church, we may
expect that, in the great majority of cases, that
form of Government which has descended with
the Christian Truth itself, will also be religiously
maintained, wherever the Truth itself as it is in
Christ is maintained; and that *thus* accordingly
the right Church-principles will be best secured
by inculcating right Gospel principles. Such is

the tenour of St. Paul's instructions to Timothy as to the mode of edifying the Church. He reminds Timothy of the grace of the Lord in coming into the world to save sinners—of the " One Mediator between God and man, the man Christ Jesus, who gave himself a ransom for all*." He speaks to him of the " good minister of Jesus Christ," as one " nourished up in the words of faith and of good doctrine†." He bids him " remember that Jesus Christ was raised from the dead, according to his Gospel ‡," clearly intimating that the doctrine of Christ Crucified had been the substance of his preaching ; as he elsewhere explicitly says, " We preach Christ Crucified." He sets forth to him " God manifest in the flesh, justified in the Spirit, seen of angels, preached unto the Gentiles, believed on in the world, received up into glory ;" as the " great mystery of godliness,"—the great truth to be taught in order to holy living against seducing innovations,—the doctrine by which he should " both save himself and them that heard him §."

Following our Lord Himself as the Way,—the only Way,—we shall also lay hold of the Truth.

---

* 1 Tim. ii. 5.   † 1 Tim. iv. 6.

‡ 2 Tim. ii. 8.   § 1 Tim. iv. 16.

Coming to Him we obtain the Truth at once beyond the reach of doubt. Those who rely on secondary means for arriving at the Truth, have at most only probability to depend on ; compared with which, the Word of the Lord Himself is as the clear and full light to the shadowiness of the twilight. In controverted questions, indeed, and all matters of difficulty in the study of Scripture and its doctrine, it is necessary to call in the aid of the skilful and judicious interpreter to guide the judgment of the generality of believers. And whether in such questions and difficulties, or in receiving and applying to our edification, the truths necessary to Salvation,—the instructions and exhortations of the ministers of Christ ought to be listened to with deference and obeyed with gladness. For the authorized ministers of Christ are of his appointment, to accompany his word —to dispense to his household the meat which He has Himself provided for them. Let not the Scriptural Christian therefore reject the aid of human guides to the truth, or speak of such guidance as is supplied in the ministry of our own Church, as otherwise than most useful *in all cases*, and in some cases *even necessary* for a right judgment respecting the Truth. But to look to

the authority of the guide as infallible,—to regard
it as essential to the filling up of the deficiencies
of Scripture,—to the stating of what is only suggested by Scripture,—to the fixing of interpretations of Scripture,—to the ruling of points left
ambiguous in Scripture,—thus to look to the
authority of our human guide to the Truth,—is
in fact to look to some other source of the Truth
than to Christ Himself. It is at any rate to
depend on *secondary* means, instead of going at
once, as we are desired, to the fountain of Truth
itself. " Lord, to whom shall we go ? " was the
earnest question of St. Peter ; and his faith gave
the ready answer, " Thou hast the words of eternal life*." Such also should be the first and
last thought of every disciple, in every age of the
Gospel, in his inquiry after the Truth.

This immediate and direct reference to Christ
would be a sure anchor to us against the waver-
ings of disputation, and the scepticism arising
from it. Why has the Roman Church claimed
for itself an infallible authority ? and why has
the assertion of such an authority proved so
important, both for securing its members, and
for gaining over proselytes ? The reason is plain.

* John vi. 68.

That Church has raised disputations by its attempts to arbitrate questions beyond the written Word, and created a necessity for laying the restless spirit which it has excited. The great question which it first proposes is, not where the Word of God is to be found,—not where Christ is,—but who are the proper guides to the Truth? involving the hearer, at the very outset of his profession, in the perplexity of deciding between the conflicting claims of different guides. For itself, it cuts the knot of the difficulty by declaring its own infallibility. For its members and proselytes, it suggests a ready relief, by tempting them to acquiesce in a claim which saves the disquietude of all further investigation. Now, in going at once to Christ revealed to us by his Word, giving up ourselves entirely to Him by faith, and accepting all his doctrine in simplicity, we look at the Gospel with a singleness of eye and heart. We then feel that we have taken our stand on a rock, and that we can hear the beating of the storm, and the tossing of the waves around us, without disturbance of spirit.

Advocates of Rome object to us, that we have no resting-place when we quit the assumption of an infallible Church; and they point to the wild excesses of some Protestants as instances of the instability of our footing. We do not own such excesses as any cases in point. They are instances of persons who are *not of us*,—who have gone from the Protestant principle of Faith in Christ only, and have set up other ways besides Christ, —formed for themselves other guides, instead of taking Christ Himself for their first and proper and only authoritative Guide. Instances occur of the like restlessness on the part of members of the Church of Rome. But this spirit is there suppressed by the concession of the infallible authority of that Church ; or is diverted into channels which give it vent ; as by the institution of monastic orders creating employment for the uneasy and the busy within its bosom. When, on the other hand, a comparison is instituted of the several Communions among Christians, and we are called to choose from among them our guide in the interpretation of God's Word, we are challenged to an unwholesome exercise of private judgment. We are then led to view the several Communions among Christians as only so many various theorists on the matter of Revelation. The question then practically comes to this ; which offers us the

greatest security? The Communion which answers such a requirement is obviously the Church
of Rome. For this may be the right one, say its
advocates, even according to the admission of
those who differ from it; but *must be* the only
right one, if it is itself to be believed. By denouncing as wrong and full of danger all that are
separate from it, it holds itself forth as at any
rate the *safest* guide. Scripture certainly does
not call upon us *thus* to judge for ourselves.
It bids us prove all things, and hold fast that
which is good,—to reject, that is, whatever does
not belong to the revealed Word. But it directs
us to *one Truth* only,—the Lord Jesus Christ and
his doctrine. Holding Him as the Truth therefore, and whatever is not of Him,—whatever
derogates from the exclusiveness of his Mediation, or the honour due to his name, and the
reverence of his Word,—as false,—we can most
consistently deny the imputation of making it
a matter of indifference what a man believes,
because we do not admit an infallibility in the
Church. We can still truly affirm that, as there
is but one Lord, so there is but one Faith; according to the 18th Article, which says; "They
are to be had accursed that presume to say that

every man shall be saved by the law or sect which
he professeth, so that he be diligent to frame his
life according to that law and the light of nature.
For Holy Scripture doth set out unto us only the
Name of Jesus Christ whereby men must be
saved."

Lastly, let us consider the remaining point of
view, in which our Lord here, as also in other
passages of Scripture, would have us think of
Him. He is not only the Way and the Truth,
but He is also the Life. " As the Father hath
Life in Himself," he says elsewhere, " so hath
He given to the Son to have Life in Himself *."
Of that Life inherent in Him, He gives also to
His disciples, that they may live by Him and in
Him ; first, by his justifying righteousness raising
up those that were dead in trespasses and sins,
and then, by the gift of His Spirit quickening
them with the inward holiness of a new life unto
God ; as it is said by St. John, " In Him was
life ; and the life was the light of men †." Whatever illumination we obtain,—whether in being
turned from a state of sin and condemnation to a
state of righteousness and pardon, or in inward
strength and comfort of the Holy Spirit,—it is

* John v. 26.   † John i. 4.

all derived from the Life of Christ,—from Christ dwelling in our hearts by faith. He is thus " our Life." In Him truly we " live and move, and have our being." How shall the Christian then not freely use his privilege of coming at once to Christ his only Mediator,—the only proper direct channel of grace,—the only Person through whom the Father will receive him, and by whom the Holy Spirit, the Lord, and Giver of Life, descends to him? How shall he be kept back to wait on other mediators and intercessors, when Christ Himself has said, *Come to Me*? He has been brought up in the simple way of Christ,—taught to regard justification by faith only in Christ, and sanctification by the Holy Spirit the gift of Christ's intercession and prayers, as cardinal principles of his religion. How shall he be tempted to resort to other mediators and intercessors to help him on the way to Christ, when Christ himself is standing at his door, nearer to him than any other mediator can be, readier and more willing, and more powerful to help, than any other mediator can be? No other mediator has ever invited us to call upon him ; no other has ever promised to give the desired succour ; no other is entitled to be addressed with the attribute of sovereign Divinity as the Hearer of Prayer, or adored in the House of Prayer, the Lord's own House. Why then shall the Christian turn aside from the Throne of grace itself, to ask for an officious and unwarranted intercession of others?

Why however should we not obtain every help, —the kind services and prayers of all we can,— to second our addresses to the Throne of grace? some will say. If we may not pray to Saints and Angels, may we not pray with them, or at least ask their prayers? if we may not invoke or call upon them, may we not call to them, or repeat their names in our prayers?—Now were it a case of intercession with man, then we might solicit all the aid within our reach, to enable us to obtain the object of our supplication. But when He is God and not man whom we approach, —when it is the grace of spiritual life that we are asking,—all other assistance is superfluous, if even it were not wrong. But it is wrong also, as interposed between the Giver of grace and the soul which is to receive grace. It encumbers, instead of speeding the soul in the approach to the Saviour. To speak of this secondary mediation as not derogating from the sole mediation of Christ, because we need only ask the *prayers* of

Saints and Angels,—because we need not invoke their aid, but only call to them,—this appears to be only a solemn trifling with words. For what is it to pray to a saint for his prayers, but to pray for his aid? What is it to call to him in acts of devotion, but to make him an object of religious supplication? And has not our Saviour Himself said, *I will pray the Father?* Has He not, whilst proclaiming Himself "the Way, the Truth, and the Life," reserved also to Himself the prerogative of commending our prayers to the Father, and being addressed in prayer as an Intercessor?

But if we may not interpose the mediation of Saints and Angels between the Saviour and the Christian soul, for the same reason also we must not delegate the Saviour's office to his ministers on earth. They are the ministers of God indeed in things pertaining to *men.* They are to preach God's word, to teach, and exhort, and admonish, and comfort, in God's name,—to watch over the fold as God's shepherds,—to superintend the household as God's stewards,—to administer the sacraments of the Gospel, as the appointed dispensers of the life and strength which He gives by those holy ordinances. But they are not the ministers of *men* in things pertaining to God, under the Gospel. There is but *One* who stands before God in man's stead, even the Lord Jesus Christ. All other ministers are His ministers, doing service for Him, and officiating in His behalf,—calling on men to be reconciled to God, and accept that Life which He freely offers them. Thus St. Paul, characterizing the ministration of men, says, " That God hath given to us the ministry of reconciliation ;" adding, " now then we are ambassadors for Christ, as though God did beseech you by us ; we pray you in Christ's stead, be ye reconciled to God *." But, on the other hand, when he would characterize the ministry of Christ, he says, " For every High Priest taken from among men is ordained for men in things pertaining to God, that he may offer both gifts and sacrifices for sins †."

Had this simple view of the ministerial office among men been strictly maintained, the Church would never have witnessed the gross error of the *opus operatum* attributing an intrinsic efficacy to the sacramental rites in themselves. Nor would the tenets of Transubstantiation, and Con-

* 2 Cor. v. 19, 20.
† Heb. v. 1. See Outram De Sacrif. lib. i. c. 19. p. 220.

substantiation, or any other attempt to explain the mode in which the Body and Blood of Christ are received in the Lord's Supper, have found a place in Christian Theology. For what was the occasion of these tenets, but the assumption of a power on the part of Christ's ministers which did not really belong to their office? The *hoc facite* would not have obtained the interpretation, "*sacrifice this*," if Christian Ministers had not disregarded the essential difference between their priesthood and that of their Lord. Nor would the expression of *making* the Body and Blood of Christ have ever been used by them, had it been duly remembered, that the Lord had not appointed his ministers to *do* anything in behalf of his people as in their stead,—for that He had done all that was necessary for them *Himself*,— but only to publish *his* Salvation,—to proclaim what *He* had done,—as stewards to dispense that bread of God, which He broke for his people when He died on the Cross, and that wine, which He poured out when He shed His blood for the remission of their sins. The Roman Church speaks of a *change* as effected in the elements themselves at the Lord's Supper by the act of its ministers. The Gospel knows no other change in the Sacrament than that of spiritual efficacy for the nourishment of the faithful soul by the Body and Blood of Christ. It only remains for his ministers to dispense the benefits which the Lord has annexed to the faithful reception of this Sacrament. It is He who has already blessed the bread and wine to their sacred purpose by his institution and promise. It is theirs to dispense the blessing from time to time, by consecrating bread and wine in memory of his death and passion, and distributing the same according to his holy institution. We do not regard Him as less really present to the faithful in the Holy Communion, because we reject the notion of a corporeal or substantial Presence in the consecrated elements. For a spiritual Presence is as real and true as a corporeal or substantial one. And what more reality and truth can we desire, than the Lord Himself immediately present to us in our hearts, as our spiritual food and sustenance, —the bread and wine of our spiritual life,—our Life itself? Every devout and holy communicant, having eaten of that bread and drunk of that wine, may say with the Apostle, "I live, yet not I, but Christ liveth in me*," "To me, to live is Christ†," "Christ is my life‡."

* Gal. ii. 20.   † Phil. i. 21.   ‡ Col. iii. 4.

Let us then, Christian Brethren, be most religiously careful to preserve the simplicity of our faith in Christ. Let us not imagine ourselves secure from any violation of that simplicity, because we hold the doctrine of Christ in its essential truth, believing in his Divinity and Atonement and Intercession and abiding Presence with his Church; and because we refer all that we have, and all that we do, in order to salvation, to Him *ultimately* as its Author and Giver. But whilst we firmly hold the doctrine of Christ, let us beware of *doctrines* of supererogation, still more even than of imaginary *works* of supererogation,—the addition of other doctrines, which, though in sound deferential to the great fundamental truths of the Gospel, overlay and obscure and weaken those truths. We are apt to regard as eminently pious, those who impose on themselves certain rules of strict observance in their religious exercises and devotions,—who superadd to the precepts and counsels of the Gospel counsels of their own wisdom or piety. Thus have the monastic orders obtained by way of excellence the title of the *Religious*. So also are persons apt to look with awe and reverence on a complex system of religious doctrine and ritual, and to give it the credit of those devotional feelings which it accidentally awakens in the beholder. This is a great temptation coming to many from the Church of Rome. Our own simplicity looks naked and cold to those, whose imaginations have been excited by the mystic elevation and symmetry of its scheme of doctrine, and the solemn pageantry of its ritual. They feel themselves drawn towards it by the interest which it excites. They begin to think, that to our soundness of foundation something at least may be *added* of that attractiveness of doctrine and ritual, which there invests with a charm even what they cannot, must not, approve. But *decipit exemplar vitiis imitabile.* If there be real faith any-where,—if there be real devotion,—if there be real love of God and charity towards man,—wherever there is any virtue, or wherever there is any praise, —let us admire and imitate it, though it be from enemies that we learn it. But let us not be be-guiled of our simplicity in Christ. Let us guard against slight and gradual aberrations from the pure faith. The slightest deviation from right often involves the most serious and fatal wrong. And however desirable reconciliation of differ-ences may be, there is far more fear of compro-mise and adjustment than of bold and decisive

yet temperate opposition. O let us not seek, if
we have gone astray from the Faith in any particular, or have forgotten any instruction of our
Lord, to return by the hand of the Church of
Rome, the great mother of corruptions and dis-
sensions. But let us go at once to Jesus Christ.
Let us retrace our way to the "Rock from whence
we were hewed" and the "hole of the pit from
whence we were digged;" and let us ask of Him
forgiveness, and illumination, and strength, and
comfort in the Holy Ghost; and He will assuredly
take us back to Himself, and cause us to return
to the point from which we may have departed.
Let us stedfastly remember that He is the Way,
the Truth, and the Life, and that no man cometh
to the Father but by Him. Brethren, let us
patiently and devoutly wait on Him. So, if our
faith have become weak and our love cold, He will
renew our strength, He will kindle us with new
warmth; then shall we "mount up with wings
as eagles; we shall run and not be weary; we
shall walk and not faint." It was by thus waiting
on the Lord Himself that our Church renewed
its strength at the Reformation. Thus, too, when
in the early part of the last century the embers of
our altars became languid and dull, the flame was

kindled up by the Spirit of the Lord reminding us of Him, and calling us to Him, who is the Way, the Truth, and the Life. And thus only may we hope that the same Blessed Spirit will revive a true Gospel-zeal among us ; if we but follow his guidance simply and earnestly to the Lord Himself. Woe is unto them who seek any other way. " Woe to the rebellious children, saith the Lord, that take counsel, but not of me ; and that cover with a covering, but not of my spirit, that they may add sin to sin ; that walk to go down into Egypt and have not asked at my mouth ; to strengthen themselves in the strength of Pharaoh, and to trust in the shadow of Egypt ! Therefore shall the strength of Pharaoh be your shame, and the trust in the shadow of Egypt your confusion*."

* Isaiah xxx. 1–3.

R

SERMON VIII.

THE FAREWELL CHARGE.

PREACHED IN THE CATHEDRAL OF CHRIST CHURCH,

On SUNDAY, January 22, 1843.

R 2

SERMON VIII.

THE FAREWELL CHARGE.

---

2 Tim. iv. 1–5.

I charge thee therefore before God, and the Lord Jesus Christ, who shall judge the quick and the dead at his appearing and his kingdom; preach the word; be instant in season, out of season; reprove, rebuke, exhort with all long-suffering and doctrine. For the time will come when they will not endure sound doctrine; but after their own lusts shall they heap to themselves teachers, having itching ears; and they shall turn away their ears from the truth, and shall be turned unto fables. But watch thou in all things, endure afflictions, do the work of an Evangelist, make full proof of thy ministry.

WE are forcibly reminded in this most interesting passage of the parting word of exhortation and blessing addressed by Moses to Joshua. It would seem indeed that the Apostle, in thus writing to his beloved son in the Gospel, had this former occasion, so like that in which he was himself now placed, immediately before his eye.

Moses had received an intimation from the Lord, that the course of his ministry was done, and that he was to go up to Mount Nebo and die. But he was not to depart without first appointing his successor, and giving that successor a solemn charge in the presence of all Israel. It was not enough that he should exhort the people themselves to remember the mercies they had received at the hand of God, and both encourage and warn them with solemn admonitions. But he was commanded to give a charge to their future leader,— to prepare him for rightly entering on those duties which now devolved upon him,—and strengthen and comfort him in order to the due discharge of them. So now " Paul the aged," being apprized by revelation that the time of his departure is at hand, gives a farewell charge to Timothy, whom he is about to leave as successor to a portion of his labours in the Gospel ; in the presence of the Christian Church ; as Moses had in the presence of Israel and in the Tabernacle before the Lord ; and embodies that charge in a writing composed for the instruction and edification of the Church at large. Each comes to the subject with a mind impressed deeply with the thought of his own removal now at hand ; not only ex-

ecuting a commission from the Lord, in appointing a successor to his office, but at the same time
bequeathing a charge near to his own heart to a
loved fellow-labourer and friend. The burthen
too of their respective admonitions is the same.
Both have their fearful forebodings of mischief
about to happen to the objects of their pastoral
care, when they should be taken away from them.
The Lord had revealed to Moses that the people
of Israel would fall away from their faithfulness ;
and that, in consequence of their idolatry and disobedience, many evils and troubles should befall
them. "For I know," he says, "that after my
death ye will utterly corrupt yourselves and turn
aside from the way that I have commanded you :
and evil will befall you in the latter days ; because
ye will do evil in the sight of the Lord, to provoke
him to anger through the work of your hands*."

In the foresight of these impending evils, he
exhorts Joshua to "be strong and of good courage ;" for that the Lord would be with him,—
the Lord would not "fail him or forsake him ;"
he should not therefore "fear or be dismayed."
So too the Apostle Paul founds his solemn call
to exertion on the part of Timothy, on the fore-

* Deut. xxxi. 29.

sight vouchsafed to him of the impending troubles of the Church. " The time will come," he says, " when they will not endure sound doctrine ; but after their own lusts shall they heap to themselves teachers, having itching ears ; and they shall turn away their ears from the truth, and shall be turned unto fables."

The coincidence that I have remarked between these two most interesting occasions,—the legislator and leader of Israel transmitting his office to his successor, and the Apostle of the Gentiles consigning the prosecution of his labours and afflictions in Christ to his beloved son Timothy,—may suggest some useful observations both for the right understanding of the passage of Scripture now before us, and our own practical edification, whether as ministers or hearers of the Gospel.

First, let us observe the correspondence of the circumstances of the two cases. Both charges were given by persons specially raised up by the Providence and Grace of God for the offices which they respectively fulfilled, and who were providing for the future administration of a new order of things which they had themselves instituted and established. As by the hand of

Moses the Lord brought out of Egypt the children of Israel for a peculiar people to Himself, and set them apart as His Church on earth; so by the especial ministry of the Apostle Paul He called the Gentiles out of the darkness of the Heathen world to his marvellous light, and established them as a visible Church in the world. Under God, they were founders and fathers of the holy societies for which they are now anxiously taking thought on the eve of their departure. As Moses could appoint no one as his successor who would in all points be exactly what he had been to the people,—so neither could the Apostle be entirely represented in the Churches which he had planted by any one to whom he should entrust the future care of them. They might have, as he says to the Corinthians, "ten thousand instructors in Christ, yet could they not have many fathers*;" none could altogether be to them what he had been—the father who had begotten them his sons in Christ by the Gospel.

The charge accordingly which St. Paul gives to Timothy, as well as that of Moses to Joshua, respects the means for continuing, and rendering

* 1 Cor. iv. 15.

effective, the systems of religious faith and conduct already established.   The charge cannot be
supposed to relate to new doctrines or new institutions, but simply to the method by which the
doctrines already taught might be explained and
enforced, and the institutions already framed
might be worked out and applied to existing circumstances.   St. Paul appears desirous accordingly of stirring up Timothy to earnestness and
zeal and courage in acting on what he had been
taught and had received, rather than of instructing him anew.   The stress of his exhortation is, to
remember how the Apostle himself had taught
and acted in every place—to hold fast the form
of sound words, or outline of wholesome doctrine
heard from him—to keep the good thing committed unto him,—to guard what he had received
from the Apostle, as a precious deposit to be kept
inviolate and entire.   His words in the text are,
" Preach the word ; be instant in season, out of
season ; reprove, rebuke, with all long-suffering
and doctrine."   All these directions relate to the
preaching of the Gospel of Christ, as a message
fully delivered ; as the word spoken by the Incarnate Son, and now published by the voice of His
Evangelists and Apostles.   It is only required

that this word should be faithfully expounded
and taught to those to whom it should be sent.
As he elsewhere says, with an admirable simplicity touching the whole truth of salvation by the
blood of Christ as the sum and substance of the
Gospel, "Remember that Jesus Christ of the seed
of David was raised from the dead according to
my Gospel* ;" according, that is, to the uniform
tenour of his own preaching. Again, speaking,
as he proceeds, of the same truth as the support of the Christian under all trials, he adds ;
" of these things *put them in remembrance.*" So,
too, he refers Timothy to his own example for a
plain direction of the mode in which he would
have him preach the word ; " But thou hast fully
known my doctrine, manner of life, purpose,
faith, long-suffering, charity, patience," &c. He
warns him against the example, on the other
hand, of those who were " ever learning and
never able to come to the knowledge of the
truth,"—teachers who were seeking to improve
upon what the Gospel had simply declared, and
recommending themselves by their semblance and
profession of superior knowledge, instead of seeking the secret approval of God by " rightly di-

* 2 Tim. ii. 8.

viding the word of truth," and setting forth in all
its parts and bearings the truth already revealed
and known. In short, *continuance* in the things
which he had learned and had been assured of,—
continuance, as opposed to *innovation* or *fancied
improvement*, (which last are characterized by the
Apostle as marks of unsound profession,) is the
great burthen throughout of the charge addressed
to this his beloved son in the Faith.

In thus admonishing Timothy, St. Paul was
but doing what Moses had already done, as I
before observed, in regard to Joshua. We have
only to turn to the account of the manner in
which Joshua enters on his divine commission,
to illustrate this. When, after the death of
Moses, the Lord spoke to Joshua, promising him
the strength of His perpetual presence, he lays
this injunction upon him : " Only be thou strong
and very courageous, that thou mayest observe
to do according to all the law, which Moses
my servant commanded thee : turn not from
it to the right hand or to the left, that thou
mayest prosper whithersoever thou goest. This
book of the law shall not depart out of thy mouth ;
but thou shalt meditate therein day and night,
that thou mayest observe to do according to all

that is written therein: for then thou shalt make thy way prosperous, and then thou shalt have good success*." According to this command was the conduct of Joshua. Whilst he was called to be the servant of the Lord in the place of Moses, he remembered that he had been the " minister of Moses ;" as the Scripture describes him. He laboured only to carry out the instructions of his master; leading the people in the way in which Moses had led them ; and executing simply the trust committed to him in the name of the Lord; not innovating, or delivering any new commandment beyond what he had received, or endeavouring in any way to establish his own authority in the place of his to whom he succeeded.

But if this be a correct view of the nature of the charge here delivered by the Apostle to Timothy, how mistaken must be the view of some, who represent the teaching of the successors of the Apostles, as the perfecting of the scheme of doctrine delivered by the Apostles themselves, —or at least as a development of the truths placed in their hands by the Apostles ; and who invest

* Josh. i. 7, 8.

the Church after the age of the Apostles, with
absolute authority to fix what shall be believed
by the Christian, and to exact from the faithful
an obedience to its word as the word of God!

You are aware, that those who claim for the
Church of a later age this privilege of giving a
supposed perfection to the elements of doctrine
deposited with the primitive Church, when pressed
with the objection, that they thus admit innovations of doctrine beyond that originally delivered by our Lord and his Apostles, resort to
the expedient of saying, that the perfection given
subsequently to the Christian doctrine was, not
the introduction of *new* doctrine, but the *expansion* of the old—not a positive increase, but a
dilatation of the parts—an explicit form given to
that which was before involved, as the full-blown
flower disclosed from the germ or the bud.

If this were really the case, there could be no
more objection to attributing such a power of
expanding the truth to the fourth or any subsequent century of the Gospel, than to the proceeding of any of us at the present day, who attempt
by our sermons or expositions to explain in fuller
statements the truths contained in Scripture.

This is in fact nothing more than to fulfil what the Apostle calls *rightly dividing* the word of truth. But it is a license beyond this which is really claimed and exercised by those who refer us to the fourth or any later century as the period of the maturity of Christian doctrine. We know as a matter of fact, that in the fourth century, the period of ideal perfection of the Christian scheme of Truth, doctrines were added, which could not in any proper sense be called mere *expansions* or *more explicit* statements of the Faith once delivered to the saints. Such, for example, were the doctrines of Purgatory, of Prayers for the Dead, and a real Sacrifice in the Eucharist,—of the veneration of Saints and relics,—of the merit of Penances, and of a Life of solitary seclusion. None of these doctrines or institutions can be regarded as otherwise than *additions* to the primitive faith and worship.

Some doctrines, it is true, did in the process of time receive expansion, in the way of more explicit or more guarded statement, as discussion arose on questions arising out of them, and as it became necessary to define more accurately the boundaries of truth and error. Such was the case with the doctrine of the Holy Trinity and that of Original Sin. But even these more explicit statements of the truth on these subjects cannot properly be said to have given a *perfection*, which it had not already, to the Christian scheme of doctrine. In the case of the doctrines thus expanded, the truth itself contained in them remained the same as before. Nothing *new* was taught beyond the Faith once for all delivered to the Saints and consigned to the writings of the New Testament. The same truth was only thrown into forms more adapted for teaching it free from error, as the occasions of the Church required, and for protecting it from perversion.

Happily, under the superintendence of the Divine Head of the Church, the several discussions which took place during the third and fourth centuries chiefly, did result, as an exact study of them will prove to the impartial inquirer, in preserving the sameness of the truths about which they were employed. Had we been looking on as mere spectators with the ordinary feelings of men on the course of those discussions, we might have trembled for the result; observing the forwardness and heat of debate which too often mingled with the sacred matter discussed. We might have looked on as on a ship tossed by the waves of a stormy sea, seeming to have no steady course, and at every moment in danger of being lost in the depth to which it plunges. But though we might have been full of fear, the Lord was in the storm and at the helm. He was all the while guiding the Church. The ship which seemed to waver, and almost founder in the midst of the waters, was eyeing its path steadily and safely to the haven where it would be. Thus has the sacred truth on the fundamental articles of the Christian Faith escaped, unharmed and entire, from the conflicts which it has had to encounter in its progress.

So, let me observe by the way, it always will be. Our faith assures us, that the truth, as it is in Jesus, shall not fail. And therefore even in our present distress, in the struggle which the truth is now passing through within the precincts of our own Church—whilst some are putting to our lips the cup of Circe, and bidding us drink deeply of the transforming draught, and others are looking on, wondering where all will end, with lukewarmness or neutrality,—amidst the open desertion of our communion by some, and the no less evident desertion of its principles by others,—still the result, we need not doubt, will

be salutary. It may please the Lord to visit us
for awhile, not in peace, but with a sword and
with fire. He may permit dissension to spread,
and a man's foes to be those of his own household. But peace is his bequest to his faithful
disciples. Let us only abide on his promise,
and the clouds which now darken our horizon
will break away, and a brighter sunshine will
follow.

To return, however, to the point from which
I digressed.

It is clear that a perfection of the *Truth* itself,
and a perfection of its *systematic statement*, are
two very different things: and the latter being
all that we can attribute to the discussions of the
ages subsequent to the Apostolic, we cannot with
propriety refer to those ages for the perfect standard of Christian truth. To do so, is to invert
the case. The true notion of the Church, considered as the depository of Christian truth and
holiness, is, that it came forth in perfect stature at once in Him who is the Word of God,
Himself its Author and Finisher; and that He
transmitted it as a whole and perfect body of
Light and Life to his Apostles, to be by them
in like manner transmitted to their successors,

and so communicated without change to his Church in its perpetual generations, as that which lives, not like earthly things by growth of substance, but ever flourishes in the native vigour and maturity of its first existence. It is in God's Revelation of his grace as in the acts of his Creation. He formed " every plant of the field before it was in the earth, and every herb of the field before it grew;" and the heavens and the earth came forth perfect in their generations " in the day that the Lord God made the earth and the heavens." Such was his revealed word, when He had once fully declared it. It came forth in its full stature and proportion; not the seed or germ; but the perfect plant, needing no time for its growth and development.

Thus does our Lord speak of having told his first immediate disciples " all things which he had heard from his Father;" evidently denoting by this expression the whole Gospel-truth. Thus St. Paul declares that he had kept back nothing that was profitable for the souls of his hearers—nothing, that is, of the doctrine of salvation through Christ; not having " shunned," as he afterwards says more expressly, " to declare unto them all the counsel of God*." Thus, too, does he here speak to Timothy, agreeably to what I have before observed, of "*continuing*" in the things which he " had learned of him ;" not of *adding* to his learning in the faith, but of making faithful use of what he had been taught. In like manner, the Apostles generally appeal to the Christian *recollections* of those whom they address. The whole tone of their instruction is that of persons who had ever taught the same truths from *first to last* ; and who had nothing to communicate to the most accomplished disciple, beyond the self-same deep knowledge of the mystery of God in Christ with which they had already fed each humble soul, whether weak or strong in the understanding of this world's wisdom,—that mystery which, incomprehensible as it is to all, instils strength and comfort as fully into the soul of the weakest member of the Church as into that of the strongest, if there be only the willing hearty disposition to receive it. What is St. Paul's admonition to Timothy throughout, but this? " Put them in remembrance." " If thou put the Brethren in

* Acts xx. 20. 27.

remembrance of these things, thou shalt be a good minister of Jesus Christ, nourished up in the words of faith and of good doctrine whereunto thou hast attained*." So St. Peter, in a passage where he expresses a feeling not unlike that of St. Paul in the text: " Wherefore I will not be negligent to put you always in remembrance of these things, though ye know them, and be established in the present truth. Yea, I think it meet, as long as I am in this tabernacle, to stir you up by putting you in remembrance; knowing that shortly I must put off this my tabernacle, even as our Lord Jesus Christ hath shewed me. Moreover I will endeavour that ye may be able after my decease to have these things always in remembrance†." The only perfection of doctrine accordingly known to the Apostles, is the primitive teaching of the Lord and of themselves from Him. He that most faithfully remembered what he had been taught would be, in their view, the best-instructed teacher, the most perfect expositor of Christian truth, the most faithful pastor of the flock of Christ.

Nor are we to suppose that this view of the office of a successor to the Apostles excludes all

---

* 1 Tim. iv. 6. † 2 Pet. i. 12–15.

that may be called improvement in exposition
of the truth. On the contrary, it leaves an opening for constant improvement in this subordinate
department. When St. Paul commends Timothy
for his acquaintance with the Scriptures, and remarks on their importance " for doctrine, for
reproof, for instruction in righteousness," he
clearly meant to encourage him still in the diligent study of the sacred oracles, and suggest
them to him as a fit manual for the due discharge
of the duties which he was committing to him.
As Timothy was led to the knowledge of Christ
by the reading of Scripture; so would he be confirmed and strengthened in that knowledge by the
continued use of Scripture. Studying the sacred
oracles as a Christian, he would now see a light
thrown on many passages which before seemed
less plain. By the general light of Scripture,
comparing spiritual things with spiritual, he would
gain a more accurate insight into the several parts
of Revelation, and their mutual illustration in
their bearings on one another. And thus he
would become more richly instructed in the wisdom proper to his holy office, and " wax riper
and stronger in his ministry."

This kind of advancement in the knowledge

and exposition of Christian truth, as it would be competent to Timothy, is in like manner open to all Christians now, and especially to the Christian minister. The Christian minister of all ages is referred by this example to *the Scriptures*, for improvement in the knowledge and practice belonging to his office. Thus may he by the advantage of his position, enjoying the benefit of the labours of others and the increased experience of the Church, become a more skilful expositor of the truth in its various lights than his predecessors, —more able to wield " the sword of the Spirit which is the Word of God,"—more richly furnished with the stores of Christian argument, and the means of Christian appliance, so as to bring home the one unchanging and unchangeable truth as it is in Jesus, to the hearts and minds of men with effect. Such is the kind of advancement in religious knowledge which Bishop Butler represents in his ' Analogy' as attainable by Christians now, where he says ; " As it is owned, the whole scheme of Scripture is not yet understood ; so, if it ever comes to be understood before the 'Restitution of all things,' and without miraculous interpositions ; it must be in the same way as natural knowledge is come at ; by the continuance and progress of learning and of liberty ; and by particular persons attending to, comparing, and pursuing intimations scattered up and down it, which are overlooked and disregarded by the generality of the world*."

And, O Brethren ! that all who have a dispensation of the Gospel committed to them, did faithfully use this blessed means of improving their religious knowledge,—that, as, according to our Ordination-Vows, we " are persuaded that the Holy Scriptures contain sufficiently all doctrine required of necessity for eternal salvation through faith in Jesus Christ ; and are determined out of the said Scriptures to instruct the people committed to our charge, and to teach nothing as required of necessity to eternal salvation, but that which we shall be persuaded may be concluded and proved by the Scripture,"—so we would " be diligent in Prayers and in reading of the Holy Scriptures, and in such studies as help to the knowledge of the same, laying aside the study of the world and the flesh†!" Then would all erroneous and strange doctrines, contrary to God's word, be effectually banished and driven

* Butler's Analogy, Part 2. Chap. iii.
† Ordering of Priests.

away from amongst us : then indeed should we
" wax riper and stronger in our ministry." Vain
is it for us, to propose this or that age of the
Church after the time of the Apostles, or this or
that Communion for our rule and pattern. This
is not the way in which we have learned Christ,
or can learn Him. Until we go in simplicity to
those living oracles which testify of Christ, and
where alone we have the whole doctrine and institution of Christ, we cannot be said to have
done " all that lieth in us, according to our
bounden duty, to bring all such as are or shall
be committed to our charge unto that agreement
in the faith and knowledge of God, and to that
ripeness and perfectness of age in Christ, that
there be no place left among us either for error
in religion or for viciousness in life." To compare ourselves with other ages of the Gospel, or
other Churches, may be an useful stimulant to
our zeal : but we can obtain no sure criterion of
our soundness in the faith by such a comparison.
All ages and all churches have but one criterion
of this—the Holy Scriptures. These alone will
infallibly assure us of what is primitive in doctrine ; telling us not merely, as the test of Catho-
licity does, *what is in fact* the profession of the

Churches throughout Christendom, but of what (if they be living branches of Christ) *must be* their profession.

I am of course not speaking of the Scriptures arbitrarily and rashly interpreted, or accommodated to the opinions of individuals. Such an use of them cannot be too much reprobated. But I mean the Scriptures, as a manual of direction to the humble member of our Church, seeking to ascertain the truth of his profession and establish himself in the faith.

And in these times, it is especially important to bear this in mind. Now, if ever, should we enforce the necessity of recurring to the guidance of our inspired oracles, when so much has been done, and is doing still, to unsettle the minds of our members as to the claims of our own Church on their loyalty and affection—to tempt them to look beyond its pale for a purer, more reverential, more spiritual faith and worship, like the citizens of Plato's Ideal Republic, knowing no peculiar tie of blood amongst their own people, but sinking all home attachments in the wide membership of the Catholic Church at large. In such times, I say, the reference to the Scriptures as the sole rule of faith—the sole criterion of right and wrong in religion—becomes especially necessary. By other means, you may more luxuriantly indulge the feelings of awe and tenderness and mystic devotion. But these are feelings which require to be controled and subdued in their application to true religion. Were it our business to give free scope to such feelings, one need look no further than to the wild forms of superstition. Heathen superstition presented large materials for these feelings to act upon; and did in fact keep hold of its votaries principally by interesting such feelings. It was the following of an evil example in the heathen rites, when the like excitement was sought among Christians by the introduction into the Church of the "Discipline of the Secret;" and when it became a practice with Christian writers to speak of the holy and comforting Sacrament of the Lord's Supper under the awe-inspiring name of the "tremendous mysteries." The Gospel of Christ needs none of these spurious attractions. That our Church should not offer any indulgence to morbid or excited feelings, is among the marks of its faithful adherence to the Gospel. And he that studies the Scriptures will perceive, that, whilst they call every pure and kindly and noble feeling into the service of the faith, their address is emphatically to the soberminded and simple—to the holy and humble men of heart; and that he has no occasion, accordingly, to go from the simple faith and worship received and established in the Church of England, in quest of the perfect religion of the Christian.

Setting aside, then, all liberty of innovating or improving on the scheme of religion, we shall see what was the nature of the power committed by the Apostle to Timothy. He was to fulfil what the Apostle himself, removed as he soon would be from the sphere of his labours, could not execute in person; to establish regulations in the Churches under his care for the maintenance of the Faith by the appointment of teachers and forms of public worship, and a government and discipline for the correction of false doctrine and schism and scandals. As Joshua was left to settle the children of Israel in the land of Canaan, and to divide to the Tribes their respective portions of the inheritance; so was the duty committed to Timothy of applying the general principles laid down by St. Paul to the particular circumstances of the Ephesian Church. In this respect, accordingly, the successors of the Apostles possess a power which they have not in the matter of doctrine. Whence it is laid down in our Articles, that every particular Church hath power to ordain or decree rites and ceremonies, so that nothing be established contrary to the Word of God.

Here then is a point on which the appeal to antiquity cannot stand. The proper authority in the matter of rites and ceremonies and internal discipline of the Church, is the Church itself which has established them. And they that would introduce other forms, in the stead of those which the Church has adopted and sanctioned by its use, are not only intruding their own private judgment in a matter of government where it has no place, but also are exacting a particularity in this respect which the Scriptures do not enjoin. They in fact proceed on the principle of those objectors, in the time of Hooker, to the forms of our Church, who complained, that any ceremony should be allowed in the Church without *express* authority of Scripture in its favour. These, in like manner, would put Doctrine and Discipline on the same footing. Only, as their favourite appeal is to Antiquity for what is true in the matter of Doctrine, so is it to Antiquity also that they appeal for what is right in the matter of Discipline. Both parties, however, equally abridge that liberty which has been given to the chief pastors of every Church, to order the internal regulations of it as may best suit the circumstances of the case.

We have thus far considered the nature of the charge given by St. Paul to Timothy. I would in the next place direct your attention to the circumstances to which the charge refers. Great dangers were impending over the Church, and had all but fallen upon it, when St. Paul addressed the language of vehement exhortation contained in our text to the Bishop of the Ephesian Church. These dangers, we should observe, were from false teaching—false teaching, too, arising out of the bosom of the Church itself; as we learn from another passage of Scripture, where St. Paul tells the Elders of Ephesus, that " even of themselves should men arise, speaking perverse things, to draw away disciples after them*."

The same was the character of the dangers which threatened Israel, (to carry on the comparison with which I began) when Joshua received

* Acts xx. 30.

his charge. The dangers to Israel were also from themselves. The great difficulty presented to Joshua was not in fighting with their enemies and leading them to victory, but, as it had been to Moses, in guiding and governing the people themselves over whom he was placed. They were ever prone to faction—ready to follow any leader who should offer himself to them. This their whole history shews, even to the latest period, down to the coming of our Lord and the destruction of the city. Their corruption in particular by their own pastors is expressly mentioned. "The prophets prophesy falsely," says Jeremiah concerning them, "and the priests bear rule by their means; and my people love to have it so: and what will be the end thereof*?" And we see the result of this process of internal corruption, by the condition of religion among them at the time of our Lord's appearing. The true religion of the Law was then overlaid by a mass of traditions; and the doctrines of the masters in Israel had superseded the commandments of God.

What is all this but a history of the wilfulness of human nature, under even the clear light of a

* Jer. v. 31.

Revelation from Heaven ? It is no wonder therefore, that we have seen the same thing reproduced
in the Christian Church. It is no wonder, that
the Apostles of our Lord foreboded its reappear-
ance, and earnestly warned their successors in
the government of the Church to check the first
symptoms of the evil. The Judaizing teachers
were the first to infect the Church with this
plague ; and it is to them accordingly that he
expressly alludes. But the Judaizing heresy,
and the Gnosticism into which it developed, were
only preludes to the great apostasy of the
Roman Church, which adopted and systematized
the early corruptions. In alluding therefore to
the Judaizing or Gnostic errors, the Apostle
appears to speak with a solemnity and energy
beyond what the occasion itself might seem
to require, and befitting rather that fearful consummation of apostasy from the pure faith which
present symptoms indicated as a future result. For Judaism and Gnosticism, as sects
or names, have passed away. But the evil itself,
denounced by the Apostle, remains. Even of
ourselves do persons arise speaking perverse
things. Even now are men not willing to
" endure sound doctrine," but " heap to them-

selves teachers, having itching ears*,"—ever
ready to hear some new doctrine, whether it be
really new, or, as a revival of the ancient, new to
them. And it is but too true still, that many
"turn away their ears from the truth and are
turned unto fables;" delighting in that which
excites their feelings; making of their religion
a beautiful abstraction for the imagination, or a
thought of rest for the wayward heart; using
it for a luxury of thought and feeling, instead of
receiving it in its positive reality, as a doctrine
of sober truth though full of mystery, and a
homely discipline of life and conduct. It is
against the general nature then of all seductive
teaching, that the Apostle must be conceived to
express his warning in the text.

And shall we not be warned by it, Brethren?
Only observe the solemn call which he makes on
Timothy, and in him, on all in authority as pastors and teachers of his word, in the first place,
and then on all members of the body of Christ.
As Moses calls Heaven and earth to witness his
declaration of God's mercies and judgments to
Israel; as he went with Joshua into the tabernacle of the congregation, and before the pillar

* 2 Tim. iv. 3.

T

of the cloud, bade him be strong and of good courage in the mission on which he was sent; so the Apostle here adjures Timothy in the presence of " God, and the Lord Jesus Christ, who shall judge the quick and dead at his appearing and in his kingdom," to fulfil his ministry. And what is his instruction to that end? *To preach the word,*—never to relax in preaching the word of God,—to be instant in season, out of season, in preaching that word,—to reprove, rebuke, exhort, with all long-suffering and doctrine. The only sure remedy according to the Apostle's direction is, to preach the word,—that word, which is mighty to pull down the strongholds of Satan,—which, if plainly and boldly preached, will carry its rebukes to error; unmasking its ingenious pretences and sophistries, and shooting the rays of light across the dark and mystic clouds in which it shrouds itself.

There is no deceptiveness so great, so effectual in working its mischief, as that of false teaching in Religion. We see this in the success which, for a time at least, attends each new sect. The reason of this probably is, that men are disposed to believe any teacher of religion to be a good man. They may suspect him to be the dupe of his own fanaticism. But they are reluctant to believe that he can intend to deceive them : and though they may not be ready to go all lengths with his teaching, they think they may at any rate obtain some good by listening to him. This is daily exemplified in the readiness with which the most untutored and the wildest fanatics attract hearers, and form a circle around them. Numbers will follow such leaders to a certain point; and having reached that point, they become interested in the delusion, and know not where to stop, until they yield themselves up to the influence which they had at first half-resisted. Thus does our Lord Himself emphatically say, " Beware of false prophets, which come to you in sheep's clothing, but inwardly they are ravening wolves * ;" describing the danger even to the elect, lest they should be deceived. For it is not only the thoughtless that may be won by false teaching; but even of those who are the most seriously disposed some will be led astray, through their very susceptibility of religious impressions and desires after religious improvement.

Well therefore has the Apostle set forth that strong admonition in the text, to *preach the*

* Matt. vii. 15.

word, with all reproof, and exhortation to stedfastness founded on the preaching of the word.
" The time will come when they will not endure
sound doctrine," says the Apostle. " They will
heap to themselves teachers, having itching ears."
The corruption spread by false teaching will act
in rendering that teaching more generally acceptable. The teachers themselves become em-
boldened by their success, and begin to triumph
as if it were too late to check them. And many
who would otherwise, perhaps, set themselves
against the delusion, are disheartened and kept
back by the fear of unpopularity and obloquy ; or
by too easily believing that it is now too late ;
that they will do no good by exerting themselves,
but only perhaps aggravate the evil by opposition ;
—some, again, thinking it best to let the evil
alone, to suffer it to exhaust itself, or call forth
its own remedy in the reaction to which it will
ultimately lead. The Apostle accordingly prepares Timothy for a task of difficulty and suffering.
" Watch thou in all things," he adds ; " endure
afflictions, do the work of an Evangelist, make
full proof of thy ministry." He tells him that
his utmost watchfulness is required,—that he
must hold on in spite of opposition and ill-treat-

ment,—and thus do the work of a preacher of the Gospel,—thus give decisive evidence of his faithfulness as a minister of Christ.

Let us observe, then, Brethren, the great commandment here laid by the Apostle on this his beloved son and successor in the Gospel, in this his farewell charge. " Preach the word, do the work of an Evangelist, give full proof of thy ministry." As in his former Epistle he spoke of the commandment given to him, and the deposit committed to him*; so here, expressing the same thing in more distinct terms, he says ; " Preach the word, do the work of an Evangelist, give full proof of thy ministry." What else could the Apostle so appropriately characterize as " the commandment," " the excellent deposit," τὴν καλὴν παρακαταθήκην†, as " the word" which Timothy had been commissioned to preach, —but the word of God, the " great mystery of godliness," the glad tidings of Salvation through the blood of Christ ? He spoke not before of commandments, and therefore could not be understood to mean rites and ceremonies and ordinances of government, but of *the commandment,*

* 1 Tim. vi. 14. 20.

† In our version, "that good thing which was committed."

—he speaks not of deposits, not therefore of a collection of secret doctrines or traditions, but of *the deposit, the excellent deposit.* What, then, can *the commandment* and *the deposit* mean, when spoken of to one who had been ordained a minister of the Gospel, but the very commission itself which he had received ;—to preach the word of God,—to publish that word, as the Apostle, who communicated to him the authority, had published it,—to preach, that is, *Christ Crucified,*—to be the herald of that mercy to sinful man, which God had freely granted through the merits and intercession of His Son ?

This, accordingly, Christian Brethren, is the divinely-appointed means, by which we are to stand against the corruptions of false teaching, and edify the Church of God. By this means we shall both save ourselves and them that hear us.

O that these words then of the Apostle, on which I have been discoursing, may sink deeply into the hearts of us all, and press upon those of us especially who have received the like charge, to preach the word, to be instant in season and out of season, to reprove, rebuke, exhort, with all long-suffering and doctrine ! The false Gospel, —that which is no Gospel at all,—forbids us to speak of the reality of the Atoning Sacrifice of the Blessed Redeemer as the direct and primary object of faith to the soul of the sinner. It does not blot out that holy mystery from its scheme of religion; but it covers it over with rites and symbols and mystic silence, and would have men preach Christ Crucified by *their own cross*, by their *self-sacrifices*, by their *own* holiness. So did the Gnostic Gospel. It denied not a death and resurrection of the Saviour. But the refinement of its doctrine could not brook the confession of a real death of the Saviour. The Gnostic system shrank from preaching Christ Crucified. Substituting a phantom in his stead, or severing the Christ from Jesus who died, it wrapt up the truth of the real Atonement made on the Cross, in the mystic doctrine of a death and resurrection of the spiritual man by his advances in knowledge and purification from the earthliness of his nature. So it is with the Gospel of apostate Rome. It would have men acknowledge the Sacrifice of the Cross as a fact in the Christian scheme, and a fundamental fact. But it would not have it preached, as the one great dominant Truth immediately concerning every Christian man at his first entrance into the school of Christ. It would present the truth under a veil, or as a latent principle, to be reached and fully known only through the operation of the Sacraments and the intermediate ministrations of the Church. Not so however teaches the Apostle. Preach the word, is his charge to us,—do the work of an Evangelist; as a minister of Christ—as a member of Christ—live and die, with the message of Salvation through the Atoning Blood of the Lord and Saviour Jesus Christ, in the heart and on the lips. Use indeed, he would say, the means of grace. Let the ministers of Christ administer his holy Sacraments, and be diligent in all the ordinances of his religion: and let none presume to hope for the precious benefits of his death, if they slight the means which He has appointed for their increase in holiness. But let them *preach his word*,—let the Truth as it is in Him be boldly declared, after the manner in which the Apostles declared it; and we shall not take His holy Name in vain. He will not charge us with irreverence in doing what He has commanded. He will take care that the utterance of His Salvation, though it come from unworthy lips, shall be sanctified and blessed to His glory.

SERMON IX.

CHRIST SANCTIFYING HIS CHURCH.

PREACHED IN THE CATHEDRAL OF CHRIST CHURCH,

On SUNDAY, January 21, 1844.

SERMON IX.

CHRIST SANCTIFYING HIS CHURCH.

JOHN XVII. 17–21.

Sanctify them through thy truth: thy word is truth. As thou hast sent me into the world, even so have I also sent them into the world. And for their sakes I sanctify myself, that they also might be sanctified through the truth. Neither pray I for these alone, but for them also which shall believe on me through their word; that they all may be one; as thou, Father, art in me, and I in thee, that they also may be one in us: that the world may believe that thou hast sent me.

THE sublime and affecting address, of which these words are a part, is the solemn initiation or consecration of Himself by our Lord, for the especial work of his mission—the Atonement which He was about to make for the sins of his people, by the offering of Himself. Like the Levitical High-priest, He prepares Himself, first, for the holy work which He is to perform for his Church, by sanctifying Himself, or devoting Himself as a victim to the sacrifice. But, at the same time, unlike the High-priest under the Law, He needs no sacrifice in his own behalf, to purify Him, and render Him meet to appear before God for others. It is enough that He *sanctifies Himself*; that He formally separates Himself from the world in which He has been living during the days of his ordinary ministry, and, now that He is about to glorify the Father by his crowning act of self-devotion, calls forth the strength of the Godhead which dwelt in Him, by communion with the Father in prayer. The words before us may, indeed, be considered, together with all that our Lord says to his disciples on this occasion, as the commencement of the sacrifice itself: each passage, as He proceeds, bringing us nearer to the awful consummation. Thus, the institution itself of the Eucharist was an introduction to the real oblation of the Lord's Body and Blood on the Cross. It instructed the Apostles that the typical sacrifice of the Passover was on the eve of removal. For He took the bread and said, "This is my Body which is given for you:" as if He said; This is not any longer the Paschal Lamb, the sign of the Lord's deliverance from the bondage of Egypt, and type of the Lamb slain from the

foundation of the world ; but a sign of the grace to
be obtained from the breaking of my Body, now
to be sacrificed for you on the Cross. And when
He took the cup, He said, " This is my Blood of
the New Testament, which is shed for you and
for many for the remission of sins : " this is no
longer the cup of thanksgiving at an earthly feast
under God's ancient covenant with Israel, but a
sign of the grace which shall flow from my Blood
to be poured out on the Cross. The words pointed
to the real Body and real Blood of Atonement,
which He was then bearing along with Him in
his own person, to be offered on the altar of
Calvary. All former sacrifices had been typical.
Now was to be offered the One real Sacrifice of
Atonement, which all former ones had only represented. And the action which before had, in
itself, a sacrificial import, was henceforth to be a
celebration of the Atonement wrought—a work
done in remembrance of the Lord Himself offered up.

All, indeed, that our Saviour utters in this
solemn preparation for his passion, carries our
minds to Himself exclusively, as performing a
Divine work of Atonement, once for all, for the
sins of the world. It is his sanctification of *Him-*

self that we here read of throughout, in order that believers in Him might henceforth be sanctified by the Truth,—by the word of God preached in his Name,—that word which is truth. He instructs the disciples that He is sanctifying Himself for their sakes ; that *their* sanctification depends on what *He* is doing in their behalf. He tells them, indeed, that they should succeed to Him in the ministration of the Gospel. " As thou hast sent me into the world," He says in his prayer, " even so have I also sent them into the world." And to them afterwards expressly :—" As my Father hath sent me, even so send I you." He informs them that it would now devolve on them to carry on the preaching of the word, receiving their mission and authority from Him, as He had received his from the Father ; they being *his* messengers to the world, even as He had been the *Father's* messenger. But He by no means intimates, in these words, that their mission should be the same as his ; but rather, that it should be subordinate and instrumental. Whereas, his office had been direct and immediate from the Father,—a mediation between God and man, in the two natures united in his Person, and by the sacrifice of Atonement which He wrought ;

making known the Father in Himself,—in the works done, and the words spoken, by Him, who is one with the Father: *their* office on the other hand should be, to deliver to men the Gospel of the Incarnate Son; to make known the Son by whom they were sent, and through Him the Father by whom He was sent.

That the mission of his disciples was entirely distinct in its character from the ministration of our Lord Himself, appears further from what He adds in the text: " Neither pray I for these alone, but for them also which shall believe on Me through their word; that they all may be one; as thou, Father, art in Me, and I in Thee, that they also may be one in Us: that the world may believe that Thou hast sent Me." Whilst He imparts to those, who were to be his Apostles, the commission to preach the word; He prays for such as shall receive the truth preached by them, the same heavenly blessing, as for those who have received it immediately from Himself; that, as they who heard and saw Him had in Him seen the Father, and known the only true God, so those who should hereafter believe, when He should Himself be withdrawn from the world, might receive the same spiritual enlightenment,—might no less acknowledge the Son, and the Father in the Son, and the Son in the Father; and so be united in one body, professing the truth; glorifying God the Father, by faith in God the Incarnate Son.

It is nothing, therefore, peculiar to the Apostles, or their successors in the Apostolic office, that our Lord is here conveying by his prayer of sanctification for them. What He says in this passage is in exact accordance with what He said to Thomas after his Resurrection: " Because thou hast seen me, thou hast believed: blessed are they *that have not seen*, and yet have believed*." He is holding out to members of his Church, in all ages, the encouraging assurance, that the faith which they shall receive from the word preached, the word of his messengers,—shall be as effectual for their Salvation, as the faith of those was, who had seen Him and heard the word from his own lips. He confers, accordingly, here on the Apostles, no power of mediation in behalf of other members of the Church, such as He Himself possessed. He sanctifies them for the holy work, which they are about to be left to execute without Him; but it is only as He sanctifies all that truly

* John xx. 29.

believe in Him ; through the truth of God revealed to them ; through its power to change their sinful nature, and make them sons of God in Christ. Elsewhere, indeed, He gives them a distinct commission to preach the Gospel, and make disciples of all nations ; to baptize in the name of the Father, the Son, and the Holy Ghost ; to administer the discipline of his Church in remitting and retaining sins ; and, in evidence of their mission, to work miracles in his name. Also in the passage now before us He refers to " their word" as instrumental in bringing believers to Him. But here nothing further appears than that our Lord prays for the disciples immediately around Him, who were to be the bearers of his truth to the world, that they might first be sanctified by it *themselves*, and thus be rendered apt instruments for conveying that truth to the world, in order that the whole world might be sanctified ; that the world might believe that the Father had sent the Son, or that Jesus was indeed the Christ, the Saviour of the world.

Our Church accordingly recognizes no sacrificial character in any minister of the Church ; since He, the great High-Priest of our profession, has passed with the Blood of Atonement into the Heavens. It looks up to Him, indeed, as still carrying on his work of mediation and intercession there ; obtaining and granting the Holy Spirit to the prayers of his faithful disciples ; and sending down strength and help and comfort to them in all their acts of devotion, and all their temptations and struggles in the world. It regards Him, too, as blessing with his perpetual Presence the faithful labours and acts of his appointed ministers, and all faithful attendants on their ministry ; so that, though absent in the body, He is still entirely and constantly with his Church by his Spirit. But we are not taught that our Lord is so present with his Church, as that the Sacrifice which He wrought for the sins of the world should be perpetuated in it by the hands of his ministers ; or that they are sanctified by Him in such a way as that all they do in his name is done,—not to say by his Spirit,—but by Himself; as if He were still in the days of his Incarnation on earth, doing the same works, speaking the same words, exerting the same authority, by the ministers of the Church as his human organs. This is not that unity with Christ, which this and other passages of Scripture represent to us. The Church owns Him as its Head. It belongs to Christ by a living union, as the body to the Head, and therefore belongs to God: for " ye are Christ's," says the Apostle, and " Christ is God's." But it is the Holy Spirit proceeding from the Father and the Son, and dwelling in the Church, that forms the bond of union,—that makes the Church one in the Father and the Son, even as the Father and the Son are one. And this union is described to us in Scripture, under the image of the marriage tie, —Christ the bridegroom, the Church his bride ; signifying that, close as the union is, it is not an identity of thought, and will, and action, that is to be understood in it ; that each subsists in distinct personality—as well the Church as its Divine Head ; and that the operations and functions of each must not be confounded with those of the other.

We believe, therefore, the peculiar work of the Saviour—his Incarnation, with its train of consequences—his holy life and teaching—his propitiatory sufferings and death—his Resurrection, Ascension, and Intercession—to stand *alone* in the history of our Religion. We may speak of them as strictly historical truths, that have had their being in respect of our Lord Himself, and that cannot be applied to any one else ; and yet, not *solely* historical, inasmuch as they are truths of eternal religious efficacy and moral importance ; which subsist for ever, as He about whom they are conversant ever subsists, to impart life and blessedness to all who embrace them in faith, and who, following the Saviour, are conformed to Him, through all generations of the Church.

Thus, though we restrict, as taught by Scripture, all that belongs to the actual work of Atonement to the Person and agency of the Lord Himself, we are far from restricting its grace and efficacy to any one period. On the contrary, we hold that an ever-flowing fountain of grace is opened for us in Heaven ; that we have, in our one great High-Priest, a very present help to all that call upon Him ; that, by virtue of *that one Sacrifice* which He has made, new members of his body, from time to time, obtain pardon and justification, through faith in its power to save them ; that again, by virtue of that same Sacrifice, all who approach God in prayer in his Name, in the Sacraments of Baptism and the Eucharist, and other ordinances of religion, or who seek to acquaint themselves with Him by the study of his revealed truth, receive those especial assistances which He has annexed to the several means of grace.

In particular, we may observe, with respect to the grace annexed to the communion of his Body and Blood in the Sacrament of the Eucharist, that we here acknowledge a Real Presence of Christ to the faithful receiver; though we are assured, at the same time, that the Body of our Lord is not on earth, but in Heaven, there abiding until His second Advent to Judgment. We acknowledge, in other words, that He is spiritually and effectually present to the faithful; for that such receive the consecrated emblems in that Sacrament, not as signs only according to their earthly nature, but as signs effectual to that end for which the Lord ordained them; effectual for the supplying of that heavenly sustenance, which the Body and Blood of the Lord would impart to our souls and bodies, could they be actually received in bodily substance.

Thus it is, then, that we consistently maintain a *real spiritual Presence* of Christ in the Eucharist, though we deny a corporeal carnal

Presence. We doubt not the efficacy of the grace of his passion, though his passion itself is a by-gone event; though having died unto sin once, he now dieth no more. Though that Body which once was broken, can be broken no more, and that Blood which once was shed, can be shed no more; we doubt not, I say, still, the efficacy of the grace of his passion to penetrate all distance of time and place; and, without any conducting medium, without intervention of any thing but the use of the appointed means on which his blessing and promise rest, to quicken our dull souls with new life, and assimilate us in spirit to Him who is our food.

Hence our Church cautions us, in the Homily on this subject, to " take heed in celebrating this feast, lest of the memory it be made a sacrifice ;" and, following the words of Scripture, speaks of this Sacrament as " the communion of the Body and Blood of the Lord in a marvellous incorporation, which by the operation of the Holy Ghost, (the very bond of our conjunction with Christ,) is, through faith, wrought in the souls of the faithful: whereby not only their souls live to eternal life, but they surely trust to win to their bodies a resurrection to immortality." Again, directing to the worthy receiving of the Sacrament, the Homily calls on the communicant not only to have a general faith in the Atonement of Christ, but to make a particular application of that faith to himself. It exhorts him to believe, as it goes on to say, " so that thou acknowledgest no other Saviour, Redeemer, Mediator, Advocate, Intercessor, but Christ only ; and that thou mayest say with the Apostle, that ' He loved thee, and gave Himself for thee :' for this is to stick fast to Christ's promise made in his institution, to make Christ thine own, and to apply his merits unto thyself.   Herein thou needest no other man's help ; no other sacrifice or oblation ; no sacrificing priest ; no mass ; no means established by man's invention."   So strictly are we enjoined by the language of our Church to look to no secondary agency for bringing down the Presence of Christ to us in this holy Sacrament.

And if in this sacred rite, in which the Lord especially vouchsafes his Presence, we are required to go immediately to Him, and believe Him to be present on the sole strength of his promise,—much less must we be tempted to think, that He has authorized his ministers to present Him to us in a more sensible manner, by any rites or ordinances of the Church, or to set up the Church before the world as the living impersonation of the Saviour.

And yet, this is the view which the Roman theory involves of the nature of the Lord's Presence with his Church. In the Roman doctrine of the Eucharist, a corporeal Presence is taught, as necessary to realize the promise of Christ in that Sacrament. For without such a Presence, the Church of Rome holds there could be no Real Presence of Christ, as an object external to the mind of the receiver. So in the Church at large, it consistently maintains there could be no sound profession of the truth of an Incarnate Saviour born into the world and living and dying for the salvation of man, unless there were an actual presentation of that truth in a visible society, in which, as in his body, He dwells before men now on earth, as once He dwelt in the flesh. In fact, the Church is regarded in the Roman theory as instinctive with the Lord's Divinity, in a way analogous to that in which his actual body was during the days of his Incarnation on earth. So long as Christ lived and taught, as both God and man, in the flesh, so long, according to that theory, was the

Church concentrated in Him, its King, and Priest, and Prophet: but when He ascended into Heaven, and endued the Apostles with power from on high to carry on the work of evangelizing the world, then began that order of things which has subsisted to this day in the Church. The Apostles, it is stated, were then fully constituted in his place, to continue what He had begun; to establish and spread, by the Divine Word imparted to them, the Kingdom of God on earth. They, indeed, were human: but so also was that nature which the Lord assumed for the accomplishment of his ministry. His ministry would have been defective, had it been simply human. By the union with the Divine nature, the frail and fallible was rendered, in all its operations, Divine and perfect. So the Apostles, as men, it is argued, were weak and fallible; but, as inspired and guided by the Divine Word, they were rendered unerring in all they said and did for the furtherance of the Gospel, and mighty in the power of their Priesthood. And what the Apostles were, that also, according to the Roman theory, are their successors for ever,—those namely who from them have received that commission, which they, as successors to the entire office of Christ, were empowered to transmit to their immediate successors, and those successors again to others after them, to the end of the world.

This is the true account of that supremacy of power and teaching, which Romanists attribute to their Church. It is here no question of degrees ; or of comparison between the deference due to the Scriptures on the one hand, and the ministry of the Church on the other, in the diffusion of the Gospel and exposition of the Faith. There can be no doubt, if our Lord Himself were still on earth, teaching with his own voice, and building up his Church with his own hands, that He must be looked to as the supreme, absolute Authority ; and that the written word must be interpreted and applied as He should direct. As his enlargement of the Law of Moses, and interpretations of the Old Testament, are authoritative and infallible,—so also must his subsequent teaching have overruled all previous statement in the written revelation of the New. Now, if the Apostles be regarded as entire successors to Christ's office, so that whatever they rule in their place, must be received as ruled by Him—whatever act they perform as accompanied by the power of his Divinity,—what has been observed on the supposition of his continuing on earth in his own person, must apply equally to them, and to those after them who receive from them the same power. Whence it would follow, that the Christian is bound to have recourse to the ministers of the Church, as the vicegerents of Christ Himself—as the appointed dispensers of grace, and teachers of his word ; believing whatever they believe, and doing whatever they enjoin ; persuaded that, as without Christ there is no Salvation, so without that society, in which alone his saving Presence is perpetuated, there is no Salvation.

Before such a living organ of Christ, the Scriptures necessarily sink in importance to the Christian soul. They are reduced to nothing more than the teaching of the Church at the time when they were written. It is granted, indeed, that they contain the substance of the truth, but not that explicit form of it in which a subsequent age of the Church has unfolded and stated it. Consequently, to take them as they stand in their original form, is, according to this view, to overlook the authoritative expansions or limitations of their meaning which they have successively obtained. It is to mistake hints and outlines for a finished structure ; statements, sufficient for the needs of the Church at the time when they were put forth, as if they were adequate for the purpose of a later age : whereas successive occasions have called upon the Church to pronounce more definitely than the Scriptures have done on many points of doctrine. By these later decisions accordingly the Scriptures must be interpreted, and not these by the Scriptures.

Thus does what, in modern phraseology, is termed the Theory of Development very naturally obtain a place in the Roman doctrine of the Church ; and that doctrine alone gives a warrant to it. Though the Church may possess authority to teach out of the Scriptures, and lead men to the acknowledgment of the truth in Christ, and administer the ordinances of Religion, unless it be further endued with the mediatorial power, it can have no authority to impose the sense on Scripture, or require anything to be believed, or done, as necessary to salvation, but what is found in the written commandments of the Lord, or evidently taught by the inspired organs of his revelation.

That Authority which our Church asserts for itself in controversies of faith, is something quite different from the power of authoritatively delivering the doctrines of faith. This is only an Authority of order, such as every communion must possess for its own regulation and peace. And even such Authority is only permitted in our Church in subordination to Scripture, and under an admission of the possibility of error in its decisions. But when the Church assumes to itself the attributes of Christ ; when it is not content to point to Him, and lead men to Him, but professes to bring Christ to them in the acts of its ministration ; when it arrogates to itself such an union with Christ as exempts it in all its functions from sin and error ; then it must follow, that its decisions are *imperatively* binding on the members of the Church ; and, instead of being restrained by the sacred text, give a sense and perfection to the simple dictates of Scripture, maturing the elements of doctrine there contained.

This theory of Development is virtually the same as that of an authoritative Tradition of doctrines and interpretations. But it carries the theory of Tradition a step further. For a Tradition of truths might be supposed to continue the same, and to admit of no alteration or improvement, even in the form of statement. As, however, the forms of Doctrine have varied, and additions have been made in successive ages, an explanation of this fact is needed to reconcile the anomaly in a Church, such as that of Rome, professedly incapable of changing the doctrine of Christ, and boasting itself ever the same. The difficulty, then, is met by regarding the Christian Faith as a deposit in the minds of the Apostles and their successors—as a nucleus of Divine truth to be acted on by the reason, and gradually unfolded in propositions, and reasonings, and conclusions. All these are asserted to be so many *explicit* statements of what before was *implicitly* held; however multiplied, as yet no addition in *substance* to the original truth out of which they are evolved; as forms of doctrine, admitting of infinite diversification, yet remaining one and the same in the truth delineated; however new in the points touched or in the manner of expression, as yet having nothing really new in the doctrine itself developed.

The theory of Development thus serves the same office in regard to the general theory of Tradition, which Tradition serves in regard to Scripture. As Tradition is used by the Romanist to interpret the Scriptures in his own sense, so is the theory of Development employed for the interpretation of the testimony of Tradition.

For example : when it is objected, that the doctrine of Transubstantiation was not known in the Church for several centuries,—that there is no such tradition,—it is granted, that the formal statement of Transubstantiation had not been made before such a time ; that the *doctrine* itself, however, so stated, had always existed, but waited its development in that explicit form, until the occasion required such a statement of the doctrine of the Eucharist, as might secure a belief in the truth of the Incarnation.

In fact, there is no novelty of doctrine which may not be recommended on this ground, as an explanation, or development, of some previous undoubted truth, in accordance with the precept of Vincent, *cum dicas nove non dicas nova.* Such a procedure is perfectly consistent on the part of those who regard the Church as the representative on earth of the Incarnate Saviour. If the Church now fills the threefold office, which the Saviour Himself held during the days of his personal ministry, of Prophet, Priest, and King,—if it is the inspired Teacher, the Offerer of Sacrifice, and Mediator between God and His people, and the

Ruler to whom entire submission both of intellect and conscience is due—an elevation, from which the Church of Rome looks down on the Lord's heritage,—then is there no alternative but that the believer must humbly accept his faith at the hands of the Church, or, rather, of its hierarchy; that he must seek his access to God only through the Church, by the way of its ordinances, and discipline, and ritual.

It were a tedious, but by no means difficult, task, to shew how all the doctrines of the Church of Rome, even those in which that Church has declared the substantial truth of Scripture, take their peculiar complexion from this doctrine of the Church. The whole Christian faith, indeed, as exhibited by the light of this theory, is the expansion of the fundamental idea on which the Church is constituted ; a vast subjective system of doctrines, resulting from the efforts of the human mind, through successive ages, to work out this idea in its various phases and combinations.

The doctrine, for example, of Justification: —What is the peculiar form which this doc- trine takes in the Church of Rome, but an expression of the idea of the Divine Word dwelling in the Church as its body? It is no longer what the Scriptures simply teach, Justification by faith only through the merits of Christ, but grace infused into the soul by communication with the Church in Sacraments—a germ of Divine life implanted in the soul by that body to which the Lord is supposed to have fully communicated his own Divine power; and through which alone He now acts for the Salvation of men. Yet the Church of Rome affirms, that we are justified before God only on account of the merits of our Lord and Saviour. But it will not consent to affirm that we are justified by faith only. And the reason of this evidently is, its peculiar view of the nature of the Church; the idea, that the Church now stands in the same relation to the world in which the Saviour Himself stood in the days of his personal ministry; the idea, that it not only is endued with grace from Christ, for its own justification and sanctification, but that it has the further power conferred on it of *communicating* grace to its members; that virtue proceeds from it, as from the Saviour's person, to heal and to save those who come to it. It disclaims the imputation of setting itself up in the place of God, inasmuch as it ascribes the *origin* of this exalted power to the Saviour's previous merits and gift.

But still it claims to be fully invested with this power of *communicating* grace from itself; and accordingly impresses this character on its doctrines and worship.

Were this view but true—were it not at variance with that character of the Church which we learn from the Scriptures, from the first records of its early existence,—we might well be disposed to regard it with feelings of awe, as the attainment of that unity which the Lord so earnestly prays for, and inculcates upon his Church. But when we come to look at it closely, it betrays a metaphysical symmetry—the unity of idea,—rather than the concord of believing hearts,—that " one heart, and one soul," which were found in the primitive believers, in those, whose praise is recorded for our example, that " they continued stedfast in the Apostles' doctrine and fellowship, and in breaking of bread and in prayers." It aspires, indeed, to represent that unity in the Father and the Son, which Christ speaks of, in his Holy Prayer, as the perfection of his Church. But the human element predominates over the Divine in the composition of the unity of Rome. The one faith of the Christian is the object which that Church *aims* at expressing by its doctrine, and discipline, and ritual; and by it to stamp the one Divine image on the soul of each believer. The aim is noble; the conception sublime: but abortive and vain the execution. True, the Christian religion, with all its Divine truths, is employed in the work: but it is the reason of man which elaborates the scheme; not simply receiving and applying the sacred truth to the work of edification,—an use of reason which is necessarily involved in every Divine gift to man,—but reason, as the Divine Logos, analysing the ideas which the faith presents to its contemplation; drawing them forth into definitions and propositions; giving them form and expression; and so realizing for man the Divine objects of the faith impressed on the mind of the Church.

I am not, in saying this, intending to say, that the Church has nothing to do in effecting that unity for which our Saviour prayed; and that reason may not properly be exerted for this object, in clearly defining and stating the truth, guarding it from corruption, and exempting it from misconception, in the form of exact propositions. Nor does it follow, because it is denied that such propositions are the developments of ideas from the mind of the Church, that such propositions have no truth or reality in them. The Church of Christ, doubtless, has a part to perform in preserving the faith of Christ entire and uncorrupt, and in maintaining peace and unanimity among the members of Christ. And, therefore, it is only *its duty* to oppose all heretical innovations, by statements framed to exclude the particular errors arising from time to time. Again, as directly employed in the work of teaching and guiding the members of Christ, it has to provide for their use creeds and summaries of doctrine, by which their knowledge and application of the true faith may be facilitated and secured. For these objects, then, among others, the doctrinal decisions and formularies of the Church are both sound and important. Such statements, too, are not the less true because they consist, in many cases, of terms not found in Scripture. It is, in fact, an advantage for the precision of statements, that they should be terms arbitrarily chosen for the purpose, and accurately limited accordingly in their sense. The propositions which consist of such terms will have their truth and reality, if they only adequately state that portion of Scripture-truth which they are intended to represent.

We are satisfied, however, in our own Church, that all such statements of Christian truth should have the evidence of Scripture in their favour; and we then consider them as possessing an ample authority. However varying in their expression—however foreign their language—from the Scripture-statement of the same truths; yet, if they can only be proved from Scripture, or shewn to be the clear consequences of what is read in Scripture, they require for us no surer warrant. We reject, indeed, no confirmation of them from external sources. We rejoice in the concurrent testimony of the universal Church to the correctness of our views of Scripture-truth; and are strengthened in our persuasion, by knowing that the doctrines we profess are none other than what the Christians of the early ages professed. But our foundation of them all is—Scripture; and when called upon for our reason of them, we appeal to no other ground as *essential* for establishing their authority.

Here, accordingly, lies the great difference in the teaching of the Church of Rome, and our own Church. The Church of Rome asserts, that the several forms of doctrine by which the faith is expressed, are its own spontaneous effusions—

decisions and declarations of the truth, possessing a divine sanction, as proceeding from itself,
because it has the mind of Christ informing it,
and the voice of Christ speaking in it. The evidence of Scripture, accordingly, is not *essential*
to the proof of its doctrines. It is enough that
they are referred to the authority of the Church.
They are the doctrines of Christ, *because* they are
the doctrines of the Church. The Church of
England, on the other hand, disclaims any right
to *originate* articles of faith of its own motion, or
any authority to command what shall be believed
by the faithful. It only proposes, for the acceptance of its members, what itself believes to be the
doctrine of Christ, in the way of authoritative
counsel and direction to them ; and bids them
search the Scriptures whether its teaching be
true or no.

It matters not to the point, be it observed,
whether the reference to Scripture be full of difficulty, or impracticable, to the generality of Christians. This is an objection often thrown in the
way by controvertists, when it is, in fact, *beside*
the question. For the real question at issue between Rome and ourselves is,—Is there a Divine
Authority, of knowledge and power, vested in the

Church, or no? If there be such authority, then the whole system of the Church of Rome necessarily follows. Its doctrines, its discipline, its worship, are but the developments of this principle. And those who accord this principle to the Church, must, if they be true to their profession, sooner or later, admit and adopt the whole scheme of religion taught and practised in that Church. But if there be no such *divine* authority vested in the Church, then neither can its teaching or its power be regarded as authoritative *in itself*: its doctrines and its power must rest on other evidence than its own assertion of them; and that evidence drawn from some confessed Divine source, such as the Scriptures are *proved* to be.

This line, then, should be distinctly drawn between the two Churches, as a boundary which cannot be passed by either, without an invasion of the territory of the other. What is the *essential evidence* on which each rests its scheme of religion, and which its advocates will never forego? Is it the dictum of the Church, or that of Scripture? A person may appeal to the evidence of Christian writers, and the determinations of the Church in the primitive times. But if he makes

Scripture his point of outset and return, and
brings all his researches to the illustration of
what he collects from Scripture, then is he proceeding in the spirit of the Church of England.
If, on the contrary, he uses the Scripture only as
a document written for the eye of the Church,
and all the while that he quotes its texts, and
importunes its evidence for his teaching, regards
that doctrine, for which he contends, as grounded
on Church authority,—such an one is a Romanist
in his proceeding, however he may profess his
attachment to the principle of the Sufficiency of
Scripture to Salvation.   Nor is this line of de-
marcation observed, by limiting the authoritative
power of the Church to any particular period, or
any particular Councils.   The moment that we
depart from the age of the Apostles, we quit the
period of *Divine* Authority in the Church.   And
however we may respect the writers of one period
of the Church more than those of another, or
certain Councils more than others, and embrace
the opinions and decisions of such, we must not
receive them as *authoritative*; we must not test
Scripture by them, but them by Scripture: if we
would keep clear of the Romanizing spirit, we
must receive them only as *confirmations* of the

truth ; not as primary and fundamental evidence of the truth.

At the same time, when our Church is said to be essentially opposed to Rome in restricting the Divine Authority of its ministration to the written word, it is not excluded by this restriction from an active *co-operation* with the written word in bringing men to Christ. Hence the assertion, that the Bible only is the religion of the Church of England is true in one sense, and not true in another. It is true as respects the *Divine Authority*, by which the Church teaches and acts. It is not true, if it be understood to mean that there is no other subordinate authority, auxiliary to the Scriptures, and administering to their use. For we fully hold that our Lord instituted a standing ministry, for the teaching of his word, and calling and receiving men into his Church ; for administering his Sacraments and feeding his flock. And when we deny to this ministry an Authority which does not belong to it, we do not deny it *all* Authority—we do not deny an Authority inherited from the Apostles, sufficient to assure the believer, that the word which the ministers of Christ preach is not theirs, but the Lord's who sent them ; and that the Sacraments and other ordinances of

Christ, which they dispense, are duly administered, and, therefore, attended to the faithful with those blessings which the Lord has connected with their due celebration.

It is the more necessary that we should study accurately the boundary which separates the Authority of our own Church from that of Rome, as unhappily there is in these times (and, perhaps, in all times, more or less, from the natural leanings of the human heart), a disposition to represent the Authority claimed by the two Churches as the *same in kind*; or, at least, to make the difference consist only in the fact that, in the case of our own Church, this high Authority has not been corruptly exercised : for that the Church has kept itself in union with the Church Catholic which cannot err or sin, and has, therefore, avoided errors ; whereas the Church of Rome, by permitting a traditionary system to grow up, and practically infect its teaching, has so far deviated from the Church Catholic, and given a sanction to corruptions of doctrine and practice.

That, in fact, has come to pass which a preacher from the University pulpit, some sixty or seventy years ago, predicted would be the result of indifferentism on the subject of religious profession,

—from men losing sight of that just Authority which must belong to the true Doctrine and Institution of Christ.

"The truth is," he says, "should men once take up the persuasion, that not only the instructors, but the institutions in all religions are the same, they could have little scruple, upon a suitable temptation offered, against becoming proselytes to *any*; nor might those who should be really willing, have it in their power to make the Romish religion an exception in this case. If its absurdities and idolatries must shock the rational and thoughtful part of the nation ; and if the humane and good-natured must be startled (as well they may) at the great barbarities formerly exercised, and the yet greater attempted by its professors in these kingdoms ; yet, let it be remembered, that it has much pomp and pageantry in its worship, to attract the lover of state and magnificence ; it pretends to have infallible guidance for the doubtful, and secure repose for the unsettled ; it offers indulgences to the libertine, and deals out pardons to the debauched, on very easy terms. And to how considerable a part of our people, when once let loose from the principles in which they have been educated, it might soon address itself, under one or other of these characters, in a conjuncture of real danger, I think every lover of his country (could we urge no *higher* motive) might do well to consider*."

These observations were made at a time when Dissent from the Church had greatly increased, through that irregular impulse of religion which the rise of Methodism had given to the mass of the people ; and it seemed, as at the commencement of the Reformation, that, together with the great good effected in awakening men from their slumber of irreligion, the principles of Church-communion and unity in the faith would be lost sight of by many, in the transport of their zeal ; or explained away, through the fallacy of judging that the *proceeding* must be right throughout, where so much essential good had been done. This consequence, we know, did take place to a great extent. But a reaction has followed, as is commonly observed in the case of all great excitements. The religious movement has not subsided, but it has taken an opposite direction. Inquiring minds have sought a station of rest amidst the agitations of Sectarianism, and have found it only in the extreme of an infallible

* Fothergill's Sermons, vol. i. p. 138.

Church-authority: and others, won by the attractions which a scheme of such imposing pretension offers, have readily given themselves to the support of the specious delusion. Persons are but too apt to dislike those that differ from them, and especially in religious opinion, in proportion to the greater interest of the subject: and the feeling against Dissent, aggravated by its increase of power and extent, has naturally laid hold of that which gave expression to it in the most intense form. Hence that disposition towards the Roman view of Church-authority which has been manifested among us. For that view involves in it a hatred of dissent: of dissent, not only on account of its errors of doctrine, but *because it is dissent*; because it is then regarded as a wilful rebellion against the authority of Christ Himself, like the rebellion of Korah, Dathan, and Abiram, against the Lord's Authority in Moses and Aaron; or like the secession of the Ten Tribes, and the setting up of the kingdom of Samaria against the Theocracy in Israel; and assumes, accordingly, the nature of impiety and sin.

That this feeling unhappily exists to a great extent among us, we cannot deny; and that it has met with a congenial support in the high notion of ecclesiastical supremacy, which has been, of late, so sedulously insinuated into the minds of the rising generation of this University especially, by a party, itself based on that notion, and the living energizing expression of it.

The ascendency, however, of a principle, even the temporary ascendency, such as it has enjoyed during the flourishing days of this party, shews its true character. Ἀρχὴ τὸν ἄνδρα δείξει is true of principles as of men. We might not have been disposed to take the warning which the long experience of the world has given in the case of the Church of Rome: because it might have been supposed that the principle could be inculcated under the shade of a *reformed* Church, apart from its obnoxious accompaniments in the former instance,—apart from the corruptions of faith and practice which have followed in the Church of Rome. But we have now seen that these corruptions are its natural and proper results; that we cannot take up an extravagant, unscriptural theory of the Church, without taking along with it its unscriptural consequences; that, if we become Romanists in principle, we must be Romanists throughout; believers in the doctrine of the Mass, and of Purgatory, and of Invocation of saints and angels, of Justification by the Sacraments, of the Merit of good works, and other corruptions of the Church of Rome; and that we must also become assimilated to it in conduct, having words of peace and gentleness on our lips, and persecution in our hearts.

The developments of the last few years have strikingly brought this fact before us; and we may learn, therefore, that there is no security to us in the soundness of our doctrines, if we admit any tampering with the principle of Church-authority: that while we are building up the walls of our city on high, and fortifying it against attacks from without, we are but giving a rallying-point to a faction within us; a citadel to be seized by an oligarchy at home, as occasion may offer, from which they may exercise their despotism safely, and model the existing constitution of things to their pleasure. We should know, too, how dangerous it is, to invite, for succour against our adversaries, the alliance of a principle which is, by its nature, too strong for us; which will not retire within its own dominion, when it has accomplished the work for which we have called it in; but will turn its triumph against our enemies, (as history has often shewn in the case of states obtaining the aid of some more powerful state against their neighbours,) into the means of mastery over ourselves.

In conclusion, therefore, I would earnestly impress upon all, what it has been the main object of this discourse to point out, the duty of acquainting themselves thoroughly with the principles of Church-authority, held respectively by the Church of Rome and the Church of England. There is no concord between them. They lead, and necessarily must lead, to schemes of religion different in spirit and in conduct.

According to our own Church :—Christ is with the Church sanctifying it by his Spirit ; sanctifying it by the word of God, which is truth ; perpetually present with it, seconding the labours of his ministers in bringing men to vital union with the Father and the Son, by the Spirit working with their ministry of the word. We look, therefore, for a constant superintendence, and direction, and assistance of the Spirit of Christ in all that is done by the members of the Church, as well as by its ministers, in fulfilling their respective vocations according to his commandment ; by the ministers of the Church, in their peculiar function of dispensing the Gospel committed to them ; by all members of the Church, in believing and obeying the Gospel dispensed to them. And a Church thus directed, we believe to be fully sanctified ; though not rendered infallible, or free from sin, at least, in its present militant state ; yet so effectually sustained by the Spirit of Christ, that, through his grace, its faith shall not fail, nor the gates of hell prevail against it. All its doctrines are, therefore, proposed as the dictates of the Holy Spirit ; to be taught by its ministers, not as their word, but the word of the Spirit given them to teach ; to be received by its members, as the lively oracles of the Spirit, which the Spirit Himself must bring home to their spirit, in order to their salvation. In like manner, in dispensing the Sacraments, it offers them to the *faith* of the receiver, as grace to be received by that faith which is the gift of the Spirit ; and not as dependent on the operation of the ministers of the Church, further than that the institution of Christ —what He has appointed for their due celebration —must be strictly observed, if we would hope for the blessing annexed to his institution.

But the Church of Rome, as I have before pointed out, speaks as the organ of Christ Him-

Y

self. It claims to be sanctified by Him as the Word of God dwelling in itself; to be as truly the representative of the Word of God in the world, as the Incarnate Word, Jesus Christ Himself, was whilst on earth. As He was God and man, so the Church, in their view, is God and man working in one visible body; the continuance, without interruption, of the teaching of the Lord; not an institution of *remembrance* of the Lord, of His teaching and His Passion, but a prolongation of both; a successive repetition of them, only modified by the different circumstances of the case; the successive generations of the Church now accomplishing, again and again, what the Lord Himself once accomplished in his own Person. Christ is thus represented, not as the foundation, according to Scripture, on which every Christian must build *at once*, all his faith, and all his hope; but rather as the basis on which the ministry are to erect their system of justification by the Sacraments of the Church; as the cause and origin of their mediatorial power, and of the faith exacted for their teaching.

Let the two principles of Church-authority be thoroughly examined; and I doubt not it will be seen, that there is no true resemblance between them—no coincidence; that there can be no sincere approximation of them.   To maintain our cause, accordingly, whether against Dissenters, or against Rome,—the way is not to take up a position by the side of Rome, the real mother of all dissent; but to strengthen our own position; to lengthen the cords, and strengthen the stakes of that truly Christian and Apostolic Church to which we belong; to imbue ourselves entirely with its spirit of moderation and charity; and to exemplify that spirit, whether we be teachers or hearers of the word, in all our profession and conduct.   So we may best hope to advance towards that unity for which the Lord prayed in that last solemn address to the Father, which has formed the subject of this day's consideration. So may we trust that we truly inherit and faithfully transmit the blessing, which the Lord pronounced on his Church, when He said, " Neither pray I for these alone, but for them also which shall believe on Me through their word; that they all may be one; as Thou, Father, art in Me, and I in Thee, that they also may be one in Us: that the world may believe that Thou hast sent Me."

SERMON X.

THE FAITHFUL STEWARD.

PREACHED IN THE CATHEDRAL OF CHRIST CHURCH,

On SUNDAY, December 15, 1844.

SERMON X.

THE FAITHFUL STEWARD.

---

1 Cor. iv. 1, 2.

Let a man so account of us, as of the ministers of Christ, and
stewards of the mysteries of God. Moreover it is required in
stewards that a man be found faithful.

As we draw nearer to the actual celebration of
our Lord's coming in the flesh, we are reminded
more and more forcibly by the services of the
Church of the necessity of preparation in order
duly to welcome the glad event.

The first Sunday of this holy season impressed
on us the general exhortation to Christian vigilance and sobriety of mind ; telling us, that it was
high time to awake out of sleep, to cast off the
works of darkness and put on the armour of
light ; for that we must think, as we look to the

day of Christ's appearing, of our salvation drawing nigh—of the night as far spent, and the day at hand.

The second Sunday in Advent sent us to those Holy Scriptures which testify of the Lord; that through them we might become acquainted with Him; learning from them all that His holy Prophets have declared beforehand of his coming, and all that He has told us by his own preaching, and all that his Evangelists and Apostles have set forth concerning Him and the way of eternal life through Him; so that we might not from ignorance of the Scriptures be slow of heart to believe in Him, but, as persons taught of God, look to his appearing with a faith firmly grounded on His Word.

The third Sunday, that at which we are now arrived, leads us to reflect on the importance of the ministration of the word and ordinances of Christ, and of the right use of the means of grace which we enjoy generally through the Spirit of Christ abiding with the Church.

Let us then, Brethren, turn our attention especially on this occasion to this view of our preparation for the coming of Christ; and so let us follow in the steps in which this day's service would lead us, and endeavour to render them, through God's assistance, effectual steps towards the Saviour to whom they point.

The analogy between the first and second coming of Christ, on which the whole service of Advent is framed, is strikingly brought before us in the service of this particular Sunday. It is made the basis of the peculiar exhortation of the day. As a messenger was sent before the face of the Lord to prepare the way at his first coming, so are the ministers and stewards of his mysteries required to prepare and make ready His way, that at His second coming to judge the world we may be found an acceptable people in his sight. We are required accordingly by this day's service to consider, not simply how we shall avail ourselves of the ministrations of the Church for the fit disposition of our minds in order to the approaching festival and the high and solemn thoughts connected with it, but how those ministrations themselves shall be best directed to their great object; how they shall truly correspond with their type, the preparing of the way of the Lord by the Baptist, and be in themselves a preparation for his coming to judgment.

For this purpose no more appropriate words of Scripture can be selected, than those which form the commencement of the Epistle of the day. "Let a man so account of us," says St. Paul, speaking of himself and his fellow-labourers in the Gospel, "as of the ministers of Christ, and stewards of the mysteries of God. Moreover it is required of stewards that a man may be found faithful." Though he wrought miracles and spake with tongues, and derived his authority for the work of the ministry immediately from the Lord Himself, he refers to none of these qualifications as the grounds of his claim on the respect of the Corinthian Church, but would be tried simply by his faithfulness in the discharge of the trust reposed in him as a minister of Christ and steward of the mysteries of God. He remembered how the Lord himself had characterized his ministers in the same language, when He said, "Who is that faithful and wise steward whom the Lord shall set over his household to give them their meat in due season?" This was the estimation, accordingly, in which St. Paul desires that himself and his fellow-labourers in the Gospel should be held by the people. Were they acting the part of ministers of Christ—of servants set

over the Lord's household—of stewards entrusted
with the dispensation of the Divine Word; were
they found to be faithful in the discharge of this
sacred trust—this stewardship of the Gospel;
were they using that authority which the Lord
had given them in his household for its proper
purpose—the feeding of his people? Were they
dispensing the Lord's meat to the several members of the household—ministering the word of
God, so that it might be received by his people
to their spiritual sustenance and comfort in the
Faith?

What then, in a word, is the pattern here proposed to us by St. Paul, of that ministration of
the Church which may be truly regarded as a
ministration in Christ's behalf to the people?
In a word, it is simplicity of teaching and ministering the word of Christ. There were other
teachers in the days of the Apostle, calling themselves Christian teachers, who, like the Sophists
of old among the Greeks, professed to inform
their disciples in all wisdom; to advance them
from the rudiments of Christ, in which they had
been disciplined by the Apostle, to more spiritual heights of divine knowledge. These were
not ministers of Christ, or stewards of the myste-

ries of God, in the Apostle's sense. He was
skilled in that learning which these pretenders
to wisdom put forth as their recommendation to
the Christian converts; but he put this away from
him in his capacity of a minister of the Gospel,
and "determined to know nothing" in all his
preaching "save Jesus Christ and Him Crucified." He considered only what might tend to
the edification of the Church on that foundation
of Christ which he had laid. The false teachers
of the Gospel cared not how they might perplex
and subvert the faith of their hearers, by the various questionings to which they might give rise
in the freedom of their speculations. Witness
the sundry difficulties with which the Corinthian
Church was troubled, by the mischievous importunity of those perverse teachers who had gained
popularity among them during the absence of the
Apostle,—difficulties, which occasioned the Apostle so much grief of heart, and which extorted
from him those eloquent testimonials of his fervour of spirit in their behalf,—his two Epistles
to the Corinthians. Whilst he discusses and
removes these difficulties in regard to the several
particulars which had been brought under his
notice, it is to be observed, how anxious he is

throughout, to cut off all occasion for them, and to restrain the professors and teachers of the Gospel within the strict limits of a Gospel profession and Gospel teaching. A feverish excitement had been produced in the Corinthian Church as to the doctrine which they should chiefly follow ; some attaching themselves to this teacher, some to another. All this had been occasioned by the variety of doctrine introduced ; unsettling the minds of the members of the Church, disquieting even the soundest of them, and obliging them to have recourse to the counsel of the Apostle in their perplexity. To remedy this state of confusion and disorder is accordingly the great object of his Epistles to the Corinthians ; and we may thus regard those Epistles on the whole, and in many express passages very distinctly, as a warning from the Holy Spirit of the evil of unstable doctrine—a warning directed first and chiefly to the ministers of the Church, and then to the members at large.

I shall proceed in the sequel of this Discourse to develop the truth of this warning, more especially in its application to ourselves.

According to St. Paul, he is no true minister of Christ—no faithful steward of the mysteries of

God,—who is reckless on this point, or who by the tenor of his teaching risks the unsettling of the minds of his brethren in Christ.

Obviously, among the characteristics of a teacher, and especially of a teacher of Revealed Truth, stability of view in regard to the great matters of his teaching must hold a chief place. It is vain for a steward of the Lord to pretend to dispense the Lord's meat to the household over which he is set, if he knows not where to find it, or what it is; if he has first to inquire as to what his Lord intends to be given to the members of his household, or what is good and wholesome for them. His time will be employed, and his thoughts distracted, in these previous inquiries; and he will omit to give them their meat in due season. And, at best, with what misgivings and questionings among themselves, must those who have to receive the food of spiritual instruction and comfort at his hands, receive it from one who presents himself before them as a man of unsettled doctrine! He will be to them as that character described by St. James, the "double-minded man, unstable in all his ways*." And how shall they learn of him who, whilst profess-

* Jam. i. 8.

ing to teach others, has not himself acquired the fixedness of a true faith?

Controversialists of Rome, looking to the differences of opinion manifested wherever the light and freedom of the Reformation have spread, or to what they call the "variations" of Protestants, and observing that even our own Church has not been exempt from the agitation of disputes, have drawn a favourable contrast of their own uniformity and unchangeableness with the imputed variableness of other Churches. But whatever grounds there may be for the imputation of variableness in other Protestant Communions, there is no justice in such a charge against our own Church. No Church has a more stable body of doctrine than ours. The formularies in which the Church lays down the rule of its teaching, are not ambiguous in themselves. Nor has the Church, from the time when it first felt the necessity of separating the truth from the corruptions which had grown around it and overlaid it, ever departed from or varied its original confession. Persons have arisen from time to time among us speaking perverse things, and drawing others after them, as in the primitive Churches planted by the

Apostles themselves. Persons, too, dissenting from the doctrines of the Articles, have represented the Articles, if not as directly favouring their views, as at least admitting their construction, or as having no definite meaning. Still the Confession of the Church remains the same; a standing witness against all attempts at innovation within its pale, in like manner as the Scriptures remain a stable rule of faith, notwithstanding all the heretical opinions which may be imputed to their teaching. If all received the teaching of our Church in the simplicity in which it is addressed to them, there would exist no ground of complaint of the varying doctrine of its ministers. There might doubtless be still many minor differences among them on points not necessary either to Salvation or to Communion. But on all the great truths set forth in our formularies, all would substantially be of the same mind and speak the same thing. Then should we, with the fuller blessing of the Spirit descending on us as one body in Christ, realize our holy mission in the world in more fully spreading the knowledge of His truth and Salvation.

The blame, then, that we do not accomplish this design of our Lord in raising us up to our

eminence in Christendom, is not to be cast on
the constitution itself of the Church to which we
belong, but on ourselves individually, that we do
not act up to the spirit of its system,—that we
act rather on our own estimate of it, and not on
its simple dictation. Persons take from it only
so much as falls in with some framework of
their own, or what impresses their feelings, or
accords with their habits of thought and taste.
Others trace out certain general ideas as the
pervading truth of the system, rejecting all
that is peculiar and characteristic; and so
practically slide into indifferentism, under the
outward profession of a definite scheme of doctrine.

All such modes of proceeding on the part of
ministers of the Church, must be accompanied
with instability of doctrine. Teachers of such a
kind, pursuing no simple path themselves, can
only (so far as their teaching has any effect, and
is not counteracted by the spirit of the Church
itself and its hold on the judgments and feeling
of those who are true to its spirit,) unsettle the
minds of their hearers, and produce in them a
distrust of the truth itself. The hearer is tempted
to suspect all teachers, when he finds himself

disappointed in those in whom he has been
previously disposed to place reliance, and to
whom perhaps he has hitherto looked up as
his guides, and examples in sound profession
of Christian doctrine. In some instances, he
may be even tempted to the renunciation of
all authority in matters of religious belief; and
against the natural bias of feeling, (for doubtless in religion especially the heart of man
does instinctively seek for communion and
counsel,) to throw himself entirely, in despair
of other human means, on his own independent
judgment.

And it is well if this distempered feeling does
not extend also to the matters proposed to belief,
and produce also, as I have said, a distrust of
the truth itself. When persons have for a long
time enjoyed a repose of mind with regard to the
great fundamental principles of their religious
profession; when their whole system of faith
and conduct has gone on the assumption of certain truths which they have never even thought
of questioning; and they now learn that what
they have hitherto regarded as axioms and pos-
tulates in their system are no longer to be held
so, but that even these must be modified or

admitted with exception ;—how must they be tempted to doubt whether anything whatever is true,—whether truth can absolutely be found, —whether anything is objectively real,—or whether at most anything can be ascertained in the matter of Religion beyond the probable !

If, for example, a member of our Church hears from its ministers that the Scriptures are not the sole source and authority of the doctrines which he must receive, but that he must obey the teaching of the Church by the mouth of its ministers, and that he rejects that teaching, as such, at the imminent peril of his soul,—what is this but to overthrow to the mind of the simple Christian, what he has been accustomed to hold as the firm and immovable basis of his religious profession ? Ask any simple-minded member of our Church to what he looks for his knowledge of divine things,—for his rule of Christian belief, and Christian life,—and he would doubtless refer you to the Bible. He may not perhaps be able to read his Bible—he may have received the truth from the dictation of others—from the ministers of the Church. Still, if he can give any answer at all to the question, it will be, that he believes the whole word of God to be contained in the Bible : so thoroughly has this persuasion been steeped into the minds of English Churchmen, that all things belonging to Salvation are contained in the written word of God. The uninstructed may not be able to explain or justify the principle: but they testify to its existence and prevalence. It is in fact the root from which has sprung the pure and vigorous stock of the religious profession of this country. Every branch of Christian doctrine which spreads itself forth among us, rejoicing in the sunshine and the dew of God's blessing, derives its strength from this principle. We have not obtained it as a graft from another tree. But by God's Providence and Grace, the Gospel has been planted in this country, not without its own stock and its own root,—the Scriptures— the word of God.

What, then, I would again ask, must be the effect on the simple hearer thus rooted and established in the doctrine of Christ, when he finds the minister disputing the point which he has all along taken for granted—laying the axe to the very root—disparaging the use of the Bible as

the only source of Christian instruction to the
people, and representing it as a dark and sealed
volume without the living interpretation of the
Church ? He may be told indeed, at the same
time, that the Scriptures *contain* all things
necessary for salvation. But how will this declaration satisfy him, when he finds it must
be understood very differently from what he
has conceived of the instruction of the Bible ;
inasmuch as, according to the explanation given
him, Scripture supplies only the elements and
germs of truth, which the teaching of the Church
develops and perfects ?

Again, the preaching of the Blessed Atonement through the blood of Christ is, to all who
have been trained in the doctrine of the Church
of England, the beginning and the end of all
preaching of the Gospel. As it is the Scriptural
confession of our Church, that " no other name
is given under heaven whereby we can be saved
but only the name of the Lord Jesus Christ ;"
so have its members hitherto been taught, that
in Him is an ever-flowing fountain of life and
grace and mercy for all sin and uncleanness
—that though a man sin again and again, still,
if he but turn to God, repenting heartily of his

sin, and determining, through God's grace, to forsake it utterly, and looking to the promises of God in Christ for forgiveness, he shall obtain forgiveness for Christ's sake.

What will the perplexity then be to the Christian hearer, when he finds his teacher forbearing to speak of the Atonement of Christ; keeping it back as a mystery too holy for the ears of an ordinary Christian congregation; as a truth deposited with the ministers of the Church to recur to in their ministerial acts, and only to be applied by them through those acts; and not the immediate object of faith to the penitent sinner,—not the immediate and proper ground of his justification before God? He has learnt from his Bible that " the blood of Christ cleanseth from all sin"—that " through Christ we have access to the Father "—that " if any man sin, we have an advocate with the Father, Jesus Christ the righteous, and that He is the propitiation for our sins," and many such declarations. In the prayers of the Liturgy, he is led to confess his sins, and hope for pardon through Christ; in every petition and thanksgiving, to rely on the mediation of Christ for the acceptance of his offering ; in partaking of the spiritual food of the Lord's Supper, to seek the benefits of the Atonement made once for all on the Cross. What, then, if he is told that he has already received the benefits of the Atonement—that he has had his portion in the Sacrament of Baptism—and if he has exhausted it by his sins —if he has fallen from the grace then received— he has lost his justification—he has no other means of recovery but the baptism of tears, the penances of self-mortification and self-sacrifice —the second plank after shipwreck,—to save him from destruction; that, true as the Atonement of the Cross is, it avails only to give efficacy to the means of restoration prescribed and administered by the hands of the ministry ; not to recommend the sinner to mercy, but to render the acts performed by him in his penance, by a virtue derived from it to them, propitiatory and meritorious ?

What must be his bewilderment of thought with regard to the doctrine of the Atonement, when he is led through this labyrinth of statement ? He had received that doctrine in simplicity. Mysterious in itself he knew it to be. But the profession of it at least, as inculcated on him by the Scriptures, and the accustomed teaching of the Church, was simple. He thought he had only to come to Christ and he should be saved—to believe in his heart that Christ had died for his sins, and had been raised again for his justification,—and he should be saved. But if what he now hears be true, he has mistaken his way: he has yet to learn the Gospel. He has been taught that the righteousness wherein he must be found, if he would be justified, is a righteousness not his own, even " the righteousness which is of God through faith," since " God made him to be sin for us who knew no sin, that we might be made the righteousness of God in him*." " Such we are," says Hooker, in setting forth the doctrine of Justification professed by the Church of England, " such we are in the sight of God the Father, as is the very Son of God Himself. Let it be counted folly or frenzy, or fury whatsoever, it is our comfort and our wisdom; we care for no other knowledge in the world but this, that man hath sinned and God hath suffered; that God hath made Himself the Son of man, and that men are made the righteousness of God†." But now the hearer learns from some, that this

* 2 Cor. v. 21.   † Discourse of Justification, p. 437.

view of Justification is but the fruit of private judgment exercised on the Scripture—a doctrine unknown to the Church before the Reformation —a Lutheran heresy and not a Catholic truth ; for that the righteousness which justifies man is a quality infused and inherent in him, admitting of degrees, varying with the varying state of the individual, capable of being diminished and lost, or increased more and more, to the attainment even in this life of the condition of the perfect saint. What the simple Christian had all along regarded as an immovable objective truth on which his conduct could have no influence or effect, (for what could undo the gracious act of a Saviour's love, what could augment or abate the saving efficacy of his Passion?), is now represented as a state of the soul, a disposition and habit engendered in the individual man. The simple Christian knew indeed that he needed the grace of the Holy Spirit working in him and with him, to enable him to avail himself of the great Salvation wrought for him,—that, " being freed from sin, and made a servant of God, he must further have his fruit unto holiness*,"—that he must be sanctified inwardly, in order to his re-

* Rom. vi. 22.

ceiving the eternal inheritance bequeathed to him by his Saviour. But though he knows that faith, and holiness springing from that faith, are wrought *in him* by the Holy Spirit, he has not confounded these internal workings of the Spirit of Sanctification with the external act of the justifying grace of his Saviour. This he does not regard as in any way belonging to him, or existing in him personally, but simply as imputed to him—as counted to him for righteousness through faith. Where then shall he find any standing-place in his religion, when his mind is disturbed on this fundamental point; when the question, already settled in the Articles, is agitated by some in his own Church, as to wherein Justification by Faith consists—and the truth is by some explained away, as meaning nothing more than Justification by the Gospel, in opposition to Judaism or any false religion, or is interpreted in a sense the reverse of the doctrine of the Reformation, namely, that Justification by Faith means, not that the salvation of the sinner is a principle of life *without* him, but a principle working *within* him?

Again, amongst the vital improvements which the Reformation has established in the modes of

religious thought and feeling of the members of
our Church, is the conviction, that forms and
ceremonies constitute no essential part of the
Christian's faith. Our Church has trained its
members indeed to have respect to the order
and decency of their public worship, and to observe such rites and ceremonies as it has appointed in the exercise of its lawful authority for
their edification. Not only in the Articles is
this shewn, but in the excellent observations on
this subject in the Preface to the Book of Common Prayer, it is expressly stated on what
ground all ceremonies are established in the
Church. " As those be taken away," it is said,
" which were most absurd, and did burthen
men's consciences without any cause, so the
other that remain are retained for a discipline
and order, which, upon just cause, may be altered and changed, and therefore are not to be
esteemed equal with God's law. And, moreover,
they be neither dark nor dumb ceremonies, but
are so set forth that every man may understand
what they do mean, and to what use they do
serve ; so that it is not like that they, in time to
come, should be abused as other have been.
And in these, our doings, we condemn no other

nations, nor prescribe anything but to our own
people only : for we think it convenient that
every country should use such ceremonies as
they shall think best to the setting forth of God's
honour and glory, and to the reducing of the
people to a most perfect and godly living, without error or superstition ; and that they should
put away other things which from time to time
they perceive to be most abused ; as in men's
ordinances it often chanceth diversely in divers
countries*." In conformity to which declaration
concerning ceremonies, it is previously stated in
the same Preface concerning the alterations introduced, " that most of the alterations were
made, either, first, for the better direction of
them that are to officiate in any part of Divine
Service, which is chiefly done in the Kalendars
and Rubrics ;" and, as it goes on to state, for
the simplifying of some expressions, and adapt-
ing them to the time, and for a more perfect,
better rendering of some passages of Scripture.
Such then is the spirit which our Church has
carried into its ritual, and which the practice of
nearly three Centuries has deeply fixed in the
minds of its members.

* Preface to Common Prayer.

What, then, will be the perplexity on this
head also, when members of the Church find controversies about ceremonies and rubrical directions keenly agitated in the Church, as if they
were matters of vital doctrine,—when ministers
of the Church are not only contending in argument about such matters, but commencing variations from existing usages in the manner of performing divine service, and exciting attention to
changes of vestments and position in the performance of public worship? It is not like the
contest about the use of the surplice at the time
of the Reformation, when the people were necessarily called to the consideration of what
should be retained, or what discarded, of those
things which had been associated with the corruptions of the Faith. The vestment controversy
was then forced on people's minds, and was far
from unreasonable at that time ; though too
great importance was attributed to it even then.
But now that the minds of members of the
Church at large are settled on this point,—now
that the decent ceremonial of the Church is held
in just esteem, nay, cherished by the chief part
of its members with strong feelings of attachment—an attachment confirmed by their expe-

rience of its tendency to edification—it must surely be most unwise to raise so unnecessary a controversy,—to disturb a feeling of wise and happy contentment, but which, when once roused from its quiescence, will not be easily quelled, nor perhaps until it has spent itself in acts of destruction which the movers of the storm would deprecate too late.

But what I am chiefly remarking here, is the evil itself of unsettling the minds of people on these matters,—leading them to think that *these* must be much more important things *in Religion* than they have been accustomed to think them ; and perplexing them with doubtful disputations ; turning their attention, for the time at least, from the substance of the faith to the externals —from the things indispensable to Salvation to things indifferent—from the service of the heart to the service of the body.

But amidst the various forms which unstable teaching may assume, none is more mischievous, both to teacher and hearer, than that which oscillates between rival systems, —which professes in outward communion the doctrine of our Church, and infuses into it practically another spirit,—a spirit alien from its own, and

which it utterly refuses. How can that person
do otherwise than produce difficulty and dissatis-
faction in the minds of others to whom he has
access, who laments over the want of spirituality,
as he thinks, in our Church—who professes
himself ill at ease under its authority—and
scruples not to avow his admiration and affection for another Church,—one, for example, who
wavers on the confines of Rome, which he seems
at every moment ready to pass, and is only kept
back by the force of the circumstances in which
he stands—only not a member of the Church of
Rome, because he is by position a member of the
Church of England? For what simple member
of our Church is there who, though uninstructed
in the controversies between the Churches of
England and Rome, does not know enough of
the disagreement between the two Churches, to
be persuaded that there can be no real union or
fusion of their respective systems of faith and
discipline? It will be a hard task, may we not
say an impossible one, to unprotestantize this
country, so thoroughly leavened as it is with the
spirit of the Reformation—so faithfully has the
memory of the great deliverance effected by that
event from the bondage of Rome been trans-

mitted from father to son, that it may be said to
live in all its freshness in the present generation.
What mean our Articles and Formularies and
Liturgy, if they do not attest, that we have come
forth from the corruptions and superstitions of
Rome to worship the Lord our God, that we might
not be partakers in other men's sins,—that we
might be a peculiar people unto God,—that we
might serve God after the manner of our fore-
fathers in Christ, the Apostles and primitive
disciples of the Church? Marvellous indeed
would be that awakening as from a dream, for
members of our Church to discover, that the
difference between themselves and Rome, which
they had held all along to be a fixed reality, was
no reality—that the two Churches were ac-
cordant in their principles—that the protestation
of our Church applies only to corrupt, traditionary practices, which Rome no less repudiates
in her internal system than ourselves. Members
of our Church must forget all the past—they
must think the blood of its confessors and
martyrs vainly, if not justly shed, in a sinful resistance to Catholic truth and authority—they
must condemn as uncatholic and unprofitable,
the labours of its great divines in their polemics

against Rome—they must contradict the very
language of their Articles, and affirm that the
Homilies, expressly prepared as they were for
the purpose of teaching the form of sound doctrine established by the Reformers, do not contain
" a godly and wholesome doctrine," nor one
" necessary for those times." All this it must
forego and abandon, if they are to believe that
they are essentially at one with Rome. Fruitless
therefore we may say will be the result, the ultimate result, of any endeavour to unprotestantize
the members of our Church. But still the very
endeavour will not be without its mischief,—probably great and long-continued mischief. The
weak and the timid will be shaken—the warm
and enthusiastic will be excited—the gentle and
the moderate will be startled—on all sides there
will be disquietude and trouble. More particularly must this be the case, if members of the
Church are impressed with the idea, that parts
of the system of the Church are at variance with
each other—and that, not by the crimination of
adversaries, to which the reply would be comparatively easy, but by the teachers themselves
of the Church—if it is represented to them that
our Articles are unsound so far as they are

2 A

Protestant, and our Liturgy sound so far as it may be understood to convey the doctrine of Rome. What, I say, must be the confusion introduced by such a method of teaching? What can be the present effect, at any rate, of such instability on the part of the authorized instructors of the people, but to introduce questionings among them respecting the sincerity of the teachers and the soundness of their doctrine?

If, then, there is any one quality more indispensable than another in the minister of the Gospel, it is stability of profession—the not looking to the right or to the left, as his eye may be captivated by some point of light in another system. I speak not with reference to the religion of Rome only, but to any other class or sect of believers out of the limits of his own Communion. I illustrate from Rome chiefly, because our chief dangers at present come from that quarter. He must have that single eye in the profession and teaching of the doctrine of the Church, which our Lord requires of all that belong to Him, in whatever they think or do in His service. He must be thoroughly persuaded in what he undertakes to teach as a minister of the Church of England, that the doctrine is true with-

out extenuation or any reservation whatever. By
this only can he be faithful to his charge, faithful
to his engagement as a steward of this portion
of the Lord's household. For it is not a mere
general commission that he has received—it is
not an indefinite general trust that has been con-
fided to him. He has received a special charge
from the Church of this realm to superintend this
peculiar household of Christ,—" to minister the
doctrine and Sacraments and the discipline of
Christ as this Church and realm hath received
the same, according to the commandments of
God ;" so as to " teach the people committed to
his cure and charge with all diligence to keep
and observe the same*." The Church, accordingly, asks its future minister whether he *thinks*
in his heart that he is " truly called according to
the will of our Lord Jesus Christ, and the order of
this United Church of England and Ireland." It
requires of him a firm persuasion, not simply that
he is " truly called according to the will of our
Lord Jesus Christ ;" but that he is called to that
particular limitation of his general duty which
"the order of *this Church*" prescribes. And when
the Ordination Service speaks of *this* Church, it

* Ordering of Priests.

2 A 2

clearly means the Church as then reformed and re-
established. He therefore that would faithfully
fulfil his Ordination Vow, as well as answer the
express requisition of faithfulness in the steward
of the mysteries of God, must, I would earnestly
repeat, be single-minded in his zeal—must teach
the doctrine and discipline of Christ, as this
Church and realm hath received the same, in
simplicity and godly sincerity, ἐν ἁπλότητι καὶ
εἰλικρινείᾳ Θεοῦ. The wavering itself of a minister of the Church is an evidence to such a
person, that he cannot teach to the edification of
the Church. What firm and consistent doctrine,
I repeat, can he deliver who is himself unsettled ;
perhaps doubting, whether he is not inculcating
heresy and schism, both by teaching what his own
Church requires him to teach, and by his example in remaining a teacher in it ? It is in
vain for such an one to encourage himself in
such a course, by the general plea that the
Church in which he thus equivocally ministers
has the Apostolic succession, and therefore the
authority to dispense the mysteries of God to
the Lord's household. This is no vindication
of *his* adhesion to his own Communion *in preference* to another, which, while it no less pos-

sesses the Apostolic succession, is in *his* view
superior to his own in other essential respects.
And what will be the result? His heart will be
with that other Communion. His yearnings will
be towards it. It is only in actual position that
he will be a minister of his own Communion.
And what must his teaching be, but a constant
effort to bend everything in his own Church
towards that which he really loves more than his
own? Whether it be doctrine, or practice, or
ritual, all will be interpreted by him in an alien
spirit, as it may be assimilated to what exists in
the Church which has his heart. And should
the force of circumstances retain him still in his
present position, his next expedient will be, to
infuse the spirit of that Church, from which he
feels himself thus unhappily precluded, into all
his acts in his own, and to hold himself and his
teaching forth to the public as a pattern, not
indeed of what the Church of his profession
actually is, but of what it ought to be, and
would be, if developed according to his feeling
and wish.

Far better than such unstable conduct is the
alternative of forsaking a Communion to which
one does not heartily belong; at least of giving

up a stewardship, in which one cannot faithfully minister to that household over which he is set.

But let us hope that, rather than adopt this alternative, he who may thus be tempted will, through God's grace, be led to see that this wavering state of mind is sinful, and will rouse himself to a worthier sense of his responsibilities to the Church to whose ministry he has been called ;—no longer working as one in chains, or as the exile from Sion singing the Lord's song in a strange land amidst people of another tongue,—but giving that free and cheerful service which bespeaks a heart at home in its appointed place of labour,—with a feeling towards his own Church like that of Jacob at Bethel when he said,—" How dreadful is this place ! this is none other but the house of God, and this is the gate of Heaven."

What is the chief burthen then, Brethren, of all that I have been stating ? It is this ; that if we would be accounted faithful stewards of the mysteries of God, we must strive with all our hearts to realize throughout our Christian profession the Apostolic rule ; " that ye all speak the same thing," not in word only, but in spirit also ; that we avoid all scattering of " doubtful disputations," διακρίσεις διαλογισμῶν, divisions of the thoughts of the heart, among the brethren— all occasion of offence—anything that may be a stumbling-block in the way of our brethren in Christ; that, as ministers of Christ, we do our best to avail ourselves of the existing means of grace within our own Communion, distributing faithfully their portions to those members of the Lord's household over whom He has placed us.

Such considerations too, Brethren, strongly impress on us all the necessity of duly using every means of preparation for the second coming of Christ, and amongst these, that in particular which the day's service sets before us—the ministration of the word of God by his appointed messengers, the stewards of his mysteries. Take we heed then, Brethren, how we hear—how we use the means appointed for bringing us to Christ, and strengthening us in the faith in Him. What though we have not the Lord Himself and his Apostles now speaking to us, as once they did in their own persons to the first converts to the Gospel? Though absent in the body, they yet speak to us in the lively oracles of the Holy Spirit. In those oracles we hear

the voice of the Holy Spirit continually bringing
to our minds, all that the Lord Himself has done
for us, and all that He has required to be believed and done by us, in order to Salvation.
The word accordingly which the ministers of
Christ faithfully dispense to the household of
God, is not theirs, but His, whose ministers and
stewards they are. The word so dispensed cannot be slighted with impunity. Whilst the Lord
inquires of his ministers at his coming, "Who,
then, is that faithful and wise steward, whom his
lord shall make ruler over his household, to give
them their portion of meat in due season?" He
will also inquire of us all, "Who hath believed
their report? and to whom hath the arm of the
Lord been revealed?" And our anxiety as to our
condition under the preaching of the Gospel may
well be great, when the Lord Himself has put
the question; "Nevertheless, when the Son of
Man cometh, shall he find faith on the earth*?"
Pray we therefore heartily both for ministers
and people in the words of the Collect of this
day: "O Lord Jesu Christ, who at Thy first
coming didst send Thy messenger to prepare Thy
way before Thee; Grant that the ministers and

* Luke xviii. 8.

stewards of Thy mysteries may likewise so prepare and make ready Thy way, by turning the
hearts of the disobedient to the wisdom of the
just, that at Thy second coming to judge the
world, we may be found an acceptable people
in Thy sight, who livest and reignest with the
Father and the Holy Spirit, ever one God, world
without end. Amen."

SERMON XI.

THE INCARNATION A REALITY.

PREACHED IN THE CATHEDRAL OF CHRIST CHURCH,

On SUNDAY, April 27, 1845.

SERMON XI.

THE INCARNATION A REALITY.

2 Cor. xi. 2, 3.

But I fear, lest, by any means, as the serpent beguiled Eve through his subtilty, so your minds should be corrupted from the simplicity that is in Christ. For if he that cometh preacheth another Jesus whom we have not preached, or if ye receive another Spirit which ye have not received, or another Gospel which ye have not accepted, ye might well bear with him.

WHEN our Lord in one of his Parables compared the kingdom of Heaven to " a man which sowed good seed in his field, but while men slept his enemy came and sowed tares among the wheat,"—he foretold what the condition of his Church would actually be in all ages of its existence in the world. The good seed of the Gospel would remain in it, and wholesome fruit would spring up from that seed, year after year. Still, too, together with the wheat would appear also the produce of the evil seed; the whole growing together in the same field, and waiting the final harvest of the great day, when the Lord's reapers shall go forth, and a separation shall be made,—the tares to be gathered up and burnt, but the wheat to be stored in his barn.

Such, then, is the picture of the visible Church. In it, the faithful and the unfaithful are mingled together under the common name of "the faithful;" the holy and the unholy are confounded under the high title of "saints and sons of God." The sound and the unsound believer—all who profess and call themselves Christians, amidst their infinite diversities of opinion and feeling, whether they be of the Lord's planting, or of that planting of the enemy which shall be rooted up and cast away for the burning at the last day—all come alike under the general designation of the visible Church of Christ. Man is eager to make the separation now before the time of the Lord's harvest; to declare at once who are or are not of the true Church, by certain notes of distinction even in the present world; persons or parties drawing the boundary-line according to their own criterion,—just as the servants of the lord of the field wished forthwith to separate the tares from the wheat. But the Lord appoints the harvest for the time, lest haply men should root up the wheat together with the tares; lest haply, in their zeal of separation, they should root up also those that really belong to Him. None can usurp his prerogative, and anticipate that judgment which He has reserved to Himself to pronounce. For whilst the call is sounded forth to all to come to Him; whilst all that name his sacred name are required, on their entering into covenant with Him, to " depart from iniquity ;" He alone " knoweth who are His." And his Church accordingly,—as it is in the world,—as it is a visible Society,—consists of all who are outwardly admitted into it—all who are baptized into the faith—all who own Him for their Lord, and are members, by profession, of the Body which claims Him for its Head.

This mixed condition of the Christian Church was manifest from the earliest times of the preaching of the Gospel. Already indeed had it been prefigured, even before the actual formation of the Christian Church, in the fact, that even one among the Apostles was an hypocrite and traitor to his Lord. But no sooner had the

Apostles begun to execute their commission of preaching the Gospel to every creature, and gathered the first congregations in Christ, than Satan went forth to sow his tares in the newly-planted field of the Lord. The sin of Ananias and Sapphira, and its awful punishment, were conspicuous examples and warnings to the infant Church, of the danger to which they were exposed, from the wiles of Satan, and the frailty of their own nature. Not long after the occurrence of this sad and fearful case, we have a still more appalling instance of the working of the Spirit of Evil in another form of corruption —the first example of heresy and schism in the person of Simon of Samaria. This was an example, not of solitary evil, such as was the sin of Ananias and Sapphira, but of evil essentially communicative, spreading an infection and canker through the body, of which the sores have never since been healed. Here was the case of a man who had been admitted into the Church by Baptism, and had been some time the companion of the Deacon Philip, and a witness of his labours in preaching the Gospel. But as the Lord had a Judas among his immediate disciples, so had his infant Church its traitor in this man of covetous and ambitious worldly mind ; who, whatever may have been his feelings in first embracing the Gospel, lent himself as a fatal instrument to Satan for its corruption. He it was who introduced false " philosophy and vain deceit" into the Church,—availing himself of the reputation which he had obtained among the people before his conversion, as " some great one ;" or, as he was styled, " the great Power of God," for the propagation of anti-Christian error under the shade of the Gospel. Though the narrative of the Acts gives us only some early notices of this man before his conversion, up to the time of his condemnation by St. Peter, and is silent as to his subsequent history, the testimony of the Fathers comes in to supply the sequel. And this testimony is explicit to the point, that, unabashed either by the authoritative rebuke of the Apostle, or the stern warning to repent, he went on like Judas in the perfidy which he had begun, and thus became, as they uniformly assert, " the father of all heresies."

We learn abundantly from the Scriptures themselves, that the great Enemy of the truth was active in diffusing the poison of heretical teaching throughout the Church, in the course of

2 B

the first twenty years after the Ascension of our
Lord. Christians had been taught to shrink
from persecution, by denying the cross of their
Lord, and conforming to the rites of Judaism,
and even partaking in the ceremonies of idolatry;
to look to the Law for their justification, instead
of simply to the Righteousness of Christ by
faith; to deny the historical truth of the birth
and life and death of Christ, resolving the substantial realities of the Gospel into mythical and
allegorical representations; and in working out
this profane ideal of religion, to explain away
the doctrines of a Resurrection and a Future
judgment.

The outset and progress of these errors, the
Fathers, as I have observed, trace up to Simon
of Samaria. And the errors attributed to him
are precisely such as correspond with those
which the Scriptures indicate as existing in the
Churches planted by the Apostles. Thus, when
St. Jerome says, that " whilst as yet the Apostles
were alive in the world; whilst as yet in Judea
the blood of Christ was fresh; the Lord's Body
was asserted to be a Phantom*;" he clearly
points out the prime article of the Corruption

* Adv. Lucif. tom. iii. fol. 66, ed. Erasm.

which Simon began, and of which we trace the development in the several particular corruptions alluded to in the Epistles. This main error sums up and involves all the rest as its natural consequences; though it is probable that not all who held the whole, or any part, of the derived corruptions, were committed to a belief in the original impiety. Let the simple truth of the Lord's Incarnation be denied in any way; let it be removed from the solid ground on which it stands, however mysterious in its nature, as a plain fact in the history of the Gospel; let it be converted into an *idea* in the construction of a system; and, though the truth may be made use of, and appealed to, in the process of the theory—all is then delusion. The Christian who is the disciple of such a system, is beguiled from the simplicity of the faith. He is no longer the simple-hearted disciple of Jesus Christ, who came down from heaven and was made man, was born and died and rose again for us men and our salvation; but he is become the disciple of a philosophy; and there is no aberration of false doctrine into which he may not then be seduced. The heresy of Simon was but the natural prelude to the opinions of

Theodotus, of Paul of Samosata, and of Sabellius and Arius in the centuries immediately following.

Such accordingly appears to have been the form which Heresy first assumed in the Church. It did not set itself up openly against the Truth, but as something by the side of the Truth. Thus the Apostle in the text expresses his fears, not that the Corinthians would at once apostatize from the faith, but that they would be " beguiled from their simplicity," in like manner as the serpent had tempted Eve. He feared that whilst ostensibly holding the Gospel, they would be drawn off into another system; as Eve, whilst professing her knowledge of God's commands, was yet prevailed on to exchange her conviction of the truth for the lie insinuated into her mind by the Tempter.

Hence the Apostle proceeds to tell the Corinthians, how vain was the expectation held out to the believer by those who were seducing them; how they deprived the believer of his only hope, and gave him nothing substantial in exchange for it. " For if he that cometh," he says, " preach another Jesus whom we have not preached, or if ye receive another Spirit which ye have not received, or another Gospel which ye have not accepted, ye might well bear with him." Believers, he would have them know, by listening to the seducing teacher, were embracing shadows, —were exchanging the solid gifts and privileges of a real Saviour, a real Spirit, living personal Beings in whom they had a personal interest, and a real Gospel, a real message of glad tidings to every fallen son of Adam, for an empty mysticism, which gave them no Saviour to trust in, no Spirit to help their infirmities,—no joy for salvation wrought, for man pardoned, and God reconciled. Had the seducing teacher been able to point to another Jesus in the place of Him whom his theory rejected—had he possessed for them the power of imparting another Holy Spirit, such as was the Holy Ghost conferred by the hands of the Apostles—were there any other Gospel which this teacher could deliver besides that which they had already accepted,—then they might have some excuse for listening to him. As it was, there was nothing of the kind. There was but one Saviour whom the Apostles had preached,—but one Spirit whose gifts they conferred,—but one Gospel which they had delivered. Believers therefore had no grounds for admitting the strange teacher,—no pretext for submitting to

the blandishments of the seducer and forsaking
the Lord to whom they were espoused.

It is greatly worth our while to consider more
particularly, the fact of the grievous corruption
of the Christian Faith noticed in this passage of
St. Paul, as illustrating, not only the high importance of right notions with regard to our Lord's
sacred Person, that we may ascribe to Him
the honour due to his name, but also how we
should keep steadily before our view in all our
Christian profession, the Life and Death and
Resurrection of the Lord, and our pardon and
justification as consequent on the reality of these
sacred truths, and the necessity of a sincere belief of them, in order to a sound profession of the
Gospel.

It is not, then, let us first observe, a mere speculative truth, that our Lord Jesus Christ unites in
his holy Person the two natures of God and man,
being at once Perfect God and Perfect man. We
see the stress that is laid on this truth by St. Paul
in combating the errors of his times. The text
alone is an evidence to us, how he regarded any
diminution or extenuation of the truth with respect to the Person of our Lord, as a forsaking
of the faith and abandonment of the hopes and

consolations of the Christian. If, according to the doctrines of the followers of Simon, Jesus is not the Christ,—if there is any separation of the Son of Man—of him who came of the seed of the woman—from the Son of God, the Word that was with God and was God,—then is our faith vain; we are yet in our sins; no atonement has been made for us; death has still dominion over us. "We," says Origen, replying to a cavil of Celsus and referring to the heretical opinion which Celsus thought more reasonable than the true doctrine, "we do not impute mere appearance to Christ's suffering, that his Resurrection also may not be made a false one, but real; for he that really died, if he rose again, really rose; but he that only in *appearance* died, did not really rise *." And this is only what St. Paul urges in other words in his first Epistle to the Corinthians, where he says, "But if there be no resurrection of the *dead*, then is Christ not risen: and if Christ be not risen, then is our preaching vain, and your faith is also vain. Yea, and we are found false witnesses of God: because we have testified of God that he raised up Christ; whom he raised not up, if so be that the dead rise not. For if the

* Contra Cels. lib. ii. p. 70.

dead rise not, then is not Christ raised : and if Christ be not raised, your faith is vain ; ye are yet in your sins *."

Thus it was not the Divinity of our Lord that was disputed in the Church in the time of the Apostles, but the full truth of his Incarnation— the truth, which in its integrity presupposes his real and proper Humanity, as it presupposes also his real and proper Divinity. The early heretics, in detracting from the Lord's humanity, detracted also from his Divinity. But the root of their error appears to have been in their denial of his humanity. When once it was taught that there was no reality in that body which the Lord assumed,—that the Christ had descended on Jesus at his baptism, and had quitted Him before the Crucifixion,—that all was illusion, consequently, which Christ appeared to do and suffer in the flesh ; when they had thus explained away what the eye had seen and the hands had handled ; it was comparatively an easy task to carry on their doctrine of illusion to the speculation on the Divine nature of Christ, and throw the veil of mysticism over the plain revelation of his Eternal Majesty and Godhead.

* 1 Cor. xv. 13–17.

Hence may be accounted for, in great measure, those several expressions, by which the Evangelists and Apostles so jealously guard the truth of the Incarnation in its full import. The preachers of Christ in the New Testament seem ever on the watch to keep off all profane intrusion on the mystery of the Incarnation, whilst they simply and explicitly assert it; revealing to us not only that God was our Saviour, but that God became man in order to effect the Salvation of man. The opening of St. John's Gospel and of the Epistle to the Hebrews clearly have this design. Evidence to the same point results from all those passages, in which our Lord is spoken of as a man, and his sufferings and death are set forth: as, for instance, when St. Paul proclaimed at Athens, that God " hath appointed a day in the which He will judge the world in righteousness by *that man* whom He hath ordained*;" or when our Lord himself convinced Thomas of the truth respecting his twofold nature, by requiring that doubting disciple to touch Him with the hand, and thus ascertain, that it was no phantom, but Jesus in very truth whom he had seen and conversed with, that now stood before him again in the proper form of man.

* Acts xvii. 31.

All such passages are utterly misapplied when they are appealed to, as they are by some, in proof of the sole humanity of our Lord. Their proper evidence is to the *whole* doctrine of the Incarnation; to prove, that He whom the Apostles preached was the true Immanuel, the Word made flesh and dwelling among us.

Now such texts of Scripture as that which we are considering this day, taken in connexion with such as those just adverted to in which the Scriptures are so express on the truth of the Incarnation, strongly enforce the practical importance of this most holy truth in regard to our whole profession of the Gospel. They teach us that to lose sight of this Truth, or in any way to obscure it, in any respect to tamper with it or attempt to explain it away, is to depart from Christian Faith and Hope. If we give up this holy Truth in its *simplicity*, we give up our ground of Salvation; we have then to look for another Saviour, another Comforter, another Gospel. Those Corinthians for whom the Apostle expresses his fears, lest they should have been corrupted from their simplicity in Christ, probably thought that they were attaining to greater perfection in their acquaintance with the Gospel, by removing the

objections of the carnal mind against the doctrine of the Cross, in denying the literal truth of
the Incarnation. But in their pursuit of fancied
truth, they abandoned the real truth to believe
a lie; in denying Jesus to be the Christ, they
denied the Father who had sent Him ; and from
being disciples of Christ in name became in fact
disciples of Antichrist*.

How awful then is the warning to all ages of
the Church that we hold rightly the truth of the
Incarnation of our Lord Jesus Christ ! It is not
a question, we see, of sound doctrine on a single
point of our religion only—it is not an isolated
matter on which we may be right or wrong, and
the rest of our religious belief remain unshaken.
It is a question whether we are Christians *indeed*
or no,—whether we are building our hopes of
Salvation on a rock or on the sand and amidst
the clouds. The Prophets of the Old Testament
foretold that God should Himself effect our salvation,—Himself dwelling with us—Himself the
Lord our Righteousness; and the Evangelists
and Apostles in the New Testament have set
forth in plain description the truth shadowed out
in the Old. Where then is the room for profane

* 1 John ii. 22.

speculation on the subject? Had the voice and
guidance of Scripture been simply followed, who
would have hazarded the thought but that He
who came down from Heaven to save us, was
God Himself, God the Son, the only begotten of
the Father, full of grace and truth—(descriptions,
which belong to no created being, however high
in the celestial hierarchy)—and that He, in assuming our nature, became very man, the seed
destined to bruise the serpent's head—really suffering and dying, and really raised again in the
flesh for our salvation?

But Satan tempted Christians here, as he
tempted Eve; and unhappily beguiled some to
deny the Lord that bought them, even in Churches,
as we find, planted and watered by the hands of
Apostles. As he marred the work of Creation, so
he spread his wiles around the work of Redemption. He suggested to Christians to be ashamed
of the Cross of Christ; to deny that God had
really become man for their sakes. And from
that first lie against the Gospel has flowed the
stream of falsehood ever since. The sacred land-
mark once removed,—as at the first temptation
of Eve there followed every form of atheistic and
polytheistic impiety and wickedness in the world,

—so here have followed the manifold devices of
the curious and carnal mind speculating on the
revealed mystery of the Incarnation.

Let us be deeply thankful, Brethren, that God
in his mercy has been pleased to vindicate the
sacred truth from these various corruptions, in
giving us so plain a statement of it in the Scriptures.   It is in the Scriptures that we find it, at
once, in the depth of its mystery, as well as in
its simplicity, and further, in its full practical
importance,—the point to which I am endeavouring especially to direct your attention.   For the
Scriptures, as I have been observing, not only
plainly state the holy truth, but they inculcate
on us its vital connexion with our Salvation.   As
I have said, it is no mere question of a point of
doctrine ; but it is a question, whether a Saviour
has been given to us—whether we be Christians
or no—whether we have the Spirit of Christ
or the Spirit of Antichrist.   For " hereby know
ye," says St. John, " the Spirit of God: every
spirit that confesseth that Jesus Christ is come
in the flesh is of God: and every spirit that
confesseth not that Jesus Christ is come in the
flesh is not of God: and this is that spirit
of Antichrist, whereof ye have heard that it

should come; and even now already it is in the world*."

Some may imagine that the force of these expressions bears chiefly, if not solely, on the times when the corruptions referred to were in their ascendency. But they belong to all times. The text shews us what importance St. Paul attributed to those corruptions; how necessary he held it, in order, not to a right faith only, but to any faith whatever, that the believer should maintain his simplicity in Christ. And this simplicity we see consisted in guarding against all innovations and fancied improvements on the doctrine of the Incarnation.

But is it not possible, it may be asked, to avoid the gross error of the early heretics in regard to the Person of our Saviour, and yet not to escape from that danger against which the Apostle warns the Corinthians in the text?

To consider this, let us in the next place therefore observe how the Incarnation of our Saviour is stated in Scripture in conjunction with the Death and Passion and Resurrection, and the Atonement for man, and Justification from sin, thereby effected. We shall thus see, that in

* 1 John iv. 2, 3.

order to hold the doctrine of the Incarnation in its full Scriptural sense, it is not enough to believe in it only as a truth which unites man to God as it were *physically* (if such an expression may be used), and thus derives the grace of Justification and of Sanctification from the mystical union itself,—though great blessings may indeed flow to us from that union alone,—but that we must receive the doctrine in its moral bearings also, as an account of the means by which the consequences of sin were removed, pardon was vouchsafed to guilty man, and righteousness and peace and life were brought back to a world lying in wickedness and misery and death.

Now the Church of Rome appears rightly to maintain the doctrine of the Incarnation in what I have ventured to call the physical sense, but to disregard it, or at least not to assign it its full import and weight, in the *moral* point of view. When we consider the Roman theory of the Church we shall see this clearly. The Church in the view of that Communion is the necessary channel through which all the graces and benefits belonging to Salvation flow to the Christian. All blessings indeed are by them acknowledged to be *primarily* derived from the Mediation of

Christ. But they are not supposed to be given
to the individual, apart from the Church to which
the gifts and graces derived from Christ are consigned. In order to their reception, the individual
must first be made a member of the Church. He
must place himself entirely and unreservedly in
the hands of the Church. He must receive from
it without questioning what he is to believe,—
obey all its commands,—entirely depend on its
ordinances and ministrations, for grace to justify
him, grace to sanctify him, grace to repent truly,
grace to absolve him from his sins, grace to
strengthen and refresh him, grace to depart in
peace when God shall call him from the world.

Now what does this theory of the Church
presuppose?—It presupposes that the Word of
God is now dwelling among men as the Word
once dwelt in Jesus Christ Himself,—that the
Church in its successive generations represents
the Incarnate Lord, and carries on his work
in the same manner as when He ministered on
earth—that the Church is the visible habitation
of the Word of God, as once the Lord Jesus
Christ Himself was the Word seen and heard by
those to whom his personal ministry was addressed. Nothing short of this supposition can

fully satisfy the Roman doctrine of the Church. For no promise of the illuminating guidance and aid of the Holy Spirit can be sufficient to bear up the weight of that mediatorial office which this doctrine attributes to the Church. Were it even conceded that the particular promise to the Apostles that the Spirit should guide them into all Truth, extends beyond the Apostles to their successors in their commission; still it would not follow that anything more might be claimed on the strength of it, than that the Church should constantly possess the Truth; that the superintendence of the Holy Spirit should preserve the Truth from generation to generation; and that those who should be guided by the Spirit would be led in all ages to the Truth. Nor can more than this be inferred from that general declaration of our Lord—" Lo! I am with you alway, even unto the end of the world!" From this we only learn that Christ will never be wanting to his Church, and that therefore it shall not utterly fail to the end of time. The maintenance of the truth then, and the perpetuity of the Church, do not imply the existence of that high prerogative, which is claimed for the Church by the Roman Communion.

Some higher ground must be sought for the foundation of their doctrine. And nothing short of the assumption, that the Church is in the fullest sense the representative of the Incarnate Saviour—the Word of God dwelling among men —speaking and acting with a living Divine Authority,—can fully serve the purpose.

This fundamental notion will at once account for that mediatorial office which the Church of Rome assumes in its several functions. It offers sacrifice, because (as it holds) Christ yet continues by his ministers, his living organs, the Sacrifice of the Cross: his representatives on earth, when they celebrate the Mass, represent the Sacrifice of the Cross. It interprets the Scriptures, because the same authority of teaching continues in it, as in the Apostles when they received their commission to go and teach all nations. It delivers the " unwritten word " of God, and develops the faith according to the exigencies of the Church, because the Word of God still lives in the Church, and expounds and develops itself through the dogmatic decisions of its ministers. The Church also, according to this theory, must be infallible; or otherwise error might be attributed to the Word of God.

But thus to regard the Church as the *representative* of the Word made flesh, is to overlook the true relation of our Lord to his Church. It is, as I have said, to uphold the truth of the Incarnation in the physical point of view, but to neglect that moral view of the subject which gives it its perfection. For the Church was founded on the Cross of the Lord. It was a purchase made by his Blood. It was not until He had " given his soul an offering for sin," and " poured out his soul unto death," that He " saw his seed ;" it was not until, as " a corn of wheat," He had " fallen into the ground," that He " brought forth much fruit;" not until " He was lifted up," that " He drew all men after him." The blessed work begun in the Incarnation was only completed, when the Lord died and passed through the grave and gate of death to a triumphant Resurrection. For then only did Man, who was dead through Sin, live again through Righteousness in the sight of God. Hence the Apostles in preaching Christ ever preach Christ Crucified. St. Peter in those first sermons recorded in the Acts, which gathered so many souls into the Church, sets forth the Crucifixion and Resurrection of Christ as the foun-

dation of the Gospel*. St. Paul, in giving his
charge to the elders of Ephesus, enjoins them to
feed the Church of God which He had "purchased
with his own blood †." Discoursing of Justification to the Romans, he speaks of " the Redemption that is in Christ Jesus, whom God hath set
forth to be a propitiation through faith in his
blood ‡." Again, he dwells on the act of Christ's
dying for the ungodly,—of our being "justified
by his blood,"—being "reconciled to God by the
death of his Son §,"—of our having " by Him received the Atonement ‖." To the Corinthians he
declares, that " he determined not to know anything among them save Jesus Christ and Him
Crucified **." And what is all his 15th Chapter
to the Corinthians but an argument for the Resurrection of Man, drawn from the Death and
Resurrection of Him who took our nature upon
Him, and in that nature overcame Sin and Death,
and gave us the victory? What, again, is the
whole Epistle to the Hebrews but a preaching
of the Cross—a demonstration by the light of the

---

* See also Acts x. 39.   † Acts xx. 28.
‡ Rom. iii. 24, 25.   § Rom. v. 10.
‖ Rom. v. 11.   ** 1 Cor. ii. 2.

typical sacrifices of the Law, of the inestimable value of the Blood of Atonement poured out on the Cross ; as that without which the Incarnation would not have fulfilled its purpose, and which gave to that beginning of the work of Salvation its crown and completion ? So that we may truly say on the authority of Scripture, that any view of the foundation of the Church of Christ, which does not include the notion of pardon and justification by the blood of Christ as primary and essential, must present a partial and inadequate view of the great truth of the Incarnation. This is the real external basis of the Church,— that which gives it an eternal objective existence, independently of our fleeting thoughts and feelings,—independently of what we may know or think or believe about it,—that God the Son in his own Person became man,—took the manhood into God—uniting in his one Person the natures of God and Man,—and really died and rose again for our Salvation.

This foundation of the Church, it was the blessed mission of the Reformation to restore to due estimation in the eyes of Christian men. Long had they been blinded that they could not see it, by the superstitions and corruptions of the dominant Church. Luther and his brother Reformers, when they taught with such vehement earnestness the great Scriptural Truth, that man is justified by Faith only, laid bare the breadth and depth of the Foundation on which the Church stood. They shewed how it was rooted and grounded in the eternal immutable counsels of God before the world was. They traced up its origin and principle of life to the "Lamb slain before the foundation of the world." They no longer suffered men to regard themselves as Christians, and in the way of Salvation, because they had received the word of God from the existing Church, however duly constituted; but only because God had in his eternal purpose given his only-begotten Son to die for their sins. The foundation had been narrowed by the Church of Rome, in making *itself* the representative of the Word of God dwelling among men. Men were thus led to look to a Body which *existed in time*, instead of referring themselves to that "Body" of the Lord which, though actually offered up in the fulness of time, had been "prepared" from all eternity*. Instead of holding forth the Church to the regard of men, as

* Heb. x. 5.

" the pillar and ground of the Truth," (which is
its proper Scriptural character,) or as the Body, of
which Christ is the Head, and which has no life
or existence apart from its Head, (which is also
a Scriptural character of it,) the advocates of the
Roman system make the Church usurp the place
of Christ Himself on the earth. The Church,
in their view, is not simply the support and
security of the Truth, but the Truth itself; nay
more, it is with them what Christ alone truly is,
the Way, the Truth, and the Life. In their view,
it is not the Body of Christ, in the sense of its
being the communion of believers in Christ
united by one Holy Spirit and looking up to
Christ as their Head, but a perfect Body as it
exists in the world,—perfect, as being the Divine
Word embodied in living members, and thus, as
I have before stated, representing God and man
united still in the world, and made capable, accordingly, of Divine acts from the Divine Principle
dwelling within it, informing it, and elevating its
human principles to an intimate association with
the Divine*.

But this, I repeat, is to narrow the foundation of the Church. It is indeed to raise up an

* This is more fully shewn in the subsequent Sermons.

imposing edifice, calculated to strike awe and admiration into the beholder. And no wonder is it, that the ideal of such a Church should fill the imagination,—should present to the eye of speculation the form and beauty of Holiness. But it stands not on the breadth of the Rock of ages. It beguiles the admirer from the simplicity that is in Christ. Like the Gnostic system, it avails itself of the fundamental truth of the Gospel that " God was in Christ, reconciling the world to Himself." But like that system, though in a different way, it dissipates the truth in the erection of its own fabric.

For where is the doctrine of the Atonement by the death of Christ found in that system? Can we call it part of the *foundation* of the system, when the Christian is required *first* to be a member of the Church that he may receive the benefits of the Atonement *through* the Church? Can the Church be said properly to be *built on* that which can only be applied to its members *by the Church*? If the Atonement, as we contend on the Scriptural principles of our Reformed Church, is an essential part of the doctrine of the Word made flesh, and the Church therefore only exists as it is built on the Atonement, it is a

mere fallacy to assert that the benefits of the
Atonement are only wrought through the Church.
For in order to be members of Christ's Church,
—to constitute a member or a portion of that
Body,—we must first be on the Foundation; we
must have received Jesus as the Christ; we must
be among those who have "received the Atonement."

Then as to the place which the Atonement
holds in the Roman system, it is plain that it is
not as the Foundation.   For it finds its place
there in the offerings of the Mass; which is
described by the Council of Trent as a sacrifice
truly propitiatory for the dead and living.   It
finds its place again in the works of penance
prescribed in satisfaction for sins—in the sacrifices of almsgiving and acts of self-mortification,
—in the merit of works of supererogation, and
the intercession of Saints and Angels.   So that
whilst it is quite true that the Atonement is held
and maintained by the Roman Church, it is no
less true that it is not held in its proper place;
it is not the proper *foundation* in that system.   If
we listen to the preachers of that Church, we do
not hear them put it forward *as the foundation*;
they preach rather the explanation of the doctrine

of the Mass as that which contains for Christians the grace of remission of sins; they preach the necessity of belonging to the Church and of obedience to the Church in order to Salvation, rather than the necessity of personal faith,—justification by Baptism and not by faith only,—the meritoriousness of works as performed by the Christian, and not the sole merit of the Lord Jesus Christ. And, however it may be asserted that in all their preaching the doctrine of Christ Crucified is implied, still it is not as the foundation,—it is not as a basis external to the Church, but as something contained in the Church and dispensed through it, and which does *not exist* for *man* but *in and through* the Church.

Now a Church such as our own, built on the Foundation of Jesus Christ and Him Crucified, and thus fully maintaining the whole truth of the Incarnation, will ever be impressing the Atonement of the Cross on its members, as that without which there is no entrance into the kingdom of God, whether in heaven or in earth,—into the Church invisible glorified and triumphant in heaven, or the visible Church militant here in the earth. It will be ever repeating the preaching of the Lord Himself, when " He opened the understanding of his disciples that they might understand the Scriptures, and said unto them, Thus it is written, and thus it behoved Christ to suffer, and to rise from the dead the third day: and that repentance and remission of sins should be preached in his name among all nations, beginning at Jerusalem *." It will not therefore, with the Church of Rome, suffer the Atonement of the Cross to be regarded as absolutely depending for its benefits to the sinner on any ordinance of the Church ; or as no longer available in the case of grievous sin after Baptism; and so throw the penitent back in despair on the promises of the Old Testament, and the forlorn hope of the baptism of tears, and the fearful expectation of the cleansing of the day of judgment. But it will ever bring at once to the penitent the consolations and encouragements and hopes of the Gospel. It will not abate from the difficulty of a true repentance, remembering how strongly Scripture speaks of that difficulty, and how awful a thing it is to crucify the Son of God afresh by our sins. But it will not withhold the balm provided for the wounded conscience. It still holds up the Cross to the penitent, and bids him

* Luke xxiv. 45.

hope for mercy; for that God became man, and accepts those who come to Him in Christ, not for their righteousness, but for the righteousness of His Son who gave Himself for them.

Then the members of a Church which thus preaches Christ in simplicity, must feel their attachment to the Church, and to each other, strongly enforced by this constant reference to the love of God in Christ as the common ground on which they stand. They must respect the teaching and the ordinances of a Church, which thus goes directly for wisdom and strength to the fountain opened for all sin and uncleanness. They will not lightly esteem its authority, whether in controversies of faith or in rites and ceremonies of its appointment, when they see its stedfastness and constancy in the doctrine of Christ,—how it denies itself and its own pretensions, so it may confess the faith of Christ Crucified and glory in his Cross. Nor will they hold it a matter of indifference whether the Apostolic order be observed in such a Church or no. But they will cherish with affection and reverence the example and model of the primitive Church, built on the foundation whilst it was wet with the Saviour's Blood, and delight in beholding in its

ministers a holy institution preserved in perpetuity from Apostolic times.

Such was the spirit in which Ignatius wrote to
the Church of Philadelphia, when, enforcing obedience to their spiritual rulers, he coupled with
that admonition the remembrance of the High
Priest, through whom they had access to the
Father. " Good," he says, " are the Priests ;
but better is the High Priest, who alone has been
entrusted with the hidden things of God,—Himself being the door of the Father, through which
enter Abraham and Isaac and Jacob, and the
Prophets, and the Apostles, and the Church."
Again, writing to the Trallians, after having
earnestly exhorted them to dutifulness to their
Pastors under Christ, and insisted on the necessity of the regular ministry in order to the very
name of the Church, he subjoins, " Be deaf then,
when any one may speak to you *without Jesus
Christ*, who is of the race of David, the son of
Mary ; who was truly born, and eat and drank,
was really persecuted under Pontius Pilate, was
really crucified and died, whilst beings in heaven
and in earth and under the earth were beholding ; who also was really raised from the dead ;
his Father raising Him up, in like manner as his

Father will so raise up also us that believe in Him in Christ Jesus, without whom we have not the true life." The testimony, indeed, of the Apostolic Fathers is throughout to the same effect. It is precisely of the same character as that of the Apostles themselves. It is throughout a preaching of Christ Crucified—not a mere preaching of the Religion of Christ in general under that name, but a preaching of the Cross expressly *.

Brethren! the Apostle Paul had his fears lest the minds of his own converts at Corinth should be beguiled from their simplicity in Christ: and shall we have no fears for ourselves? To those very people respecting whom he expresses these fears, he had faithfully preached Christ Crucified. It was among them that he had made this truth the burthen of his preaching, determining, as he says, to know nothing among them but Jesus Christ and Him Crucified. Not four years had elapsed after a long sojourn which he had made at Corinth, occupied in preaching the Gospel incessantly and with great success, when this very Church in which he had so laboured was rent

* See a passage of Polycarp to the Philippians, c. iii. p. 470, where he calls the Faith "the mother of us all," and that on which Christians are "built."

with schisms of a fatal character; one party
calling itself of Paul, another of Cephas, another
of Apollos; the chief part happily remaining
sound, but still a considerable portion beguiled
from their simplicity in Christ. These schisms
too, let us observe, were not mere followings of
certain eminent persons in the Church. The
names were a mere pretext for the heresies
which the parties had adopted. They had forgotten the truth, that Christ was crucified for
them,—they had quitted the foundation laid
among them. They had begun to look to the
holiness of men—to respect the persons of men
—to think themselves holy and religious, because they were following the instructions and
counsels of men esteemed spiritual and perfect
among them. Thus they had formed factions
in the Church, breaking the unity of the Catholic
Church founded in Christ. And let us further
notice the character of the heresies themselves
into which they had fallen. There were among
them, those that denied the Resurrection of the
Body—the true Christian Resurrection,—who
fell back from their Christian enlightenment on
this momentous doctrine, into heathen speculations and mystic refinements respecting the

Immortality of the Soul. " How say some among you," says St. Paul, " that there is no Resurrection of the dead ? " It was not that they denied any Resurrection, but a Resurrection of the *Dead*; as we learn from another place, where we are told of some who taught that " the *Resurrection was past already* *;" that it consisted in a spiritual process by which the disciple while living passed into a higher state of being, exempted from the pollution of the animal and earthly natures. This is apparent from the whole course of St. Paul's argument, directed as it is to the proof of a real Resurrection of the Body. Some of them again appear to have regarded Christ as only a Teacher or Head of a Sect. For we find that while one said, " I am of Paul" or " I am of Apollos," another said, " I am of Christ†:" unless we are to understand by this assertion, that some thus contended for the Gospel against the party-disputes raging around them. This was totally to pervert the Gospel—to cast away the Atonement—to forget, that they only lived before God as they were the Body of Christ and as the Spirit of Christ lived in them. Under this perversion, given over as they were to the

* 2 Tim. ii. 18.   † 1 Cor. i. 12.

leading of a carnal spirit in renouncing the spirit of Christ, persons were ready even to disown Jesus as the Christ,—even to advance to that height of blasphemy as to " call Jesus accursed*,"—calling themselves (according to their fanatical distinction between Jesus and the Christ) the disciples of *Christ* who came down from heaven, but not the disciples of *Jesus* who *died on the Cross.*

And how then does it appear that these several heresies and divisions had arisen? I repeat from abandoning the simplicity of the faith in Christ, the Incarnate Lord. Such is the tenour of St. Paul's Epistles addressed to these Christians. All his instructions and reproofs tend to bring them back to that simplicity. All turn on the fundamental truth of Christ Crucified. What is his argument against divisions, but that Christ was Crucified for them? What his argument against their carnal affectation of spiritual gifts, but that as believers in Christ, owning Jesus as the Lord, they had all received one Spirit— were all made members by the Holy Ghost of one Body in Christ? What his argument for the Resurrection of the Body, but that " Christ died for our sins according to the Scriptures, and that

* 1 Cor. xii. 3.

2 D

He was buried and rose again the third day according to the Scriptures* "? Would we learn, therefore, from Apostolic example, we must, like St. Paul, seek to maintain sound doctrine and order in our Church by holding fast and maintaining " the simplicity of the faith that is in Christ."

We have heard it said among us that we ought not openly and unreservedly to preach the Atonement of Christ,—that it is not an elementary truth of our religion, but a truth only for those that have been long and carefully trained in the teaching and discipline of the Church.

Not so says the example of the Apostles and their immediate successors in the Church; if there be any justness in the observations which I have been submitting to you. And what, I may add, is such a position but an adoption of the error of the early heretics ? It is not indeed to remove the Lord Himself into the abstractions of a theoretic system. But it is to remove a great truth connected with his mission from its positive place in the Gospel, into an ideal fabric of religious truth. For a minister of the Gospel to shrink from the plain avowal of the doctrine of the

* 1 Cor. xv. 3, 4.

Cross, because it may be profaned by the general hearer, is a proceeding, not very unlike that of avoiding the objections of a carnal and worldly wisdom, by denying the simple truth of the Incarnation. Accordingly, we are told that when Scripture speaks of preaching Christ Crucified, self-mortification, self-sacrifice is the doctrine intended; for that each member of the Church takes up the Cross of Christ in bearing his own cross, and represents the Lord's Cross in his own sufferings and mortifications. Again, when Scripture speaks of "Justification by Faith," this means, it is said, that the Christian Religion *as a whole*, in opposition to Judaism and to Natural Religion, is the only means of Righteousness and acceptance with God. If this is not to explain away texts of Scripture, and substitute interpretations consistent with a preconceived theory for the obvious meaning, what else can be? Let it be granted that the Doctrine of the Church held by the Roman Communion is true; and then all those texts of Scripture which speak of the Cross, must obtain an interpretation consistent with it. The Roman Church has taken on itself to be the representative of the Saviour on earth: and consequently, if we follow its guidance, we can only

2 D 2

look to the Cross as *represented* under the veil of
its ordinances and its forms of Doctrine and Ritual. These are to the member of that Church,
since the Ascension of Christ, the absolute rule
of his profession of the Gospel: since they are
to him real manifestations of the Divine Word,
varied only by the circumstance that the Word
is now revealed by the Church, and not by the
personal ministry of the Lord Himself.

But we have not so received the Gospel. Our
Church has led us at once to the foot of the Saviour's own Cross, and taught us to regard ourselves as members of his Church, because we hold
to Him as our Head, believing, that " whosoever
shall confess that Jesus is the Son of God, God
dwelleth in him, and he in God*." Thus, if we
believe in Christ truly, resting all our hopes of
Salvation on the promises of grace and mercy
through Him, we are encouraged humbly to trust
that we are living members of his Body.

But, will a Christian impressed with this truth
think of himself as an isolated independent individual? or that he has no necessary connexion
with the whole Body of which he is a member?
This would be to forget, that Christ, when He

* 1 John iv. 15.

had given Himself for the sins of the world, instituted a Society on earth—a Society, not only founded on Himself, but compacted and knit together by his Spirit for the edification of its several members ; that, on his departure, he breathed his Holy Spirit into that Society, and gave it a perpetual existence, with the Holy Spirit for its guidance and comfort; and appointed a standing Ministry, and the preaching of the Gospel, and the two Holy Sacraments of Baptism and the Eucharist, and united Prayer in his name, with his blessing on these institutions, to be of constant observance in the Society. Such indeed is that description of the design of the Church given by St. Paul to the Ephesians ; where, having spoken of that essential unity in " the one hope of their calling" which characterizes the Church, he adds its holy design, as being " for the perfecting of the Saints, for the work of the ministry, for the edifying of the Body of Christ ; till we all come in the unity of the Faith, and of the knowledge of the Son of God, unto a perfect man, unto the measure of the stature of the fulness of Christ *." Nor will the Christian, resting on Christ Crucified, be insensible to the fact, that,

* Eph. iv. 12.

as his natural life was not given to him but in Society, and by means of his natural parentage,—though *God alone* was his Creator, and his Father in Heaven his true Father,—so neither is his second birth, his life in Christ, given him but in that Society which exists by Grace, and through its spiritual parentage,—though he is "created" anew solely by grace " in Christ Jesus*." He will be humbly thankful therefore for the privileges of his Christian Baptism, and Christian nurture under the ministrations of the Church and its ordinances, and strive to keep himself in the communion of the faithful, by communicating with them in shewing forth the Lord's death in the Sacrament of his Body and Blood. Further, not only will the Christian reverently cooperate with his brethren in Christ, " continuing stedfastly in the Apostles' doctrine and fellowship, and in breaking of bread and in prayers †," but looking unto Jesus Crucified for sins, he will flee from all sin ; he will die unto sin and live unto righteousness,—knowing that " he that committeth sin is " not of God, but " of the Devil ‡."

Let no man therefore, Brethren, beguile us of

* Eph. ii. 6.　　　† Acts ii. 42.　　　‡ 1 John iii. 8.

the simplicity of the faith that is in Christ. The
corrupt teachers at Corinth accused St. Paul to
his own sons in the Faith, of a want of spiritual
knowledge and power in teaching. They complained of his method in the Gospel, as poor,
and inadequate to the needs of the people—of his
presence as base, and his speech as contemptible:
and because he did not inculcate their fanatical
contempt of the body, they said, he "walked
according to the flesh *." They set off against
the Apostle's system the advantages of their own
seducing doctrine—an imaginary science of perfection, leaving far behind it in its flights the
humbling doctrine of Christ,—captivating in its
mysticism, and awe, and seeming, but fallacious,
purity of exemption from everything carnal and
material. What did the Apostle reply to these
accusations against the Gospel which he had
preached? Did he labour to shew, that his doctrine, too, was full of a refined and elevated
wisdom,—that it made men as gods while living
on the earth—setting them far above the material world, and rendering them incapable of
its pollution? Far from this. He condemns the
pretensions of these false teachers and sophistica-

* 2 Cor. x. 2.

tors of the truth as utterly delusive, and strongly
asserts his own Apostolic mission and character.
But what does he say of his own Doctrine? It
is not, he owns, after the wisdom of men. It
was not such as to satisfy the expectations of the
Philosopher and the Rhetorician, or the cravings
of a morbid imagination. He calls it " the foolishness of preaching,"—what men accounted
foolish and weak, though it was the wisdom
and power of God,—the simple doctrine of Christ
and his Cross. He is content to lay down the
truth of Christ Crucified again and again, without
extenuation, as the sum and substance of his
preaching, and only to demand of the Corinthians
that they should receive it with simplicity.

The only question then for us, Brethren, is ;
Have we received this truth in its simplicity?
Is it taught and enforced in our branch of the
Catholic Church, as the Apostle would have it
taught? The question is one of large bearing :
for it leads us to review our whole standing in
the faith and profession of the Gospel. For, we
must see also that we are rightly building on the
foundation, and carrying out its strength and solidity into all the parts of our building. I would
conclude then in the words of St. Jude, which

strongly contrast the true with the sophistical profession of the Gospel: " But ye, Beloved, building up yourselves on your most holy Faith, praying in the Holy Ghost, keep yourselves in the love of God, looking for the mercy of the Lord Jesus Christ unto eternal life*."

* Jude 20, 21.

SERMON XII.

THE WORK OF CHRIST.

PREACHED IN THE CATHEDRAL OF CHRIST CHURCH,

On SUNDAY, October 25, 1846.

SERMON XII.

THE WORK OF CHRIST.

JOHN XIV. 26.

But the Comforter, which is the Holy Ghost, whom the Father will send in my name, He shall teach you all things, and bring all things to your remembrance, whatsoever I have said unto you.

IT is impossible to study with attention those deeply affecting passages of Scripture, such as the text, speaking of the mission of the Comforter, without being forcibly struck with the earnest, anxious manner, in which our Lord connects the dispensation of the Spirit for the building up of his Church, with his own departure from the world to the Father in heaven. The intimation of the coming of the Comforter is only given at the very close of our Lord's own ministry, and is conveyed in accents of consolation to his disciples for the loss, which, He tells them, they were soon to sustain by his removal from their society. It forms the burthen of a solemn parting admonition to them,—such as a dying friend would give to those who had hitherto been most affectionately bound to him and to one another,—not to forget how they had been united, and to continue in the same love when He should be taken from them. He had called them, as he passed by the wayside; and they had gathered around Him, forsaking all at the instant, and confiding themselves at once to his guidance and teaching; amidst his persecutions; even up to that moment when the hour of darkness was fast deepening its shadow. And now that He is soon to be withdrawn, the same word —the same inspiring, "Follow me"—is sounded in their ears, though in another form; revealing to them a new and more intimate invisible bond of union with Him when absent, in the succeeding mission of the Spirit.

They had indeed the Holy Spirit already given them, according to their capacity and their need, at that time when the Lord thus spoke to them. For, it was only through the Spirit that they had been led to believe in Christ, and to love Him as they had hitherto done. But the Spirit had not yet been manifested to the world in them. They had only received his secret influences and inspirations of goodness, strengthening them, and keeping them in the faith. They had not been distinctly placed under the teaching and guidance of the Spirit, whilst Jesus Christ Himself was with them in the flesh. Neither, again, when after his resurrection He breathed on them, and communicated to them the Holy Ghost, ordaining them to their ministry, did they then receive of that fulness of the Spirit which was promised to them in the words of our text. By that special gift at their ordination, they were indeed blessed with power, and prepared to go forth on the Lord's errand, at the instant that they should receive the fulfilment of the promise of their Lord. But after that, they had yet to wait for the actual fulfilment of the promise ; until the Spirit should be poured down on them ; and they should know, that a new order of things was begun under the dispensation of the Spirit.

The mission of the Comforter, accordingly, on the day of Pentecost, in order to be rightly estimated, must be regarded as constituting a distinct epoch in the annals of the Gospel. It was the beginning of the building of the Church on the foundation laid by Christ. Christ, the great Master-builder, had then finished his work; and the time was come when another Almighty worker should enter on his labours. There remained nothing more for the Son of God, who was also the Son of Man, to achieve. The bloody Sacrifice which He had undertaken to perform, was accomplished, when He gave himself to death, and rose again from the dead, leading captivity captive, and destroying the power of sin in his body. This was a work, which by its blessed efficacy reached once for all to a whole world lying in sin; so that there is no sin, either in the past generations of man before the offering was made by Christ, or in the generations following to the end of the world, but is expiated by the one oblation and satisfaction made on the Cross.

Depicting the intensity of that struggle with the enemies of our Salvation, together with the glories of the triumph, " Who is this," asks the prophet, " that cometh from Edom, with dyed garments from Bozrah? this that is glorious in his apparel, travelling in the greatness of his strength?" Then he gives the Redeemer's an-

THE WORK OF CHRIST.

swer : " I that speak in righteousness, mighty to save." Again he asks, " Wherefore art thou red in thine apparel, and thy garments like him that treadeth in the wine-fat ?" And again the Conqueror of death and sin answers, " I have trodden the wine-press alone, and of the people there was none with me : for I will tread them in mine anger, and trample them in my fury, and their blood shall be sprinkled upon my garments, and I will stain all my raiment*."

So St. Paul, throughout his whole Epistle to the Hebrews, presents the work of Christ under the same aspect, as standing *alone*,—admitting no succession, no repetition ; so that for those who by their impenitence refuse the blood of Christ, or who having been enlightened, apostatise, and crucify Him afresh by their sins, there is no hope ; as renouncing Him, they must perish in their guiltiness ; for there remaineth no more sacrifice for sins.

Such, then, is the absolute intrinsic efficacy of the work of Christ—his Sacrifice and Atonement for the sins of the world.

But though the Lord had thus laid the foundation of his church in his blood, and had finished

---

* Isaiah lxiii. 1–3. Ep. for Monday before Easter.

2 E

his work which the Father had sent him to do,
He had yet to superintend and direct and bless
the work, to be carried on in the building of
the Church on his Foundation. It was expedient, therefore, that He should go away—that
He should be at the right hand of the Father,
at the fountain of grace in heaven, there to
present himself as a Priest fully consecrated,
to intercede for those whom He had atoned
for on earth, and bring them to Himself; first
making them members of his Church in the
world, and then exalting them, by continual supplies of his grace, to perfect blessedness with
Him in heaven.

For this holy work accordingly He sent down
the Holy Spirit the Comforter, not to perfect
what He had done, as if it were in any respect
imperfect, or supersede his own heavenly ministrations in our behalf at the Throne of grace, but
to begin, as it may be said, a new work on the
earth; to gather a congregation of believers from
all parts of the world, without distinction of race,
without respect of persons; and unite them in
one body as a holy temple, built up of living
stones on the Lord himself, the Foundation; a
work, which the world certainly had never yet

witnessed ; and which, but for the Saviour's own work preceding, could never have been accomplished. Without Him it would have been as a building on the sand—soon to sink by its own weight, and be scattered in ruin.

And how different, let us observe, was the work for which the Holy Spirit was sent, in the actual business of which it consisted, from that of our Lord Himself. The Lord called a few around Him : preached but to few, confining his personal application to the lost sheep of Israel alone. The Author of eternal Salvation to all men, was a minister, in the days of his personal ministry, to his own people only ; intent as he was—if we may venture thus to analyze so mysterious and high a ministry as His—more on suffering than on acting ; more in combating with the Powers of darkness, than in proclaiming the redemption wrought out of their hand ; more on shewing forth in his own Person the way and the truth and the life, than on didactic exposition of the truth ; scattering, indeed, the seeds of heavenly doctrine as he walked through the cities and villages of Israel ; but all the while, bearing his Cross, and Himself going before, and opening the gate, and making straight the path through the grave to the Life Eternal.

When the Holy Spirit entered on his mission the case was entirely changed. Then was wanted a power which should diffuse itself far beyond the narrow limits of the land of Israel—which should be a word, like the sun, going forth into all lands, even to the utmost extremity of the earth, and calling all men, individually as well as collectively, to embrace the Salvation wrought by Christ; one that should be present everywhere, and through all ages, to the end of the world, with the Apostles and their successors in the ministry; giving them thought, and utterance, and holiness, and zeal, commensurate with their high calling; and enabling them mightily to convince the gainsayer and disputer of the world, that Jesus was the Christ, as also to work persuasion and comfort in the heart of each poor and contrite sinner. Thus did the gift of the Holy Spirit, at his effusion on the day of Pentecost, realize the imaginative wish of the poet; being as "a hundred tongues, and a hundred mouths, and a voice of iron," to each first missionary of the Gospel; speaking to every man in

his own tongue, wherein he was born, the wonderful works of God.

Then how different was the result! When the
Holy Spirit goes forth on his work, we see immediately the Church begins to be built up. Previously, we have only known that the foundation
has been laid. Now the walls begin to rise above
the ground, and the plan and dimensions of the
building appear to view. The little true-hearted
flock gathered out of the wilderness of Judah by
the Lord himself, which is found tarrying in
Jerusalem, waiting for the fulfilment of the promise of the Spirit, consisted only of about one
hundred and twenty,—a happy assemblage indeed,
an omen of the future glorious countless church
that shall be gathered in the fulness of time,
about the Throne of the Lamb,—but still a little
flock then, amidst the multitudes of an unbe-
lieving world. Contrast with this the effect of
the first ministration of the Holy Spirit on the
day of Pentecost, when, under his inspiration,
the Apostle Peter preached Christ to the Jews
assembled from the various countries of their
dispersion; in nothing dissembling the unwel-
come truth to Jewish ears; in nothing keeping
back the shame of the Cross; but expressly de-

claring as the sum of his doctrine, " Therefore
let all the house of Israel know assuredly, that
God hath made that same Jesus whom ye have
crucified, both Lord and Christ." On that glad
occasion, we hear of three thousand souls added
to the number of believers at once ; and the increase proceeded so that " the Lord," it is said,
" added *daily* to the church such as should be
saved." Then too, through the energetic working of the Holy Spirit, many of those who had
derided the Lord himself when personally ministering to them, and obstinately set themselves
against Him, were softened in heart. " A great
company of the Priests," we read, became " obedient to the faith ;" and, as the narrative proceeds, it informs us of believers counted by tens
of thousands ; and the word of the Lord is described as " growing mightily and prevailing."
The converts, too, are represented as " continuing stedfastly in the Apostles' doctrine and
fellowship, and in breaking of bread and in
prayers ;" whereas, even of the thousands fed by
the Lord in the wilderness, many went back,
and walked no more with Him. And now, even
in these degenerate times, so many hundred years
since the dispensation of the Spirit began, may

we not discern the fruits of the same blessed energy, in the missionary zeal which goes forth from among us to new fields of labour, and, amidst much outward discouragement and hazard, gathers harvests to the Lord where before all was barren and waste? So may we hope, that, as the Gospel is more and more spread through the world,—as the love of the Spirit works in more hearts through faith, and the multitude of labourers is sent from all parts into the field,—the work of the Spirit in bringing men to Christ shall be productive of still more wonderful effects, though by ordinary and far humbler means than those vouchsafed to the Apostles.

Do we derogate from the merit or the effect of the Lord's own work, when we thus magnify the work of the Spirit? Far from this, indeed! Rather we give Him the glory of the whole. For it is in His name that the Spirit thus works with might ; it is by virtue of His Sacrifice that the Spirit goes forth to convert the world ; it is the boon granted to the Saviour's prayer, that the Comforter first came down to the work, and to his continued intercession as the great High Priest at the Throne of grace, that the Spirit still unceasingly carries on his blessed agency in the saving of a fallen world.

The text thus leads us to refer the work of the Spirit throughout to the scheme of Salvation set forth by Christ. The Comforter, our Lord tells his disciples, would be sent " in his Name ;" not with an Authority distinct from His ; but as the bearer to the world of an Authority from Him to carry on the work ; the same Authority, which they had seen so evidently manifested in Him by signs and wonders. The Comforter again should " teach them all things, and bring all things to their remembrance, whatsoever He had said unto them." As his own doctrine had been not his only, " but the Father's who sent him *," so should the doctrine of the Spirit, whilst it should be a full instruction in all things needful for the edification of the Church, be the doctrine which they had received from Christ himself; as He elsewhere says, " He shall not speak of himself, but whatsoever He shall hear, that shall He speak :" " He shall take of mine and shew it unto you †."

This it was that rendered the Holy Spirit the

* John xiv. 24.   † *Ib.* xvi. 13–15.

representative, or substitute, of Christ—*vicarius Christi*, as Tertullian expresses it ; not, as has been before shewn, that the Spirit would stand to the Church precisely in the same relation in which Christ had stood ; but that He should revive and perpetuate the same doctrine. The disciples should experience in Him a full compensation for the loss of their Master's society ; they should hear the same voice, which they had listened to with burning hearts whilst he went in and out amongst them ; the same heavenly teaching, which but a few weeks before had been overborne and silenced for ever, as it might then have seemed, by the mad uproar of the people, should again be perceived by the inward ear ; like the still small voice heard by the Prophet, after the fire and the earthquake, and the great and strong wind, which rent the mountains and brake in pieces the rocks. The presence of the Holy Spirit thus awakening in them the image of Christ, would enable them to proceed in the execution of their commission from Him to evangelize the world. As the disciples of Christ, they would carry with them the doctrine of Christ, repeating again and again, as they addressed "themselves" to one person after another, the

same words which they had learnt from Him ;
ever preaching his Death and Resurrection, as the
ground of the sinner's pardon and acceptance
with God ; and as the simple direct ambassadors
of Christ, putting nothing in their teaching in
front of the one great master principle of faith
in Him as the only way of Salvation. They
would go forth indeed in the might of the Holy
Spirit. Without his aid, and strength, and guidance, they would feel that they were nothing,
and could do nothing. Still they would be
Christians throughout. It would be the savour
of Christ that would breathe from all their teaching. They would doubtless, too, often speak of
that blessed Comforter, through whom they were
enabled to bear true and faithful witness to Christ.
They would inculcate on all whom they would
address, a supreme reverence for the Divine
Majesty of the Holy Spirit, as the coequal of the
Father and of the Son, in the glory of the Holy
Undivided Trinity. For so had they been taught
by their Master to reverence the Comforter whom
He would send to them ; when he bade them
baptize believers in the name of the Father, the
Son, and the Holy Ghost. They would also im-
press on their hearers, what their own expe-

rience, as well as the word of their Master, had
taught them, that without the help of the Spirit
they could do nothing in the service of Christ.
Still they would labour, as we find they do, from
all that is recorded of them in the Acts of the
Apostles, or their teaching in their Epistles, to
make men disciples of Christ—*Christians*, as we
might say emphatically ; not disciples of themselves, as teachers under the dictation of the
Spirit, nor even disciples of the Spirit himself,
but simply disciples of Christ.

And it is no insignificant testimony of this conduct on their part, that the disciples whom they
gathered first out of the world obtained the name
of *Christians*.   Had this name been given to the
infant flock whom the Lord himself brought into
his fold, this would have had nothing remarkable
in it.   They might naturally have been called in
the world by that sacred Name, when they were
seen to be the followers of Him who claimed it.
But there must have been some ground in the
doctrine itself taught by the Apostles, when the
disciples whom they formed were not called by
their name, or by that of the Spirit, whose immediate instruments they were in the work of conversion, but after Christ only.   It shews that

the doctrine of Christ must have been ever on
their lips; that their teaching was identified
with that of Christ himself; and delivered no
other message but that which they had received
from their Lord. And it is no small confirmation of this assertion, that it was at Antioch that
the disciples were first called Christians;—a result, that may well be connected with the teaching of that Apostle, who called forth that marked
blessing from the Lord on his hearty confession
of his faith—" Blessed art thou, Simon Barjona,
for flesh and blood hath not revealed it to thee,
but my Father which is in heaven;" and who on
account of the same was surnamed the Rock; as
Abram became Abraham, " the father of the great
multitude;" so he, from Simon the son of Jonah,
becoming Peter, " the Rock," as the first to proclaim that faith in Christ on which the Church
should be built.

Do I seem, Brethren, to have been labouring
a point about which there is no difficulty?

Let it be granted, that there is no difficulty in
the matter, to the simple student of Scripture,
and the follower of the teaching of our own
Church.

But has there not been an attempt lately made,

to separate the teaching of the Apostles and their successors, under the dispensation of the Spirit, from the case of our Lord's own personal teaching ; and to characterize it as a perfection of doctrine beyond what was imparted before that dispensation ? and thus, in fact, to trace up Christian doctrine to the mission of the Spirit and his working on the understanding of man, instead of deriving it exclusively from the primary work and doctrine of Christ ?

It may readily occur to you, that I allude to a publication recently circulated among us, and which, as an indisputable evidence of the real spirit and tendency of the theological movement begun within these last few years, in this place, has attracted a degree of interest beyond that intrinsically belonging to it*.

According to the tenour of that publication, the Holy Spirit was not sent down to the Apostles, simply to inspire them with a wisdom and confidence and zeal and power to deliver the doctrine already fully set forth by their Master, but to suggest to them the secret undefined consciousness of Divine Truth ; to be in their minds

* Newman's Essay on the Development of Christian Doctrine.

a prolific germ of doctrine, opening more and more in the progress of the Church.

In such a theological system, the doctrine of Christ Himself is but a meagre element ; the mere unformed matter, waiting to be moulded into shape by the plastic power of the successive authoritative teachers of the Church ; through whose hands, on occasion of controversies and speculations arising to demand more explicit statements, the truth is wrought out to its perfect outline and body.

A great and most important question, accordingly, has been forced on our notice, as to the proper historical character of the doctrines professed among us ; whether, namely, they were wholly committed to the Apostles at first by our Lord Himself, and have been thus inherited by us as an original bequest of Christ to his Church in all ages, without addition, diminution, or alteration ; or whether, on the other hand, they are the gradual result of the abiding dispensation of the Holy Spirit, the accumulated truth of successive ages bringing them to maturity and perfection.

Or, as it might thus be stated, the question now before us is ; whether the body of Christian truth professed at this day in the Church, is a fixed and definite scheme of doctrine, delivered once for all at its own period, and simply transmitted in its entire form from age to age ; or whether its nature is, to have been spread over the succession of ages, and to be only what it is ultimately, by successive gatherings into it and increase of dimension.

This is the great question which we now seem called upon to consider and resolve for the satisfaction and peace of the young members of our Church, whose minds may have been excited on the subject by the appearance of the work to which I have alluded.

The question is fundamentally connected with that on which I have been speaking, the relation of the mission of the Comforter on the day of Pentecost to the mission of our Lord Himself. It turns eventually on the point,—what was the office of the Comforter thus sent ; whether it was simply to be a remembrancer of Christ,—a builder up of the Church on the foundation of Christ, — an inculcator of the doctrine and discipline of Christ,—an effectual worker with those already imbued with " the truth as it is in Jesus,"— establishing, strengthening, settling them in the

Faith,—empowering them to bear true witness to the Resurrection of the Lord, to convince the world of sin, of righteousness, and of judgment, and bow to the Cross the stubborn heart of man ; or whether the Comforter, thus sent, came to be an Institutor of the Religion which, assuming the former dispensations as its point of outset, should bear the name of Christ, as first preached by the Apostles of Christ—to be an ever-speaking oracle of Divine truth, giving forth the response of heavenly instruction in the emergencies of the Church, and expressly dictating from time to time, the sentences containing its doctrine, and imparting to such sentences, at whatever period delivered, an infallible Divine Authority.

This was the great question with which the Church had to contend in its early history ; in its struggles with the Gnostic teachers from the very times of the Apostles. For we find such teachers disturbing the Churches planted by St. Paul with complaints of the imperfection of that Apostle's teaching: disparaging the simple preaching of the truth witnessed by the Apostle ; and professing to impart to those who would listen to them, a more spiritual doctrine ; a doctrine, not originally communicated to the Apostles, but subsequently revealed ; the effect of the teaching of the Spirit.

Though, however, the early Gnostics assumed the principle of a Divine instruction imparted to the Church, subsequently to its foundation by the life and death and teaching of Christ, the principle itself does not appear to have been so formally established in their system, as it was about the middle of the second century, by the sect of Montanus. It has been questioned, what was the precise character assumed to himself by that heresiarch : whether to be the Comforter Himself, the Paraclete, (as Tertullian designates the Holy Spirit ;) or only to have received special communication from the Teacher promised under that name to the Apostles. It has, however, I think, been clearly shewn, from the passages of Tertullian which refer to the pretensions of Montanus, that he claimed only to be regarded as a prophet inspired by the same Holy Spirit, or Paraclete, who had been sent down to the Apostles*. Such a claim would proceed on the notion that the Holy Spirit had been given to the Apostles, for the *revelation of truth beyond*

* Bishop of Lincoln's Eccl. Hist. illustrated by the writings of Tertullian.

2 F

what they had received from their Master—to teach, indeed, a religion not entirely new,—for it was to be the religion of Christ,—but new in the way of additions ; as perfecting what had been left imperfect ; as settling what had been left undecided. For Montanus, if we may judge of his teaching from his disciple Tertullian, strictly maintained the creed, or rule of faith, as then received in the Church, but asserted a power from the Spirit to develop what was only implied in the records of the Apostolic teaching ; to throw a light on the obscure intimations in them ; and fill out the parts of a perfect discipline of life, too strict to be borne in the time of the Apostles, but now, as he affirmed, enjoined by the Spirit.

" For what a thing is it," asks Tertullian,* the Apologist of the system, " that, whilst the devil is ever working, and is adding daily to the devices of iniquity, the work of God should have either ceased, or left off advancing ! when it was on this account that the Lord sent the Paraclete, that, since human mediocrity could not receive all at once, Discipline should gradually be directed, and ordered, and brought to perfection by that Vicar of the Lord, the Holy Spirit. ' I

* De Virg. Vel. c. i.

have yet many things to say unto you, but ye
cannot bear them now. Howbeit, when He, the
Spirit of truth is come, He will guide you into all
truth: and He will shew you things to come.'
But above, also, He pronounced respecting this
work of His. What, then, is this administration
of the Paraclete, but that Discipline is directed ;
that the Scriptures are unveiled ; that the understanding is reformed ; that there is an advance
to better things ? Nothing is without age, and
all things wait for time. Finally, the Preacher
says : ' There is a time for everything.' Behold
the creature itself gradually advancing to fruit.
First it is a grain, then from a grain a stalk
arises, and from a stalk shoots forth a little
shrub ; next branches and leaves grow, and a
tree in full name is expanded ; next is the swell-
ing of a germ ; and from a germ a flower opens ;
and from a flower a fruit is disclosed ; that too,
for some time rude and unformed, gradually directing its age, is educated into mildness of
flavour. So also Righteousness, (for the same is
the God of Righteousness and of the creature,) was
first in its rudiments a God-fearing nature ; then,
by the law and the Prophets, it advanced to infancy ; afterwards by the Gospel it burst forth

2 F 2

into youth ; now by the Paraclete it is settled into maturity. He is the only one from Christ, worthy to be called and reverenced as a Master. ' For He shall not speak of Himself, but the things which are committed to Him by Christ.' He is the only antecessor, because He is the only one after Christ. They who have received Him, prefer Truth to custom."

Thus was that theory which has been lately propounded to us, as the only solution of the state of Christian doctrine in the Church under the ministry of the Apostles and their successors, originally the device of heretics, seeking by it to recommend their innovations as the authoritative dictates of the Holy Spirit.

And Gnosticism, and Montanism, and afterwards Manicheism, (for Manes, too, gave himself out to be the promised Paraclete, the perfecter of the doctrine of Christ ;) in this, have only been the precursors of the Church of Rome. Rome has taken up the principle of those sects, and pushed it to its natural consequences. For if it be once granted that the Holy Spirit, He who by Christ's promise is to abide with the Church for ever, was sent to be a revealer of new and as yet untaught truth in the minds of the authoritative teachers of

the Church ; there is no reason why such a revelation should be limited to one age of the Church
more than to another ; or one class of things, (as
for instance to matters of discipline only,) than to
another class, that of doctrines ; or why improvements (not to say in modes of statement or expressions only), but in doctrines themselves,
should not be found in a later age rather than in
earlier ; and so the whole present system of the
Church of Rome be justified, with all its additions to the original faith, as the highest, truest
Christian wisdom.

So necessary is it, that we should strictly observe the great landmarks laid down in Scripture,
between the Gospel itself of our Lord,—the great
immovable saving truths belonging to the Life
and Death, and Resurrection and Ascension, and
Everlasting Priesthood of Christ, with all other
truths connected with them, respecting the nature
of God and man, which together make up the
Doctrine and Discipline of Christ ;—and on the
other side, the teaching and guiding of the Holy
Spirit vouchsafed to the Church for the maintenance and application of those great truths to the
Salvation of man.

Depart once from this solid ground, and attribute the Christian doctrine to the revealing Power of the Spirit dwelling in the hearts of its human teachers, and you destroy the vital objective character of that doctrine.

Believe in the fullest inspiration, the most effectual guidance and strength, imparted by the mission of the Spirit to the Apostles ; enabling them to preach the word without error; enlightening them ; sanctifying them throughout ; and enduing them further with those miraculous gifts and powers, which they possessed by the Lord's special promise ; and you only ascribe the honour due to the Holy Comforter, and to the Father, and the Son, by whom He was sent.

But regard the truths of the Gospel as the gradual production of the Holy Spirit working in the mind of the teachers of the Church ; and you then reduce Christianity to a series of doctrinal phenomena,—possessing indeed their truth at the time of their appearance,—but not endued with any fixed unchangeable character, as the word of God which standeth fast for ever. The several objects of Christian belief then assume the varied livery of human thought ; shifting like clouds their form and colour with the rays that fall upon them. Try to realize them in the past, and they are already faded away and indistinct. They exist in the present only ; for to change is with them to live.

No limit can be assigned to the extravagances of such a theory of Christian doctrine. Under a religion which flows with the flowing of thought through the mind of man, even the most opposite statements may be held true in their turn. If the nature of doctrines is, to be the exponents of ideas, the same may be true at one time and false at another. The Church, accordingly, is described by the advocate of this theory, as converting even contraries to its purpose—taking into its system, and applying to the support of the faith, the errors of heresy and the superstitions of heathenism. We learn from him, how Montanism, at one time cast out of the Church as a fanatical innovation, puts off its heretical garb, and reappears ; no longer uttering unauthorized prophesyings and imaginary revelations ; but now a spirit of development, and infallibility, and holy discipline, in the doctors and saints of the Church. Sabellianism, again, we are told, was a premature effort in its day, "to complete the mystery of the ever-blessed Trinity ;" destined at length to be " realized in the true unitarianism of St. Augustine." And in general, " doctrines, usages, actions, and personal characters become," by the magic of this theory, incorporated with the Gospel, and are made " right and acceptable to its Divine Author ; when before they were either contrary to truth, or at best but shadows of it*." Such is the ground on which Image-worship, among other corrupt practices of the Church of Rome, divests itself of its heathenism, and is transformed into a Christian service ; and heathen philosophy, exiled from the Church by Apostles, is brought back and consecrated to the use of the Church by their successors.

And can we regard such a speculation as Christian Theology ? Is it not rather wholly a Platonic philosophy of ideas—of ideas, as types or forms of existing things, passing through various outward manifestations, as they enter into and mingle with this lower world,—the world of generation and corruption—the world of shadows,—in which nothing really subsists, but all is flowing and changing without ceasing ? Imagine ideas, according to this philosophy, at one time appearing in the form of heathen doctrine and heathen worship, or the speculations of heathen philo-

* Essay on Development, pp. 354–366.

sophy—and then only imperfectly developed ; assuming accordingly wild, grotesque, unreal forms ; distorted in shadow, or faintly pictured in legend and fable ; then, as the state of the world affords them happier occasions of development, issuing in more and more perfect forms, more according to their own proper nature, as the true and real types of things ; first, however, still in shadows and symbols under the Law and the Prophets ; then in an elementary manner at the outset of the Gospel ; afterwards expanding in their native vigour, and reaching their maturity, as the elaboration of the Church's Doctrine and Discipline proceeds ;—conceive all this,—and you have then a just view of what is now recommended to us for the Gospel of Christ, under the name of the Development of Christian Doctrine.

The most complete scepticism would result from such a mode of dealing with Christian doctrine, were not the strength of an Infallible Authority invoked to the aid of the wavering mind. A peremptory dogmatism at once silences and subdues each rising doubt. This throws its chain of ice across the flowing stream ; stays the current, however rapid and ruffled ; and fixes it, for the time at least, immovably. A complex dogmatic system exhibits in one present scheme, the several presentations, or forms of Doctrine, under which the objects of belief have successively appeared, as developed by the mind of the Church through the course of ages. Hence the profession exacted of members of the Church of Rome, to believe whatever the Church believes. Without such an acknowledgment of the absolute power of the Church to fix the matter of belief, all would relapse into uncertainty. Deny the infallibility of the Church at any period of its existence; relax but ever so slightly the despotic hold which the Church of Rome has, by this high assumption of infallibility, on the minds of its people; and the fabric must fall to pieces.

Let us not wonder, therefore, that divines of that Church are ready to sacrifice other principles at times, when pressed with difficulties on particular points, so long as this is strictly maintained. When it is pointed out, for example, how in the religion of Rome there is a vast accumulation of materials from without; additions to the pure faith of the Gospel from heathen philosophy and heathen practice; the charge is admitted; as here in this Theory of Development which I have been noticing. But the incorporation of this ex-

traneous matter into the religion, is boldly justified on the ground of a perpetuated Divine Authority in the Church, enabling it to discriminate
what should be approved, what rejected, in the
chaotic mass presented to it, and to determine
the Truth with unerring judgment.

The infallibility of the Church is thus the fundamental assumption of the Roman Church; pervading and animating its whole system, and which
it cannot part with but with its life *.

And not only is the Church of Rome committed to this assumption; but no less so are all who
would represent the doctrines of the Gospel as
issuing from the mind of the Church, and determined by its authority, and not simply as doc-

---

* "Nostra igitur sententia est, Ecclesiam absolute non posse
errare, nec in rebus absolute necessariis, nec in aliis, quæ cre-
denda vel facienda nobis proponit, sive habeantur expresse in
Scripturis, sive non; et cum dicimus Ecclesiam non posse
errare, id intelligimus tam de universitate fidelium, quam de
universitate Episcoporum; ita ut sensus sit ejus propositionis,
Ecclesia non potest errare, id est, id quod tenent omnes fideles
tanquam de fide, necessario est verum et de fide; et similiter,
id quod docent omnes episcopi, tanquam ad fidem pertinens,
necessario est verum et de fide . . . . . . Sic igitur Apostolus
vocans Ecclesiam columnam veritatis, vult significare veritatem
fidei, quoad nos, niti Ecclesiæ auctoritate, et verum esse, quicquid Ecclesia probat, falsum quicquid improbat."—*Bellarm.*
De Eccles. Milit. l. iii. c. 14. p. 1277.

trines of Christ taught in Scripture. Great, indeed, is the blessing to its members, of a Church
which professes, and inculcates by its authority,
the truth of Scripture; and we cannot lightly
disobey the voice of such a faithful teacher.
But we cannot receive doctrines absolutely on
its word, without admitting its infallibility. You
must, then, have some positive determining authority to rule each point of faith. Once, however, admit its infallibility, and you are the disciple of Rome in principle; and the transition is
then easy, as experience has shewn, to the disciple
in fact.

But with all this effort to fix the body of doctrine as developed by the Church, and secure the
faith of believers, the evident tendency of such a
proceeding is to scepticism and ultimate infidelity.
For it throws a shade over the information of
history in regard to theological questions. We
can then find no resting-place where we may ter-
minate our inquiry, and say, that we know this
or that doctrine to be the truth, by the evidence
of it there found. Scripture, and the writings
of the Fathers are, in this respect, on the same
footing. As the sacred text must be ruled by
the subsequent comment of Church-authority;

so must the evidence of an earlier Father be explained by the evidence of the later, who lived when the doctrine in question obtained its more explicit statement. To rescue the living, it seems no offence to trample on the dead. To clear the ground for erecting some sightly edifice, the sanctuary of the tomb is invaded without compunction. Thus is the inquirer utterly bewildered in his search after the truth. He walks over the ground where the monuments and relics of his faith should be found, but some one has been before him, and obliterated the traces for which he is looking.

For thus we find advocates of this theory of Christian doctrine, not only characterizing Scripture as obscure and uncertain in its language on the great mysteries of our faith, but destroying, or at least weakening, the testimony in their favour in the writings of primitive antiquity. The case of the learned Jesuit Petau, or Petavius, is probably well known, even to those who have not examined his own writings, from the distinct notice of it by Bishop Bull, in his celebrated "Defence of the Nicene Faith." In his blind zeal to cut away the ground from Protestant controversialists, the Jesuit was willing to sacrifice

the existing evidence to the doctrine of our Lord's
Divinity in the first Three Centuries of Christian Antiquity; and even to incur the reproach
of Arianism; so that it might appear that there
existed no more certain evidence in Antiquity
for the great doctrines held in common by every
sound Protestant as well as Romanist, than for
the corruptions imputed to Rome*. Following
in the same track, the recent advocate of the
Roman system of doctrine willingly concedes, that
the evidence of the first Three Centuries looks
unfavourably for establishing the truth; that the
Fathers of those Centuries are as clear for the doctrines of the Mass, of Purgatory, of the Worship
of Saints, of the Supremacy of the Pope, as they
are for the acknowledged articles of a saving
Faith, the truths of the Trinity in Unity and the
Incarnation.

No open adversary of Patristic authority could

* "Atenim complures antiquorum illorum quos auctores
ac testes appellamus, fidei nostræ, de plurimis dogmatibus,
præsertim vero de Trinitate, multum a nobis diversa scrip-
serunt," &c.—*Petav. Dogm. Theol.* tom. ii. p. 4.

He was followed in this argument by Huet, Bishop of
Avranches. Priestley attempted, on the same ground, to
impugn the Scripture evidence to the perfect Divinity of our
Lord.—See Bishop Horsley's Charge. *Controv. with Priestley,*
p. 64, &c.

have so effectually damaged that authority, and, together with it, the integrity of Christian belief, as its professed advocates have done by such an admission of its insufficiency.   For, if those who lay so much stress on Tradition for ascertaining and establishing Christian truth, are found afterwards to invalidate that very evidence of which Tradition consists, what ground do they leave to the believer? what temptation do they not hold out to those, who are not prepared at once to accept the alternative of believing whatever Rome believes, to conclude, that, as the evidence on which they have hitherto been taught to depend, fails on more mature consideration of it, in the judgment even of its advocates, the Faith itself must be precarious and uncertain*?

---

* What can it avail against the force of such a conclusion to urge as Petavius does: " Cæterum quod, in superioribus capitibus tribus, Veterum sententias ac dicta recensuimus, quæ alienum quiddam, et abhorrens a Catholica professione, saltem loquendi modo, continere videntur; non sic accipi velim, quasi nihil sincere, Catholiceque scriptum, in eorum libris exstet," &c. (*De Trin.* l. i. c. 6.)   Or as Mr. Newman does, after him; "Let it not be for a moment supposed that I impugn the orthodoxy of the early divines, or the cogency of their testimony among *fair* inquirers,"? &c.—*Introd.* p. 15.

Bishop Horsley has pointed out the occasion which gave rise to this mode of dealing with the testimony of the primitive

Such is the downward path, the *facilis descen-sus*, of those, who commit the first great error of setting up an Authority in the Church of infallible dictation over the word committed by Christ to his Apostles, and by them consigned to the Scriptures. Such an Authority cannot, as I have endeavoured to shew, be attributed to our Lord's promise of the abiding presence of the Spirit with the Church. It does not appear, at least, from the text of Scripture. And surely Rome cannot, with any reason, assert that infallible Authority for thus construing the promise of the Spirit in Scripture, when the very passages which

ages. "At the time," he says, "when Petavius wrote, the minds of the most enlightened and liberal of the Romanists were so ill-reconciled to the separation of the reformed Churches from their communion, that it was the fashion for the champions of the Papal superstition, in order to weaken the support which they were sensible the Protestant cause received from the writings of the Fathers of the three first Centuries, to take every method to derogate from their Authority. And this, it was thought, could in no way be more effectually done, than by bringing them under a suspicion of misbelief, in doctrines, which the reformed Churches, and the Roman, hold in equal reverence. The learned Petavius considered not, that he sacrificed the cause of our common Christianity to the private views of his own Church, in thus attempting to corrupt the stream of Tradition at the very fountain-head."—*Charge— Controv. with Priestley*, p. 55.

contain the promise, are those, on which the question itself of Infallibility chiefly depends.

Let the example of Rome,—the rocks and quicksands which that Church has run upon, in thus arrogating to itself a gift which the Lord has not conceded to it,—be a warning to all, how they undervalue that degree of evidence for the truth which the Lord has judged sufficient for us, in a vain reaching after an infallibility, which lies beyond our present sphere of belief and action.

It is but the same principle on which the infidel proceeds in rejecting the Gospel. The utmost that he can allege against it is, that its evidence is not absolutely irresistible; that it presents some difficulties to the speculative and critical reason; and may therefore be objected to by such as require a perfect, overpowering, demonstration of its truth*. The infidel accordingly seeks an infallibility in the evidence of the Gospel; and, from this false assumption, refuses the blessing of a Faith intended by its Divine Author to prove and discipline the receiver of it. So do those naturally miss the true Faith, who, neglecting the proper evidence of its doctrines in the certainty and sufficiency of Scripture, demand a

* See Butler's *Analogy*, Part II. cc. 6 and 8, *Conclusion*.

2 G

more distinct evidence, to enable them to discriminate between the true and the false; and are
dissatisfied with anything short of a living infallible interpreter.

Would we know Christ, and the Salvation by
Him, we must indeed seek the aid of the same
Holy Comforter, who was given to the Apostles,
to teach them, and bring to their remembrance
all things whatsoever He had said unto them,—in
like manner to teach us, and bring to our remembrance, (for we too, who have been baptized and
instructed in the Faith, have already been taught
by Him,) whatsoever He has said to us. The
Spirit has been given to the Church—let us ever
bear in mind—not to dictate to us anew what we
are to believe ; but to open our understandings,
that we may receive the testimony of Christ ;
and to cleanse and exalt our hearts, that we may
appreciate his truth and love towards us. The
fullest, most effectual superintendence of Christ
by the Holy Spirit over the Church as a whole,
and every member of it in particular, is undoubtedly a great Scripture-truth. We are assured
accordingly by our Lord, that his Church shall
never utterly perish, nor truth, consequently, nor
faith, fail out of the earth ; however iniquity, and

error, and all the powers of Antichrist, may prevail for a season.   We are to live on this promise;
not to pride ourselves, as if in perfect security of
possession of the Truth and Faith.   The gift of
the Spirit, though as Christians we already enjoy
it, is yet to be regarded as in promise ; as it was
to the Apostles looking forward to the day of
Pentecost, though they had already been made
partakers of the Spirit: " for unto every one that
hath shall be given*."

Nor let us despise or slight the Authority and
guidance of the Church in which we are provi-
dentially placed ; though we reject the theory of
an inherent Infallibility in the Church.   It was
to the Apostles in communion with each other as
disciples of Christ, that the Spirit was promised,
to teach them and guide them and assist them in
the work of the ministry.   It was on them when
assembled together as a Church, that the Holy
Spirit descended.   Let not this example be lost
on us.   Let us remember, that none liveth to
himself as a member of Christ.   He is a part of
the Body of Christ.   Then let not " the eye say
unto the hand, I have no need of thee ; nor again,
the head to the feet, I have no need of you ;" nor

* Augustin. *in Ev. Joan.* c. xiv. *Tractat.* 73.

2 G 2

any one member claim to itself to be the body.
But let us take to ourselves the counsel and
strength of the Body, in which we have been
placed by the good pleasure of our Lord—our
own Apostolic and Scriptural Communion; and
so obtain a strong ground of trust, that the Lord
will pray for us, as for his first disciples, and
keep us by his Spirit, that our faith fail not, nor
He withdraw his Truth from us.

SERMON XIII.

THE WORK OF CHRIST

AND THE WORK OF THE SPIRIT.

PREACHED IN THE CATHEDRAL OF CHRIST CHURCH,

On SUNDAY, November 1, 1846.

SERMON XIII.

THE WORK OF CHRIST

AND THE WORK OF THE SPIRIT.

MATT. XXVIII. 18–20.

And Jesus came and spake unto them, saying, All power is given
unto me in Heaven and in earth. Go ye therefore and teach
all nations, baptizing them in the name of the Father, and of
the Son, and of the Holy Ghost: teaching them to observe all
things whatsoever I have commanded you: and lo, I am with
you alway, even unto the end of the world.

I CONCLUDED my Sermon of last Sunday, with
an exhortation to you, to seek the teaching and
guidance and strength of the Holy Spirit, in order
truly to receive the Doctrine and Discipline of
Christ; not as solitary detached individuals, having no spiritual tie to others around you; but
as members of the body of Christ; as persons
united in one Communion under Christ our Head.
As the Apostles received the special illumination
of the Spirit, for the work of building up the
Church founded by their Lord, at a time when

they were joined in holy fellowship with themselves and the other disciples of the Lord; and when, having continued in their Lord's love, according to his earnest parting injunction,—having but one heart and one mind,—they were met together, (as we read,) " with one accord in one place"—the place of common worship; so should we, I urged, and would still urge, after their example, look for the promise of the Spirit to ourselves, as we abide in communion with each other; remembering, how God has placed us in his Church in the world, and availing ourselves of the benefit of this disposition of his Providence.

The work of the Holy Spirit on earth thus is essentially connected with the visible institution of the Church, the Body of Christ on earth. Unlike the work of the Son of God in this respect, it is carried on within the circle of an existing Society. The work of Christ had nothing to build on,—no circumscribed ground on which its operations were to be effected. Like the beginning of the Heaven and the earth, it was a new Creation. " God said: Let there be light, and there was light:" a new Heaven and a new earth appeared; no longer material and perishable, like the first, but invisible and immortal; wherein Righteousness should dwell for ever. On this new Creation, called into being by the Word of God, went forth the Holy Spirit, moving on the face of it with wonder-working energy, breathing into it life and holiness. And as the natural Creation became fruitful and multiplied, by virtue of his blessing, so has the Holy Spirit descended on the Creation of grace—the infant Church,— blessing it with increase; until at length the " thousands of the tribes of Israel," spoken of in the Apocalyptic vision, shall be " sealed;" and " that great multitude which no man can number, of all nations, and kindreds, and people, and tongues, stand before the Throne and before the Lamb, clothed with white robes, and palms in their hands, and cry with a loud voice, saying, Salvation to our God, who sitteth upon the Throne, and unto the Lamb *."

Glorious, unspeakably glorious indeed, will be the result, when the work of the Holy Spirit shall thus be consummated, and the Church of Christ shall come forth as his Bride, " arrayed in the fine linen, the righteousness of saints," amidst the triumphant songs of myriads of angels; and

* Rev. vii. 4–10.

when that day which we celebrate in faith and
hopeful anticipation, year after year, as now, shall
be realized in joyous fruition. What happiness!
what encouragement, Brethren, to perseverance
in our holy calling! to contemplate, even in this
our distant unworthiness, and amidst our awe at
a thought too great for our minds, the prospect
of that last glad celebration, and the hope held
forth to us, that we may at length have a name
among those that live, on the great day of All
Saints!

This is the true development,—if we may use
the word in a sound sense,—which belongs to the
religion of Christ. From small beginnings,—from
a germ of life, planted, and watered, and fostered,
and nourished by the Holy Spirit,—shall spring
up a vine, to "cover the hills with its shadow, stretching out its branches to the sea, and
its boughs unto the river:" from the pure fountain, small at its rise, shall flow rivers of water,
pouring their riches through all lands, and swell-
ing in their course into a mighty ocean. The city
of Zion, no longer bounded within the narrow
circle of its own hills, " shall be established in
the top of the mountains, and shall be exalted
above the hills, and all nations shall flow into it ;"

and " the kingdoms of the world shall become the kingdom of our Lord and of his Christ." This is, I say, the true development of the religion; because it is that held forth by the word of God to the faith and hope of the Christian. He is told by that infallible oracle, that the Church is not now what it shall be. As an individual of the Body, he knows and feels, that he is himself but in progress; that he must grow in grace; and that, though he may have made some advance in his holy calling, he is still far from having attained to the Resurrection from the dead, or being a fit citizen and subject of that kingdom which is to come. He looks forward, therefore, with faith in the word of prophecy and promise,—faith in the efficacy of that Atonement and Salvation which the Son of God has wrought for the world, —faith in the sanctifying energy of the Holy Spirit, in building on the foundation of Christ,— not doubting, that the Church now militant in earth shall finally be triumphant, and shall be presented to the Father, having neither spot, nor wrinkle, nor any imperfection whatever. He may be tempted, when he looks either into his own heart, or abroad into the world, to ask, " How long, O Lord, how long!" But he will reflect, that his own condition, as well as that of the Church, forbids the fond expectation of glory to be realized at once. He returns to his Scriptural assurance, that the Church of Christ is now in a state of progress; that it waits for its perfection, until the Lord shall have put all enemies under his feet, and death shall be swallowed up in victory.

Thus was the revelation in Christ, comprising all that the incarnate Son of God has done and taught during his earthly ministry, complete, as soon as his work was finished; from the first delivery of it, summing up and closing all the previous dispensations of the Old Testament in the final mystery of the Gospel. The Law and the Prophets were up to that time—dispensations essentially relative to another age, which should follow them—prophetic and preparatory,—destined to receive their perfection of design, and fulness of light and blessing, when God should in the latter days speak by His Son, and put an end to the types and sacrifices of the Law, and stamp an all-powerful efficacy on the preaching of Repentance by the Prophets, by the one true Sacrifice of the Son. The whole of the New Testament is but a full description, elucidation, and enforcement, in all its grand points of view, in all its bearings and consequences, of this great Truth. One Evangelist may present some parts of the Truth more distinctly or more fully than another ; or one Epistle exhibit to us the relations of the several truths into which it is distributed, more than another ; as that, for example, to the Romans, compared with any other, shews pre-eminently the relation of the Sacrifice of Christ to the fallen condition of man and to the principle of Faith. But the whole New Testament together is not an expansion of doctrine from doctrine, or series of developments, but rather, a combined view of the whole Doctrine and Discipline of Christ, as revived and impressed, through the operation of the Holy Spirit, on the hearts and minds of the Apostles, once for all, and left in writing as the one indelible Divine record for each succeeding age.

Not so, however, was the working of the Holy Spirit in bringing together the living stones of which the Temple of the Lord is built up. Whilst we speak of the Lord's work in the peculiar and strict sense, as the *Foundation*, yet subordinately to that, and in an inferior sense, we may speak of the Church as founded also on its Apostles and

Prophets; as in that Scriptural account of it; " built up on the foundation of the Apostles and Prophets: Jesus Christ himself being the chief Corner Stone*." As I have said before, the commencement was made by the Lord, the Corner Stone: then the Apostles, inspired and guided by the Spirit, proceeded to the foundation for the vast Temple, which it should be the work of ages to raise up on it. And surely, if ever there were need of the perfect Doctrine of Christ, it was at that time, when the Apostles were employed in beginning the building of the Church through the Spirit. If it was needed in the process of ages, much more was it needed *then* in its length and breadth; to be the eternal basis, on which the glorious fabric was afterwards to be built by other hands—hands, less skilled, less divinely guided for the task, than their own. Well therefore may we believe,—what I endeavoured to impress on your attention last Sunday, in discoursing on the special mission of the Spirit,—that the Church possessed from the first the knowledge of the Truth as it is in Jesus, as fully as it does now; and that the labour of subsequent ages has not added to, or cleared up, or worked out, the ori-

* Eph. ii. 20.

ginal Doctrine, but only counteracted attempts to vary and corrupt it ; not enlarging or improving the Doctrine itself, but only preventing its diminution or change in any essential respect.

Augustine indeed, and Vincent of Lerins, have been supposed by some to speak of a proficiency of Christian Truth beyond this. But when we come closely to examine their statements, we do not find that they countenance a Theory of Development.

Augustine refers to certain doctrines as not perfectly handled, until the rise of controversies had exacted the full discussion of them. He does not say that the *truth itself* on these points so controverted, was brought out and perfected on such occasions ; but only, that the points were more fully treated in the course of time and more fully explained to the Church at large. It is not of the doctrines themselves that he speaks as latent before such discussion, or as obtaining development by the action of controversy,—but of persons in the Church, (*multi latebant in populo Dei*, are his words,) capable of discerning and handling the Scriptures, and solving difficult questions, as drawn forth into the service of the Church by the need of the occasion.

Through such persons accordingly, he observes, the truth already handed down and known, when assailed by the oppositions of heresy, received defence and elucidation from the Scriptures*. The amount of what he says on the subject is: that, through such labours, the Scriptures were better understood, and their bearing on the truths in question was more fully appreciated.

Vincent of Lerins, so far from being an authority in favour of the Theory of Development, must be regarded as an opponent of it. No writer insists more strongly than he does on the *sameness* of *Doctrine* through all ages of the Church. As Tertullian instances in the growth of the tree with its fruit from the seed, to illustrate the advancement of Discipline in the Church under the dispensation of the Spirit,—so indeed does Vincent appeal to the natural growth of man from infancy to old age, in illustration of his argument. But his main object in such an illustration is evidently the opposite to that of Tertullian. It is to prove the sameness of the doctrine of the Church at different periods, subsisting, like personal identity, under any apparent changes which it may have exhibited. At the same time, he would se-

* S. August. in Psalm liv.

cure Christians against the temptation to change, which heretical teachers were holding forth to them, whilst such teachers found fault with the simplicity of Christian Faith, and offered to advance them in the knowledge of the truth. He shews accordingly, that there is a real proficiency which the Christian may have in view. The heretics, he says, treated the Christian religion, "as if it were, not a heavenly dogma, which might suffice once revealed, but an earthly institution, not otherwise to be perfected but by assiduous emendation, or rather reprehension." In opposition to this, whilst he forbids all change, whether of addition or diminution, he allows the teacher of divine truth to "polish, adorn, and illustrate" his matter by exposition, regarding it throughout, at the same time, as perfect in itself and incapable of any "variety of definition"*.

As far as Doctrine is concerned, Tertullian, even in his Montanistic treatises, takes the same view. He only argues for a development in the matter of Discipline; for a more rigid practice, a greater austerity of life, than had hitherto been required in the Church. The "Rule of Faith," the Creed, he strongly insists, is one and immovable.

* Vinc. Lirin. Commonit. pp. 331–337, Ed. Baluz.

2 H

According to this sense of proficiency, when the Apostles themselves, by the inspiration of the Holy Ghost, preached the Gospel, and afterwards committed the Faith, which they had delivered by word of mouth, to the Scriptures of the New Testament, we may say, there was a statement of the truth more distinct and full than had been given before to the world. For our Lord, though he discoursed of his religion to the people, had more clearly expounded it to his disciples, who were afterwards to bear it to the world under the guidance of his Spirit. It remained, therefore, for them to state more at large what they had already received; to explain it, and enforce it on the popular understanding, and invest it with an abiding authority. This, the Holy Spirit which was given them enabled them to accomplish: so that the Scriptures now present to us the truths of the Gospel in their fulness of doctrine and heavenly comfort; not beyond what the Apostles received, but the same truths; only those truths made more familiar, and more accessible, by their statements and expositions, to the hearts and understandings of all men of all ages of the world.

In like manner, though at an infinite distance from the authority of the inspired teaching of the

New Testament, does the Christian Church of all
ages since the Apostolic, proceed in setting forth
and expounding the same original truth to its
members.   Whether by formal decrees in Councils, or by expositions of doctrine given in Creeds
and Catechisms, or in summaries, and treatises
of Theology, or by the sermons and pastoral exhortations of its ministers, all that the Church
really effects is, to explain more clearly, and enforce more strongly, and guard from perversion
and abuse, the Word of God, as it exists in its
original depository of the Scriptures.   And a valuable service this is.   The same doctrine may
thus receive a fuller exposition and illustration
from time to time, and an accession of evidence,
from the increased study of Scripture, and a better understanding of particular texts.   But all the
while that this sort of practical improvement may
be going on in the Church, as the wisest of men
can enter into the mysteries of God no more than
the simplest who have but an honest reverent
heart ; so neither will the men of the latest age
of the Gospel have to say of themselves, that they
possess a perfection of Christian doctrine beyond
the knowledge of those of the earliest.   A later
age may possess a fuller, larger, statement of this

or that particular doctrine ; but there will be only a change of expression at most ; no change of the Doctrine ; no advancement or perfection of the Truth itself thus variously stated.

Such only is that improvement which Bishop Butler suggests,—an improvement arising, as I have said, from an enlarged study of Scripture,— a better understanding of particular passages in themselves, and in their bearing on Doctrine ; no perfecting of the Doctrine itself*.

But the Romanist theory implies much more than simple elucidation of Doctrine from Scripture, and improvement in its statement. The sort of improvement which it contemplates is, the drawing forth of Doctrine ; making explicit what was held implicitly before ; divulging what has hitherto been kept secret or reserved. For instance ; according to that theory, the doctrine of the Incarnation is developed in the fifth century into that of the deification of the Virgin Mary. It was then that she received, we are told, " the public and ecclesiastical recognition" of her " place in the economy of grace :" her " incommunicable dignity" was declared ; and a worship, only not that due to perfect Deity, was

* Butler's *Analogy*, part ii. c. 3.

assigned to her*. The sanctification, or rather the deification† of man, and consequently the

* "The votaries of Mary do not exceed the true faith, unless the blasphemers of her Son come up to it. The Church of Rome is not idolatrous, unless Arianism is orthodoxy."— *Newman's Essay*, p. 406.

Another author, a writer in the "Tracts for the Times," seems not to differ much, if at all, from this view of "the incommunicable dignity" of the Virgin Mary. "The thought of her," he says, "is inseparable from meditation on the true doctrine of the Incarnation, that our Lord was 'God of the substance of His Father, begotten before the world; and man, of the substance of His mother, born in the world.' To deny the word θεοτόκος is, of course, heresy; to shrink from it, then, is to be ashamed of the truth of God; to shrink from dwelling on the doctrine conveyed in it, that He 'abhorred not the Virgin's womb,' is secretly to have entertained some heretical counterfeit."—*Pusey's Avrillon, Pref.* Surely, however, one may acknowledge the value of the term *theotocos* in stating the truth of our Lord's proper Divinity, without acceding to the doctrine respecting the Virgin Mary, here supposed to be implied in it. The same writer seems disposed to speak of the Virgin as "purer than angels," according to the text of the Jesuit author, whose Devotions he edits for the "use of the English Church," whilst he modifies it into the expression, "pure as angels." For in making the correction he subjoins the remark, "Yet this refers to the time before the Conception. For by the Conception, indeed, any one who meditates on the Incarnation must think, that the Blessed Virgin has a nearness to God, closer than that of any other created being."—*Note on Avrillon*, p. 132.

† "Christ, in rising, raises his saints with him to the right hand of power. They become instinct with his life, of one

whole *Cultus Sanctorum* in the Roman Church,
is derived also from the same truth—from the
notion of our Lord's having sanctified a portion
of the corrupt mass of Matter by taking on Him
human flesh ; and thus further, from the same
truth, the Resurrection of the Saints of Christ to
their glorified state ; the Real Presence in the
Eucharist, as held by the Church of Rome ; the
sanctity of Relics, and the merit of Virginity.
Baptism again is asserted to have been developed,
first into a Sacrament of Penance, and, as time
went on, into a doctrine of Purgatory. These
surely are not instances of expansion, or improvement, in the statement of known doctrines,
adapted to the purpose of exposition in altered
circumstances of the Church ; but rather (as the
Theory of Development boldly asserts, leaving
the Scriptures far behind it), instances of " the
mind of the Church working out dogmatic truths

body with his flesh, sons, kings, gods. He is in them, because
he is in human nature ; and he communicates to them that
nature deified by becoming his, that it may deify them. He is
in them by the presence of his Spirit, and in them is He seen.
They have titles of honour by participation, which are properly
his.   Without misgiving, we may apply to them the most
sacred language of Psalmists and Prophets.   ' Thou art a
Priest for ever,' may be said of St. Polycarp or St. Martin, as
well as of their Lord," &c.—*Newman's Essay*, pp. 402, 403.

from implicit feelings under secret supernatural guidance."

Whilst, however, the Truth itself, as it is in Jesus, has ever been one and the same, the Church which has subsisted upon it, has been growing, both by the increase of its members in grace individually, and by its spread through the world.

From the words of our text, it would appear, that this future enlargement of the Church was distinctly contemplated by our Lord Himself in his first charge to his Apostles concerning it. What is that power which he speaks of as given to him ? It is, " all power in heaven and earth ;" power extending beyond the limits of any one country or age, and even beyond the visible universe, to the Courts of Heaven ; signifying, that the Church should not only be the " pillar and ground of his truth " on earth, but that " by the Church also should be known in heavenly places the wonderful wisdom of God." Then how vast is the charge ! " Go ye and teach all nations, baptizing them in the name of the Father, and of the Son, and of the Holy Ghost, teaching them to observe all things whatsoever I have com-

manded you;" a commission reaching far beyond the possibility of execution by the individuals themselves so sent; implying, as it did, a
personal address from them to individuals of
every nation. And that the charge was thus extensive, and indeed bounded by no limits of time,
appears still further from that wonderful assurance
which carries it out into His own infinity, " Lo,
I am with you alway, even unto the end of the
world !"

It is plain, then, that a principle of indefinite
extension was imparted to the constitution of the
Church at its very commencement. The groundwork may have seemed to human eyes, looking
on it from without, to have been straitened and
small, unequal to the burthen of future greatness
which the Lord's word had laid upon it. But He
" who layeth the beams of his chambers in the
waters, and maketh the clouds his chariots, and
walketh upon the wings of the wind," had
" stretched out the line, and laid the measure
thereof." As He was Himself the chief Corner-
stone of the building, so had He " founded it on
the seas, and prepared it on the floods," that it
should be for an everlasting habitation, a house

of many mansions, where all his saints, in the fulness of time, should be gathered in one holy home.

Let us, then, consider what provision was made by our Lord in the first establishment of His Church for its perpetual enlargement ; and more particularly, in what manner that enlargement takes place and is effected through His abiding Presence.

First, let us more particularly observe how it is that the Church may be truly said to *grow*, or, according to the current expression, be " developed" in the world ; whilst the doctrine of the Church remains one and the same, undeveloped, unchanged, and unchangeable.

When St. Paul, addressing the weak members of the Corinthian Church, speaks of them as not yet fit to be addressed but as babes not able to bear the food of men ; and of a wisdom to be received by them that are " perfect;" he will be found (if his meaning be duly weighed according to the tenor of his whole Epistle and the occasion on which he is writing,) to be speaking, not of any difference in the truths to be imparted, but of a growth in grace ; of the necessity of a growth in grace to render a man a disciple of Christ, after

THE WORK OF CHRIST

he has once received the truth. For he is complaining there of their having forsaken the simplicity of the faith,—of their having given themselves over to seducing teachers,—of their having departed from the sincerity of a pure Gospel profession, into carnal and worldly ways, into party strife, and disputations of worldly wisdom, into heresy and unclean living. They were boasting of a perfection in a wrong line, in a direction opposite to the Gospel; treating, in fact, the Gospel-truth as a mere element in their system, as an idea to be expanded in their ethereal region of thought; and soaring on the false wing of a profane speculation to a heaven of their own imagining. Meanwhile, they were grovelling on the earth, immersed in the mire of violent and unchastened passions,—returning into the ways of that corrupt nature which they had once eschewed; and that, at their very entrance on the Christian faith, when in the laver of regeneration they had not long put off the old man, and became again as little children in professing themselves Christians. In the view of such apostates from their profession, the Apostle Paul was far exceeded by themselves in the pursuit of Christian perfection. He reminds them, therefore, in his earnest expostulation, that such wisdom was foolishness with God ; that he and his brother Apostles had received "the mind of Christ," without which it were vain to speak of the things of God; that his simple preaching of Christ crucified, though with them it sounded as " the foolishness of preaching," was " the wisdom and the power of God,"—a doctrine, such as would carry them to the perfection of their calling, emptying them of mere earthly wisdom, which was really foolishness with God, and purifying them as a Temple of God, the habitation of the Holy Spirit.

So also to the Hebrews, he speaks more expressly of " leaving the principles of the doctrine of Christ, and going on unto perfection, not laying again the foundation," &c. But does he mean by this, that they are to proceed to some more recondite truth,—some more definite, more expanded views of the truth they had received ; to look down on the fields of early Christian Doctrine as from some lofty watch-tower, commanding from its survey the subject-plains of sacred truth ? Surely the Apostle had no such meaning. He never anticipated that dream of modern theorists, that the Gospel, as first revealed, was only a nucleus of the truth, destined to grow in

Christian minds, and ripen to maturity by the processes of human thought. Surely he never had this meaning when he goes on, as we find, explaining himself more fully, to speak of apostates from the Faith,—of those who crucified the Son of God afresh,—falling away from Him,—living, as if they had never been taught the necessity of being buried with Christ in baptism, and of " repentance from dead works, and faith towards God," and the truth of the Resurrection and the Judgment to come.

It is in fact little else that he here expresses, but the language of our own Church; where, after having admitted into its bosom its infant member, on the assurance of faith in the Doctrine of Christ, as that to which the child is pledged, it bids all remember that " Baptism doth represent unto us our profession; which is, to follow the example of our Saviour Christ, and to be made like unto Him; that as he died and rose again for us, so should we, who are baptized, die from sin, and rise again unto righteousness; continually mortifying all our evil and corrupt affections, and daily proceeding in all virtue and godliness of living*;" or where, again, our Church

---

* Office of Public Baptism.

enjoins on its ministers " to bring all committed
to their charge unto that agreement in the faith
and knowledge of God, and to that ripeness and
perfectness of age in Christ, that there be no
place left either for error in religion, or for
viciousness of life ;" and directs them further,
" continually to pray to God the Father, by the
mediation of our Saviour Jesus Christ, for the
heavenly assistance of the Holy Ghost, that by
daily reading and weighing of Scriptures, they
may wax riper and stronger in their ministry*."
The same is the perfection in Christian doctrine
held out to the Christian's aim by the Church
here, and by the Apostle in the places I have referred to ; as also by St. Peter, when he bids
Christians " desire the sincere milk of the word,
that they may grow thereby†." The individual
Christian is taught to live and grow in the holy
doctrine, or as our Church again distinctly expresses it, that " all things belonging to the
Spirit should live and grow in him ;" the same
unchanging doctrine being in him a living principle, expanding and maturing him to manhood
in all Christian graces, so that " the man of God

* Ordering of Priests. † 1 Pet. ii. 2.

may be perfect, thoroughly furnished unto all good works."

It was then clearly for this purpose, first, that the Holy Spirit should abide for ever with the Church, working continually in each member of the body of Christ's Church, and bringing him nearer to that perfect conformity to Christ, which is the end of his holy calling. Let each member of the body of Christ thus cherish the abiding presence of the Holy Spirit, in this respect the true *Vicarius Domini*, the real representative of Christ,—not, that is, as taking up what Christ has left undone, but as sustaining in its integrity the work of Christ; speaking his words to the inmost heart ; fixing his cross there ; quickening the inert soul with its secret influences ; and by his mysterious union with the Father and the Son in the majesty of the Holy Trinity, bringing down Christ, though absent in the flesh, together with the Father, to dwell with the contrite puri- fied heart of man :—and then may we feel a scriptural trust, that there is a work in progress, —a change proceeding more and more from dark- ness to light,—from the faltering tongue and un- steady walk of the child in grace, to the bold and consistent profession of the full-grown man of faith, who puts away childish things, and reaches on towards the measure of the stature of the fulness of Christ.

Consider, on the other hand, the contrast of the supposition, that it is the Doctrine which is developed in the Church, instead of simply the Church itself in its members.

Where can be the steadiness of profession in the man who is the disciple of a system of faith, which is continually developing itself; of which he cannot be assured at any given moment, that it is what it shall be; or what he shall believe, or act upon, at some future period of his life? Such an one converts, by his theory, the stable constitution of his religion under its ancient code of fixed laws, into a fluctuating system of government by popular decrees, the voice of a majority from time to time. He may delude himself indeed with the persuasion, that he is but following out the same ideas, and pursuing an unity of thought, under the various transformations which it successively assumes in its progress down the ages of its course. But he is essentially the disciple of change. He is embarked on a stream. He may look back to the land which he has left, and

think that it still exists for him ; but soon it is
to him only as a cloud in the far distance ; and
he is on the wide ocean, knowing not where he
may be going.

Is it matter of surprise, then, that this system
of developing Doctrine should, in many instances,
have gone hand in hand with scepticism, and
looseness of belief, and unfaithfulness to the particular communion in which the Christian has
been placed by his Lord ?   Shall we wonder that
men of morbid, dissatisfied minds, have found a
congenial refuge in the variable dogmatism of
the Church of Rome ; which gives them at once
something to hold to with positiveness, and something to change to without a shock ?   And have
we not heard of Jews, and even infidels, ministering at the altars of a Church, which proclaims
itself infallible, and seeks to invest its decisions
with the sanction of divinity ; not by the warrant of the written word, but by the mere fiat of
its own authoritative decree ?

The blame of Rationalism has been thrown on
the religion of Protestants.   Far more justly is it
due to the ascendancy of the Roman theory of
Christian doctrine ; essentially rationalistic as that
is in its fundamental assumption, that doctrines are

ideas admitting of development. Rationalism has unhappily been the bane of Protestant Germany ; but it has been fostered in the bosom of the Roman Church, and has issued from that home. Of Dr. Moehler, the modern advocate of the Theory of Development, to whose work, entitled Symbolism *, we probably owe the recent introduction of the speculation to our notice here, it is mentioned in the memoir prefixed to the translation of his work, that, even after he had been ordained a priest in the Church of Rome, and had entered on a pastoral charge, " the Church had not yet won all the affections of his heart, and the objects of his enthusiasm lay, in part, beyond her circle : his views did not entirely harmonize with all her doctrines, nor agree with all her disciplinary institutions †." Of the first theological work of the same author it is also observed, that " in this book there was much which in his riper years he no longer approved of ‡." Thus was

---

* Symbolism, or " Exposition of Doctrinal Differences between Catholics and Protestants ;" translated by Robertson : in Two Volumes. The original work has passed through several editions. It was first published in 1832. The author died at Munich, where he was Professor of Theology, in 1838.

† Robertson's Memoir of Moehler, p. xcii.

‡ *Ib.* p. xcv. also p. cxxvii.

this eminent controversialist of the Church of Rome naturally led into the Theory of Development by the frame of his own mind. It accorded with that frame of mind, and gave him an apology for the difficulties with which he would otherwise have been embarrassed. In like manner, among ourselves, the author who has followed in the track of Moehler, and recommended the same theory by the light of fanciful analogies, appears to have passed through something of the like changes to that which is described of his German predecessor. We have seen his Retractations*—not mere corrections of former errors on more mature reading and experience, but contradictions of statements solemnly made at a former period, when he was not what he has become since. We have seen him begin his career as a writer and editor of the Tracts for the Times, gradually developing an idea of indefinite approximation to the Church of Rome, without an actual coincidence. We have seen at length his confession of a change which came over him in the course of his composition of his last work ; his development into a conviction in

* Prefixed to his Essay, but separately published also some time before that appeared.

favour of the Church of Rome—a conviction superseding further deliberation.

And if more evidence were wanting of the affinity of the theory of Christian doctrine, held in the Church of Rome, to looseness and unsteadiness of principle, we have it in the instances which have appeared of men holding the whole cycle of Roman doctrine, and yet continuing members, and even ministers of our Church; nay, even professing themselves its best and most zealous servants, whilst holding to it only by the most precarious tenure; or at length, only withdrawing from its communion under the pressure of outward circumstances, and ranging themselves where their hearts had gone long before*.   If

* Bishop Burnet, speaking of the conversion of several persons in his times, says, " The method that carried over the men of the finest parts among them to Popery, was this: they brought themselves to doubt of the whole Christian religion; when that was once done, it seemed a more indifferent thing of what side or form they continued to be outwardly."—*History of his own Time*, vol. ii. p. 399. 8vo.

The conversion of Gibbon, at an early period of his life, to the religion of Rome, is an illustration of the same fact. It arose from that sceptical habit of mind, which is so fully displayed throughout his great work. With the same inconstancy, he renounced his adopted faith shortly afterwards; and in the subsequent part of his life took refuge from his doubts in a sort of indifferentism, " acquiescing with implicit belief," as he says

some, again, alarmed at the rapidity of their progress, under the captivation of a theory of a living
oracle of doctrine in the Church, have cast forth
their anchor on some shoal which they were drift-
ing past, and refused to go further; let the shifts
and expedients to which such have resorted to
maintain their position, be a lesson to others,
that there is no sure footing to those, whose religion is a flowing principle—a system of doctrine
drawn forth and moulded by the passing occasion
—not full-wrought and perfect, as it first was
taught by inspiration of the Holy Ghost to the
Apostles, and consigned to the Scriptures.

On that holy truth then, perfectly communicated to the Apostles, and by them imparted to
the Church in their preaching and the records of
the New Testament, the Church, as in its infancy,
so now in its advanced state, continues to grow:
first, as I have already stated, by the increase of

of himself in his Memoirs of his Life and Writings, " in the
tenets and mysteries which are adopted by the general consent
of Catholics and Protestants."

Bayle, the professed sceptic, in like manner, when a young
man, was for a time a convert to Romanism.

The conversion of Chillingworth may also be attributed to
the unsettled state of a mind craving after an infallible authority in religion for its direction.

grace, strength, and holiness in the individual members; each " building up himself," as St. Jude speaks, " on his most holy Faith ;" then, by the aggregate of its members, in the whole collective body. For thus, by the spread of the same unvaried doctrine, does the Church lengthen its cords, and increase by accession of members. By that same doctrine, those who were lost, are found ; the fallen are restored ; the stranger is adopted into the family of the Lord. It goes forth into the highways, and brings in the halt, and the maimed, and the blind, so that the Lord's house may be filled. So efficaciously does that power, which the Lord impressed on it at the beginning of his kingdom on earth, push itself forth, and evince itself to be Divine by the energy of its working.

What then are the means, by which the Spirit thus continually enlarges the kingdom of Christ ? What is that method, by which the one unchanging word is rendered effectual to the harvest of souls ?

In a word, we may answer, by the Church itself; by the provision, which the Lord has made in the institution of the Church, for its perpetual life and sustenance by his Spirit.

First he appointed a Ministry,—the Apostles, and those to be sent by them in successive generations.

The commission was expressly given to the Apostles alone ; but it was evidently not confined to them personally ; since, as has often been observed, the promise of the Lord's abiding reached beyond them even unto the end of the world, and extends the commission, accordingly, to their successors in perpetuity.

Then, to this Ministry thus appointed, he assigned their peculiar service. They were to go and make disciples of all nations, baptizing them in the name of the Father, and of the Son, and of the Holy Ghost ; and teaching them to observe all that he had commanded them :—or, as the commission may be summarily stated, to administer his Word, his Sacraments, and his Discipline. For though the Sacrament of Baptism, as the initiation into the Faith, is alone expressly mentioned in this place, the other Sacrament, the Communion of His Body and Blood, is doubtless included in the general observance of his commands here required to be inculcated on all members of the Church—the celebration of that being, indeed, an express command from Him, when he said, " Do this in remembrance of Me."

Simple were these instruments;—the Ministry, the Word, the Sacraments, and the Discipline of Christ ; but wonderfully efficacious in carrying on the work of bringing sons and daughters to Christ. At the call,—" Repent, and be baptized for the remission of sins,"—numbers came in, and were baptized. The word of the Lord, at first taught by oral delivery, was soon secured in its invariableness, by being committed to writing and read in the assemblies of the Church. The prayers and songs of Christian congregations rose as a daily incense to the Lord. The Lord's Supper was constantly and duly celebrated. Charity was spread abroad. The discipline of Christ was faithfully observed and administered. Offenders were corrected, or restored to the Communion of the Church, as the case might require ; first, with miraculous demonstrations of the presence of the Lord, confirming the acts of His Apostles and first disciples,—then by the ordinary power of his grace bequeathed for that purpose : and the Church thus daily became " strong in the Lord, and in the power of his might."

Such were the effectual provisions by the Lord

Himself, for the work of the Holy Spirit to be carried on, through his Ministers, in the building of his Church through all ages. Only to his first Ministers, for the far heavier burthen imposed on them of laying the first stones of the building, he gave the Spirit in greater measure than to their successors ; impowering them to speak with tongues, and work miracles ; to confer the gift of the Spirit on others, whether for the confirmation of the faith, or for the work of the ministry ; and generally, to establish the government and order of the Church for the ages to follow. When these peculiar duties of the first Ministers of the Gospel were accomplished, there existed no further occasion for the exercise of these extraordinary powers. And we have no reason from Scripture to believe that they were continued beyond the Apostles, and others, their contemporaries, on whom the Apostles laid their hands and conferred them. The authority of ordaining others to the ministry, of preaching the word, and of administering the Sacraments and the discipline of Christ, would necessarily be among those gifts of the Spirit, which they would transmit to their successors ; to be by them in their turn transmitted to others after them, as it has been to this day.   And thus, on the whole, would a complete groundwork be formed in the Church, on which the future structure might proceed, under the abiding Presence of the Lord, its Founder, by His Spirit.

But the Church of Rome has not been content with this simple view of the means provided by our Lord, for the strengthening and extension of His Church.   As it professes to have been employed in elaborating the Doctrine, and working it to a perfection beyond the simplicity of the Scripture outlines, so has it constructed an artificial theory of the method set in order by the Holy Spirit for the building of the Church on the foundation of Christ.   On what indeed has it rested for the theoretic ground and defence of its teaching, but on the assumption of a character for the Church throughout its *whole* existence, with which the Lord Himself and the Holy Spirit have not invested it ; that of a standing infallible oracle for the dispensation of the Gospel in all its parts ? *Dixi, vos Dii estis—Nolite tangere Christos meos,*—these are the phylacteries which it binds on its forehead ;—calling on all men to believe it, and follow its teaching throughout, as the voice of Christ ; as they would testify their allegiance and loyalty to Christ Himself. Accordingly, to establish this claim of infallible dictatorship over the kingdom of Christ on earth, it confounds together the work of Christ, and the work of the Spirit ; the salvation of the Gospel, and the means provided by the Lord through the Holy Spirit for the edification of the Church ; or in other words, the Salvation wrought,—the Truth revealed,— the Church, as it is the body of Christ,—and the Internal Constitution of the Church, as a provision for disciplining its members, and extending the Faith, and multiplying believers. All these, which are really distinct objects, when we contemplate them by the light of Scripture, the Church of Rome confounds, in one general all-absorbing idea of the Church, as an embodied Representation of the Religion of Christ. Rather, if it may be so stated without profaneness (for this is the real notion at the bottom of all these transcendental descriptions of the Church, found in Romanist writers, and those of kindred spirit), the Word of God is again made flesh,—again lives and dies, and is offered up, and makes Atonement, and forgives sins, and confers justification, and reveals the truth of God, under His abiding manifestation in the Church, as He did during the days of His own ministry in the flesh.

" For, by the Church on earth," says Moehler, the writer to whom I have already referred, " Catholics understand the visible community of believers, founded by Christ, in which by means of an enduring Apostleship established by Him, and appointed to conduct all nations, in the course of ages, back to God, the works wrought by Him during his earthly life, for the Redemption and Sanctification of mankind, are, under the guidance of his Spirit, continued to the end of the world *."

And again, " Thus the visible Church, from the point of view here taken, is the Son of God Himself, everlastingly manifesting Himself among men in a human form, perpetually renovated and eternally young—the permanent Incarnation of the same ; as in Holy Writ, even the faithful are called ' the body of Christ.' Hence it is that the Church, though composed of men, is yet not purely human. Nay, as in Christ, the divinity and the humanity are to be clearly distinguished, though both are bound in unity ; so is He in undivided entireness perpetuated in the Church.

* Moehler's *Symbolism, Transl.* vol. ii. p. 5.

The Church, His permanent manifestation, is at once both Divine and human—she is the union of both. He it is who, concealed under earthly and human forms, works in the Church*."

Again he adds, " In and through the Church the Redemption announced by Christ hath obtained, through the medium of his Spirit, a reality; for in her his truths are believed, and his institutions are observed, and thereby have become living. Accordingly we can say of the Church, that she is the Christian Religion in its objective form—its living exposition; since the word of Christ (taken in its widest signification) found, together with His Spirit, its way into a circle of men, and was received by them, it has taken shape, put on flesh and flood; and this shape is the Church, which accordingly is regarded by Catholics as the essential form of the Christian Religion itself†."

Nor is this the view of the Church presented us by a modern writer only of the Roman Church; it is also that of Bellarmine, who, in explaining in what sense the Church should be regarded as the body of Christ, says, " This cannot so conveniently be referred to Christ as the Head, as to

* Moehler's *Symbolism*, vol. ii. p. 6.   † *Ib.* p. 7.

the same Christ, as the hypostasis of that Body. The Church is called the Body of Christ, and not that of St. Peter, because Christ is the hypostasis of this Body, sustains all the members, and works all in all, sees by the eye, hears by the ear ; for it is Himself who teaches by the teacher, baptizes by the Minister, finally does all things through all*."

" The Church," again says Bellarmine, " is governed by Christ, as by its spouse the Head, and by the Holy Spirit, as by the soul, as is plain from Ephes. i. ' He gave Him to be Head over all things to the Church, which is His body :' and Ephes. v. ' The husband is the head of the wife, even as Christ is the Head of the Church.' Therefore, if the Church should err in dogmas of faith or manners, error might be attributed to Christ, and the Holy Spirit. Wherefore in John xvi. the Lord says, ' The Spirit of truth will teach you all truth†.' "

And what, I would ask, is such a view of the Church but a development, an attempt I should rather say at a development, of the Scripture account of the foundation and institution of the

* Bellarmin. De Rom. Pontif. i. 9, p. 635.
† De Eccles. Mil. 1. 3, c. 14, p. 1277.

Church ?   In this view, the Church as it now is,
realizes to the world the events of our Lord's life
in their spiritual purport and application : what
was transacted once in the course of our Lord's
own ministry, this, the Church is here described
as more fully expressing under its permanent
form. The scenes of Gethsemane and Calvary,
with all that preceded and immediately followed
them, have passed away, to reappear in living
representations in the Body itself, and in the
ordinances and teaching of the Church ; successively presented, as the Church is renewed,
again and again, in the persons of its members
and Ministers ; as it teaches the divine word, and
administers the Sacraments, time after time.

Where, then, scarcely is the difference of such
a theory of the Church from that of the German
idealist, who would destroy all reality in the life
of our Lord, and represent His Life and Death,
and Resurrection and Ascension, as only the impersonation of certain traditionary, or philoso-
phical ideas ?   The only difference is, that the
Roman theory admits the original historical truth
as it stands in the sacred records ; whereas the
German, without pretending to annihilate the
whole Gospel as a fiction, artfully labours to

spread a doubt over the whole, as to how much is to be believed real, or how much rejected, whilst it resolves the chief part into fable and allegory. But this difference is not so great in the result, as it seems at first. For though the Roman theory presupposes the original historical truth, it virtually destroys it. For, according to the illustration used in explaining the theory, whilst the plant expands, the germ out of which it grows disappears, and is lost in the maturity which it has attained. So does this theory make the fundamental historical truths of the Gospel but as germs to vanish in their perfect expansion, whilst it ascribes to the existing Church the realization of what was shadowed out by the life and doctrine of Christ. The existing Church then becomes the true Christ ; as in the German theory, his own philosophy becomes to the idealist his phantom-substitute for the real body of the Lord. The latter indeed, when the realities of the Gospel have faded and dissolved, like pictures painted by the sunbeam, in the cold atmosphere of his criticism, still clings to his speculative dogmatism as a reality remaining to him at least. So does the Romanist, after he has done all that subtilty can accomplish, to mystify the sacred text, and banish the Gospel from its surface, strenuously maintain, that the Gospel still survives in its integrity, in the actual developments of it which his Church presents. The former may call his interpretation of Scripture, the mythical ; the latter may more reverently term it, the ecclesiastical*. But both agree in substituting a latent sense of the text for the manifest one, and explaining the primary sense by the secondary, the direct and proper by the mystical †.

Thus the author to whom I have before referred characterizes " Prophets or Doctors " as "interpreters of the Revelation." "They unfold," he says, " and define its mysteries, they illumi-

* Something like a fusion of the two characters is asserted by Mr. Newman, when in his Essay on Miracles, prefixed to a Translation of a portion of Fleury's Ecclesiastical History, he speaks of sudden transitions in the sacred narratives, as " imparting to the sacred text that ecclesiastical or mythical character, which is so solemn and elevating, yet so unsatisfactory to the more intellectual critic."—*Newman's Fleury, Addit. Note to* p. clvii.

† It is not a little remarkable how persons sometimes betray a weakness on a point, by their very air of confidence in asserting it. Thus Mr. Newman commences his Essay with a great parade of the *historical* character of true Christianity ; when the real effect of the work is to destroy that character.

nate its documents, they harmonize its contents, they apply its promises. Their teaching is a vast system ; not to be comprised in a few sentences, not to be embodied in one code or treatise, but consisting of a certain body of truth, pervading the Church like an atmosphere ; irregular in its shape from its very profusion and exuberance, at times separable only in idea from Episcopal Tradition, yet at times melting away into legend and fable," &c.*   Such is " Prophetical Tradition," in his view ; " partly being a comment, and partly an addition upon the articles of the Creed :" and such is that mass of doctrine, which, in its " vastness and indefiniteness," he would propose to the Christian for the Gospel of Christ.

It was but pursuing the same line of thought, when the author, whilst a member of our Church, proceeded to interpret the Articles in what one of his followers called the non-natural sense ; reading them, that is, not as they are written, but as he conceived they ought to be read,—as symbolizing and representing to his mind the ideas of what he held to be Catholic Theology.

* Newman's Essay, pp. 115. 116.

2 K

In like manner we have been exhorted, according to that method of interpreting the Articles, to bring out the catholic points in the doctrines and practices of our Church, and "develop" them "as occasion may offer," and thus "realize" what our Church should be *. We have been told of an "ideal" proposed to themselves by the writers of the "Tracts for the Times," and other publications of the same school; according to which, the existing system of the Church of England might be wrought to a perfection of which it is susceptible, but which it does not actually exhibit †. Thus do they use the doctrines and practices found in the Church, as rudiments,

* "What we have not" (in the Liturgy) "is being daily restored to us, if we in patience wait for it; and for the mean time, the humble-minded will feel that all which is withheld from us, is kept back in mercy to us, that what we have is best suited to us."—*Pusey's Letter to the Archbishop of Canterbury,* p. 17. Also *Pusey's Letter to Dr. Jelf in defence of Tract* 90, p. 183.

† "This is the ideal which we have proposed to ourselves, not to alter anything in her, but to recall the minds of her children to what she plainly has and teaches, and as occasion may offer, to develop according to primitive antiquity those doctrines and practices in her, which she has, yet for some reason, not so explicitly as the rest."—*Pusey's Letter to the Archbishop of Canterbury,* p. 50.

out of which they may mature their supposed
Catholic system*. And they further intimate to
us, that we are not in a condition yet to bear all
that we ought to have ; that we must wait our
time ; and so may at length raise our Church to
that perfection, which is now impracticable, or in-
expedient to be pressed. They have themselves
gradually advanced in their teaching ; from putting forth humble efforts as younger men, they
have ripened more and more with their age into
boldness and fulness of teaching ; have drawn
nearer and nearer to that theology to which they
were tending ; have become more explicit in
setting forth what they at first implicitly, or
perhaps unconsciously, held. Yet still, we may
observe, they practise a reserve. Imitating the
Discipline of the Secret of the early ages, they

* " Now we have the rudiments of everything, but nothing
developed."—*Ibid.* p. 25.—" The Editor is glad to take this
occasion of expressing his sense of the considerateness of the
article on Confession in the British Critic (No. 66), and of the
great value of the practical hints and temperate and thoughtful cautions in Mr. Ward's recent book," (*Ward's Ideal*, &c.)
" in the chapters vi. vii. ' on our existing practical corruptions,'
and ' additional suggestions by way of remedy,' which are
most seasonable to those who are in earnest about the amend-
ment of the deep practical evils and sins of omission in our
Church."—*Pusey's Surin*, p. lv.

leave a sort of haze around their statements as
they approach the point of distinct avowal, so
that, whilst there can be little doubt of what they
would say, it remains all but said, to be completed
by the understanding or feeling of the hearer.
Thus, too, they find a plea for arguing the sameness of their teaching with that of the Church
itself; while the doctrine of the Church, under
this process of developing and realizing, goes into
an alien system; and they sophisticate themselves
into a belief that they are Church of England divines, whilst they are but fondly pursuing their
own ideal.

In opposition to all such fancied schemes of
improvement in Christian doctrine, whether by
mythical or ecclesiastical development of its
truths, Scripture strongly admonishes us to "hold
fast the profession of our faith," "the faith once
for all delivered to the saints*," "the form of
sound words" heard of an Apostle, "without
wavering;" to be "stedfast and unmoveable,"
to "continue in the faith grounded and settled,"
and the like in other places. And that the

---

* Jude 3. Τῇ ἅπαξ παραδοθείσῃ τοῖς ἁγίοις πίστει. This
description marks the *completeness* of the Faith *in the times* of
the Apostles.

Gospel has no semblance to human imaginings, —to fables and legends, and mythical forms such as philosophy of old employed to recommend or veil its speculations,—St. Peter pointedly instructs the Church, when, on the eve of his departure from the world, he exhorts, with so much stress, to faithful "remembrance" of his teaching founded on the simple Apostolic testimony to Christ ; contrasting it with the seducing words of human wisdom: "For we," he says, "have not followed cunningly devised fables,—(σεσοφισμένοις μύθοις,)—when we made known unto you the power and coming of our Lord Jesus Christ, but were eye-witnesses of His majesty," &c.*

The sacramental system of the Church of Rome, is the working out of this theory of the Church which I have already described.

The Sacraments of Rome are not simply " out-

* 2 Pet. i. 16. Our Lord indeed employed parables in his teaching. It was not, however, to darken the sense, or throw a mystic air over his doctrine : on the contrary, it was to illustrate the truth and render it more familiar to the people, that they might see and hear, and understand, if they had but the will. We cannot with truth say of the *whole of* his teaching, that it is parabolical. There are also symbolical actions recorded in the Bible, as, for instance, in the Prophecy of Ezekiel; yet it is untrue to say, as has been boldly said, that the whole Bible is " one great parable."

ward and visible signs of an inward and spiritual
grace given unto us, ordained by Christ Himself,
as a means whereby we receive the same, and a
pledge to assure us thereof ;" but, as that Church
takes to itself the Priesthood of Christ, the Sacraments become the several forms under which that
Priesthood is manifested with power *. Instead
of Justification being imputed to man, as our
Articles teach, by faith, on account of the merits
of Christ,—by a cause thus altogether external to
ourselves ;—the Sacraments, according to Roman
doctrine, are the means by which Justification is
first infused into us, then increased, or if impaired,
renewed, or if lost, restored †. They are regarded
as containing in them the virtue of Christ,—as
actual applications of His Atonement and merits
to the soul of the receiver. Their operation indeed, it is said, may be hindered by any bar in the
receiver : and there must therefore be the will, and
faith, and repentance, in order that their virtue
may take effect in those to whom they are administered. Still it is the outward action duly

---

* Respondeo, sacerdotium in Christum esse translatum, sed
Christum non per se, sed per suos ministros in terris fungi
sacerdotio.—*Bellarmin. de Pœnit.* iii. c. 3.

† Conc. Trid. Sess. vi. vii.

performed, which in each of their seven Sacraments is held to work the effect. But this can only be explained on the supposition that the Church is endued, in the persons of its ministers, with the Priesthood of Christ, and the power of communicating his virtue, so as to convey by the act grace to the receiver—grace as from the touch of Christ Himself. If Rome simply maintained that Christ had blessed His own institutions,—had promised to give life and strength by them to those who used them in faith according to His appointment,— the case would then have stood quite differently. Such an efficacy in the two Sacraments instituted by the Lord Himself, our own Church thankfully acknowledges, and doubts not, that he gives the life of grace to the child baptized in the name of the Father and of the Son and of the Holy Ghost, and imparts the spiritual sustenance of His Body and Blood to the faithful communicant*. But

---

* "The elements and words have power of infallible signification, for which they are called seals of God's truth; the Spirit affixed unto those elements and words, power of operation within the soul, most admirable, divine, and impossible to be expressed. For so God hath instituted and ordained, that together with due administration and receipt of sacramental signs, there shall proceed from Himself grace effectual to sanctify, to cure, to comfort, and whatsoever else is for the

the view of the efficacy of the Sacraments held
in the Church of Rome, far transcends this. An
efficacy depending on the institution and promise
of Christ, would not answer the requirements of
the Roman theory. The sacramental character
of the Church assumed in it, would then want
that perfect development, which it now exhibits
in ascribing an absolute intrinsic efficacy of operation to the Sacraments.

Again there is a sound sense in which the Lord
Himself may be said to do by His ministers, what
they do faithfully in His name according to His
command: that is, they have His authority to
perform that act, and they have reason, from the
promise of His abiding, to trust that His Holy
Spirit goes along with them in such faithful acts.
But there is no ground in Scripture for identify-
ing the act of Christ with the act of His minister,
and making the latter the entire representative of

good of the souls of men."—*Hooker, Eccl. Pol.* vi. p. 86.
"For we take not Baptism, nor the Eucharist, for bare re-
semblances or memorials of things absent, neither for naked
signs and testimonies assuring us of grace received before, but
(as they are indeed and in verity) for means effectual, whereby
God, when we take the Sacraments, delivereth into our hands,
that grace available unto eternal life, which grace the Sacraments represent or signify."—*Ibid.* v. 57.

the former. This, as I have endeavoured to shew,
is but a theoretic development of the doctrine of
the Incarnation, proceeding on the supposition,
that our Lord Himself is now personated in the
world by the Church, as He was in the flesh in
the days of His own ministry on earth.

Would that those who have been labouring to
bring the doctrine and practice of our Church into
conformity with the Roman-Catholic model, could
be brought to see in its true light the theory on
which they have been working, and on which they
must ultimately lean, to justify their proceeding!
If they are prepared to identify the religion of
Christ with the Church professing it—the earthly
priesthood of men with the everlasting Priesthood
of the Lord Himself—the word and the preaching
and the operation of the human instruments of
the Spirit, with the working of the Spirit Himself,
—then may they exhort us to draw near to the
Church of Rome, and interpret and apply the
doctrine and practice of our own Church by the
symbols of that Church. But then, they cannot,
with any reason, stop at such approximation and
such interpretation. They have no right, then, to
separate between sound doctrine and corruptions

of doctrine, where the whole is sanctioned by the same authority. Nothing is, then, a corruption, but what has not been incorporated into the system of the Church. What exists, and is found in the system of the Church, must belong to it; or it would not have survived. A heresy would have run its course and died away.

The author accordingly, of the Essay on Development, could see no other corruptions of religion but such as consist in the breaking up and shattering and dissolution of " Ideas." Seeking the truth in the indefinite expansion of Ideas, he was naturally led to place the false in the contrary,—in what might appear to check such expansion or be incapable of it.

If we turn from this fanciful speculation, to ask of the Scriptures, what are corruptions of religion and what are not; they send us, not to our own minds for the solution of the question,—not to the world of " ideas," to note for our guidance what ideas coalesce and are prolific in consequences, or what start asunder and refuse to be expanded; but they simply tell us, that a corruption of the Faith is a forsaking of the true God revealed to us, for the love of idols. They characterize it as spiritual adultery,—as a breaking of the chaste and holy tie by which the Church is wedded to Christ its Lord. Looking to this test, we can at once decide that the doctrine of the Mass, the worship of the Virgin, and other peculiarities of doctrine or practice of the Church of Rome, seducing the heart from Him, who only is Holy,— who only is the Lord,—are corruptions; whatever may be the consistency and perfection of the ideas involved in them.

If, however, we abandon this test, and estimate doctrines by their ideal perfection, there is no corruption, which we may not ingeniously reconcile to ourselves and adopt into our system of faith. For this excellence certainly cannot be denied to the system of the Church of Rome; that all its parts are adjusted to each other with consummate skill, and, by the mere fact of their consistency, give the semblance of truth to the whole. And it is scarcely matter of wonder, therefore, that those who have been drawn within the circle of her attraction, see nothing to object to in point of principle in her doctrinal system, and find her corruptions only in her practical degeneracy from her standard of Faith; instructing us, as they do, to distinguish between the

" practical corruptions" of the Church of Rome
and her " theoretical errors*."

But if the doctrinal system of Rome appears in
itself, apart from its practical corruptions, to be
so worthy of reception,—if what has·been ruled
by the authority of that Church is Catholic and
true,—no reason can be assigned, why some of the
doctrines so ruled should be accepted, and others,
equally resting on that authority, be refused. It
is vain, after such an admission, to object to the
worship of the Virgin, so incorporated as that is
with the Liturgy of the Roman Church; or the
doctrine of Transubstantiation; for these tenets
may be no less shewn to be equally authoritative
developments, at their proper period, of subsisting
Catholic ideas.   In reference to such an arbitrary
selection or rejection of the doctrines of Rome,
the following expostulation of the author of the
Theory of Development is not out of place :

* " It often happens that she leads her members into error
where her statements in themselves are not very unsound."—
Tracts for the Times, vol. ii. p. 192; also *Pusey's Letter to
Dr. Jelf in defence of Tract* 90, pp. 159–185. It is a main
object of Tract 90 to shew that such only are the corruptions
attributable to Rome—traditionary corruptions, by the side
of an orthodox standard of doctrine. Mr. Newman admits
corruptions of this kind even since his conversion.—See *Essay
on Development*, p. 363.

" ' Who told you,' he says, (personating one whom he supposes to deal thus with the doctrines of that Church,) ' about that gift ?' I answer ; ' I have learned it from the Fathers. I believe the Real Presence, because they bear witness to it.' " Then, citing several expressions from the Fathers on the subject, he proceeds in the same assumed character : " ' I cast my lot with them ; I believe as they.' Thus I reply—and then the thought comes upon me a second time,—And do not the same ancient Fathers bear witness to another doctrine which you disown ? Are you not, as a hypocrite, listening to them when you will, and deaf when you will not ? How are you casting your lot with the saints, when you go but half way with them ? For of whether of the two do they speak more frequently, of the Real Presence in the Eucharist, or of the Pope's supremacy ? You accept the lesser evidence, you reject the greater *."

---

* Newman's Essay, p. 20.—His Sermon on the Theory of Development, preached from the University pulpit in 1843, furnishes ample evidence, that he then held, all but explicitly, everything that he avows as a Romanist, in his Essay in 1845. That Sermon is thoroughly rationalistic in principle, no less than the Essay,—treating Christian Theology as a subjective system,—as an expansion of an Idea in the mind—a collection

Whether the particular instance here adduced, is to the point or no, it matters little. It pointedly illustrates the position of those who, having surrendered themselves to the guidance of a false principle, would too late reclaim their right of private judgment.

A reverent estimation of the Church as the Body of Christ, sustained and nourished by His Spirit, and of the Apostolic Ministry within it, working through the same Spirit for the edification of the Body ; this is, indeed, a principle strictly belonging to our own Communion, and with which the formularies of our public profession, as well as the writings of our great standard divines, are deeply imbued. But, while we thus duly estimate the blessing of that union in Christ, and the means of cementing it, which the Society of the Church bears in its bosom, let us beware of being carried away by an excess of admiration of the Divine Idea of the Church, and of being tempted to make it all in all in our religion. In such case, we shall

of impressions—efforts to realize an internal vision—representations true enough to act upon, but, so far as man can know, nothing more. Such is the Theology which has presided over the editing of the Tracts for the Times, and the propagation of which, (it is boasted by their contributors and admirers,) has done good in the Church.

surely find in the end, that we have quitted the solid ground of historical truth to walk amidst shadows, and changed the Gospel into what the corrupt heart would wish it to be, from what the word of God simply reveals it.

Be not ensnared then, I would earnestly say to the younger members of this congregation, by high-wrought representations of the Idea of the Church, and of the benefits to be derived from it as the channel of grace to the soul. Humbly and thankfully use the means of grace provided for you by Christ, in the institution and ordinances of the Church. But trust not to them to work Salvation for you, and Justification from your sins: matters too high for them, and which God has reserved in the hand of the Saviour of souls alone. Seek, indeed, grace to repent and amend your lives, and strength and comfort, by the help of every pious ordinance of the Church; yet not in superstitious feeling towards them, as if they were absolutely efficacious in themselves; lest, haply, any one should be found taking comfort to himself where there is no ground for comfort in him, and healing the hurt of his soul lightly, where the wound of sin is deep, and asks more searching remedy than any help or medicine of man can give. Be not, then, too eagerly anxious about obtaining at once that ease and comfort of mind, which belongs only to him that is well-grown in grace : for it is "perfect love" alone that "casts out fear." Strive, indeed, unceasingly after the attainment of this happy state ; but let it be by active performance of Christian Duty—Christian Duty founded on Christian Truth; by keeping constantly before the eye the mercy of God in Christ, and the blessed example of the Saviour ; and so perfecting holiness in the fear of God; working together with the Holy Spirit that has been given you, and will be given still. Be not, however, I say, too eagerly anxious to realize the comfort of the Gospel at once to yourselves. Be patient ; waiting for the consolation of the Lord to be granted in His own time and His own way. Impatience will only end in disappointment; especially if it carry any to seek counsel, but not of the Lord ; to place their consciences in the hand of man for spiritual direction ; to create to themselves unauthorized and unreal atonements for sin ; and to rest satisfied in the forgiveness of sins pronounced by human lips.

I feel it the more necessary to give this caution to the younger members of the congregation, as they have had views of the doctrine of Repentance presented to them, utterly at variance, as I conceive, with that patient waiting on the Lord which is the spirit of a true Gospel Repentance.

You have been taught to look at Repentance as a work of inward purgation of the soul,—as a second Baptism,—a Baptism of tears washing out the stain of sin—a laborious and painful process, by which the obstacles to the shining of grace into the soul are gradually removed, and the image of Christ,—the divine nature imparted to it by the Sacrament of Baptism, but since obscured and defaced, or lost by sin,—is again formed in the soul. Such is the view taken of Repentance by the Church of Rome, and those who adopt its teaching on this point as Catholic truth*.

Now in the Church of Rome, such a view of the nature of Repentance is perfectly consistent. Commencing with regarding itself as the impersonation of Christ, and developing the Sacrifice and Atonement of Christ, into an offering made by its Priests at its Altars in the Sacrifice of the Mass, it consistently proceeds to develop the method of reconciliation to God by Repentance,

* Conc. Trid. Sess. vi. c. 14; xiv. cc. 2, 3, 5. Bellarmin. de Pœnit. I. c. 4.

into a process of reconciliation to the Church by
a discipline of Penance. To be reconciled into
the Church is, then, in fact, the same thing as to
be reconciled to God. The interrogatories of the
Confessor, and the arbitrations of the casuist,
and the revenge of self-inflicted chastisements,
and the Absolution pronounced by the Priest, are
here accordingly in perfect keeping. All these
bring the penitent into contact with the assumed
living representative of Christ, the Church; to
derive from it the virtue of Christ, with which it
is conceived to be endued. And the penitent
himself, as a member of the body in which the
virtue of Christ is thus supposed inherently to
reside, represents by his own sufferings the Cross
of Christ. Christ is thus crucified in him, whilst
he crucifies his flesh by his mortifications;—and
whilst he is meriting grace and expiating his sins
by his works, he is enabled with some specious-
ness to say, that he is depending on the merits
of Christ for his salvation; for his own works are
regarded as the works of Christ*.

Not such, however, is the view of Repentance

---

* Quæ enim justitia nostra dicitur, quia per eam nobis
inhærentem justificamur, illa eadem Dei est, quia a Deo nobis
infunditur per Christi meritum.—*Conc. Trid. Sess.* vi. c. 16.

taken by our Church. As our Church commences with regarding the Sacrifice and Atonement of Christ as a work altogether external to man, and requires only, in its doctrine of Justification by faith *, that the efficacy of that one blessed Sacrifice and Atonement should be fully believed and acted on by the Christian,—so it proceeds in calling Christians to daily Confession of sins and Repentance towards God ; that they may testify their faith in Him who alone saves the soul, and their detestation of that sin which nailed Him to the Cross, and their deep sense of their own corruption of nature and need of the sanctifying grace of the Holy Spirit, that they may think or do anything in order to their Salvation. Accordingly, instead of considering Repentance in the sense of the Church of Rome, as a preparatory virtue only in order to Baptism, to be succeeded after Baptism by a sacramental rite of Penance serving to the restoration of the lost privileges of Baptism, it enjoins the same Repentance throughout the Christian course which is begun at the

* Most injuriously is this great truth represented as an ascribing of our salvation to " mental energies ;" as if we made the justification of the sinner a subjective operation, and the Romanists made it objective by ascribing it to the Sacraments. Exactly the reverse is the truth.

font, as a grace ever indispensable,—ever to be sought from the Holy Spirit,—ever blessed with the Saviour's love and the mercy of His Atonement*. At the same time it prescribes the constant faithful use of the Word and Sacraments and Ministry of the Church, to further the work of holiness in its members; only however as instruments divinely appointed, and helps, in their kind and degree, in order to the work, not as causes operative in themselves of holiness.

Strange, indeed, would it be, had our Church intended, that Private Confession with Absolution should be brought back among us, on the strength of the two cases†, to which alone the sanction of

---

* It has been weakly attempted to overthrow this great truth of the ever-subsisting efficacy of the one Atonement of the Cross, by an inference, (such as is common in the Unitarian school,) from the mere tense in which in Rom. iii. 25, it is described, as a remission τῶν προγεγονότων ἁμαρτημάτων,— evidently, to make room for the notion of Penance, as the expiation of post-baptismal sin.

The Church of Rome declares of the whole Christian life, that it ought to be "a perpetual repentance" (*Conc. Trid.* Sess. xiv. c. 9.); but it means a perpetual Penance; for its notion of *pœnitentia* there, must be taken from what it had already explained on the subject.

† The case of persons perplexed with scruples about their fitness to attend at the Communion, and that of persons at the point of death desirous of making Confession as a relief to their

such Confession is given in the Book of Common Prayer; when it has so sedulously removed everything that ministers to it. The fact, that the scandalous evils arising out of the practice were a principal occasion of the Reformation, might be sufficient to shew, that our Church had no design of countenancing the practice itself, the abuses of which were, evidently, not incidental merely, but inseparable from it, as long as Human Nature is what it is *. Would you learn, however, what our Church thinks of Private Confession, look around our places of public worship, and seek for the Confessional. You see the Font and the Communion-Table, the Reading-desk and the Pulpit; but the Confessional, that constant accompaniment of Roman-Catholic churches, is nowhere to be seen in those of our own Communion. Look

conscience. For the former case no Absolution is provided in the Prayer-Book, and none, consequently, can now, it seems, be rightly given in such a case.

* The bulls of two Popes, Pius IV. and Gregory XV., at the interval of nearly a hundred years, directed against the same horrible evils attendant on the practice of Private Confession, are an illustration of this. It cannot be said that these evils were consequent on the *compulsoriness* of the practice. They arose out of the practice itself. And the like evils have followed even out of the Church of Rome, where the practice has been adopted.

through the various services. The rubric of the First Book of Edward VI. desiring the form of Absolution for the case of the dying penitent to be used in all cases of special Confession, has disappeared in the Second amended Book, together with the rubric and prayer for anointing the sick : and no form is substituted for general cases, as in the Roman Ritual*. Look, again, through

---

* " If a minister of the Established Church were desired to pray with a sick person, and that sick person gave no intimation of a troubled conscience, or a want of spiritual relief, the minister would not be authorized by the Rubric even to *recommend* a special confession. It would be a most impertinent and unjustifiable prying into secrets, with which he is no otherwise concerned, than as the patient himself *requires* his assistance."—" Even the absolution is not given, unless ' he humbly and heartily desire it.' Of this absolution, though it is often quoted for the purpose of shewing the similarity of our Church to the Church of Rome, it cannot be necessary to make many observations. The case, in which alone it is to be used, is a case which *hardly ever occurs*. It is to be used only according to the Rubric, when the sick person has thought proper to make a ' special confession of his sins,' and then heartily *desires* the absolution. The consequence is, that very few clergymen have ever had occasion to use it."—*Bishop Marsh's Comparative View of the Churches of England and Rome*, pp. 196, 197, and Note.

Bishop Bull, in his last sickness, desired the form of Absolution in the Communion Service to be read to him, in preference to that in the Visitation of the Sick.—*Nelson's Life of Bp. Bull.*

the charge laid on the ministers of the Church at their Ordination ; and you find no injunction relative to hearing Confessions or giving Absolution*. Above all, look through the Scriptures ; and you find no instance of an Apostle confessing or absolving a penitent. Calls indeed to that Confession of sins which is the sign and earnest of repentance, and that remission of sins which Christ gives to the true penitent, proceed from the lips and the pens of Apostles. But there is no office of the Confessor, or of the Director of the conscience, exhibited in any of the Apostles,

---

* "And where that they do allege this saying of our Saviour Jesus Christ unto the leper, to prove auricular confession to stand on God's word, *Go thy way, and shew thyself unto the priest* : do they not see that the leper was cleansed from his leprosy afore he was by Christ sent unto the priest, for to shew himself unto him ? By the same reason, we must be cleansed from our spiritual leprosy; I mean our sins must be forgiven us, afore that we come to confession. What need we then to tell forth our sins into the ear of the priest, sith that they be already taken away ?"—*Homilies, Second Part of Sermon of Repentance,* p. 480, ed. 1840.

Compare with the above the following. " Well is it, if the mind can bring itself to the solemn task of discharging the heavy load, of which it will too often become conscious, under the sacred seal of confession to God's priest; for the Absolution so solemnly bestowed has often been, among us, the source of new life."—*Pusey's Surin,* p. liv. *et alib.*

or their immediate successors in the ministry : nor are any such offices referred to in the mention made by St. Paul of the ministrations in the Church. We hear of Apostles, Prophets, Evangelists, Pastors, and Teachers, instituted "for the perfecting of the saints, for the work of the ministry, for the edification of the body of Christ*;" but no mention is made of the Confessor.

There can be little doubt then, that the offices of the Confessor and the Director are to be regarded as Romanist developments of the office of the pastor and teacher of the Church. To receive indeed the Confession of the sinner who desires to make it, and to declare and pronounce such Absolution† as the ministry of God's word may impart to true penitents, whether in the public services of the Church, or privately to the dying and the scrupulous, in order to their comfort as members of the Church, and full enjoyment of its privileges, is clearly within the province of one

---

* Eph. iv. 11, 12.

† The sense in which the Church of Rome regards the Absolution pronounced by the Priest, is marked in the Missal, where, when the Priest in his turn absolves the *ministri*, the Rubric says : "*Postea Sacerdos junctis manibus facit absolutionem dicens; Misereatur*," &c. Of the same form as used before by the *ministri*, it is only said, *Ministri respondent.*

who is appointed a steward of the mysteries of
God, to dispense to the family of Christ their
meat in due season. But these ministrations are
very different from the functions, assigned to the
Confessor and the Director by the Church of
Rome. They are, in the view of the Church of
England, simply ministerial; not ministerial in
the sense that the Priest is but the hand and
mouth of the Lord in what he does and says;
but such helps and appliances as his sacred appointment enables him to give, to the members
of Christ's household over whom he has been set
by the Holy Ghost *.

Were those who are recommending to you
Private Confession, with Absolution following, to
give the full development of their views, they

* To refer to the words used in the Ordination of Priests,
and to the form of Absolution in the Visitation of the Sick, as
proofs of the doctrine of Absolution held in our Church being
the same as that of the Church of Rome, is clearly begging the
question; which is, not whether remission of sins is a power
given to the ministers of Christ, but what is the nature of that
power so given. Then to explain that power, as given at the
Ordination of Priests in the words of Scripture, by the form
of Absolution in the Visitation of the Sick, is to proceed on
Mr. Newman's principle, of interpreting Scripture as well as
the primitive statements of the Church, by the comment of a
later age: the indicative form of Absolution being comparatively modern.

must come at last to the doctrine on the subject
which Rome explicitly avows. Now indeed they
hold it forth as a counsel, rather than a positive
precept and command of our Church,—as a way
of perfection, rather than a necessary duty,—as
what the Church ought to teach and promote,
rather than what it actually inculcates,—as invested with sacramental power*, rather than as a
Sacrament generally necessary to salvation. But
if Absolution be capable of making an alteration
in the soul of the sinner†, and if it be divinely

---

* " Thus the priests of the New Testament have more power
than even this great Forerunner; for being clothed with the
authority of Jesus Christ, whom they represent, they have
power to confer this remission, and to apply the merits and
the blood of the Saviour."—*Pusey's Avrillon*, p. 163.

" Use every means for obtaining this remission, through
the virtue of Penitence and the sacramental power of Absolution."—*Ibid.* p. 164.   " Par la vertu et le Sacrament de
Pénitence." (*Original.*)   " The word ' sacramental' is adopted
from Hooker."—*Ibid. Note by Editor.*

But where does Hooker set forth " the sacramental power
of Absolution ?"   We find it in Bellarmine : "Actiones autem
pœnitentis solum concurrunt ad remissionem peccatorum effi-
ciendam, quatenus vim Sacramentalem à verbo Absolutionis, à
quo formantur, participant."—*De Pœnit.* I. c. 8.

† " What is then the force of Absolution ?" says Hooker.
" What is it which the act of Absolution worketh in a sinful
man ?   Doth it by any operation derived from itself alter the
state of the soul ?   Doth it really take away sin, or but ascer-

ordained, as a rite conferring grace, and all men
are in a condition, on account of their sins, to
need such grace, what reason is there, that
Absolution, with its attendant Confession and
Penance, should not be regarded as a Sacrament
in the sense in which the Church of Rome holds
it to be, and why it should not be laid down as
necessary for all ?

The only reason apparently that can be assigned
for their withholding the full doctrine on the subject, is, that we are not yet prepared to receive

tain us of God's most gracious and merciful pardon ? The
latter of which two is our assertion, the former theirs."—*Eccl.
Pol.* vi. p. 74.

And again : " Let it suffice thus far to have shewed, how
God alone doth truly give, the virtue of Repentance alone
procure, and private ministerial absolution but declare, remission of sins."—*Ibid.* p. 99.

So also Bishop Taylor : " The result is, that the Absolution
of sins, which in the later forms and usages of the Church is
introduced, can be nothing but declarative; the office of the
preacher and the guide of souls, &c. . . . but the power of the
keys is another thing; it is the dispensing all those rites and
ministries by which heaven is opened; and that is, the word
and baptism at the first, and ever after the holy Sacrament of
the Supper of the Lord, and all the parts of the bishops' and
priests' advocation and intercession in holy prayers and offices."
—*Doct. and Pract. of Repentance, Works,* ix. p. 265.

" Absolution in whatever degree alters a sinner's state before God."—*Pusey's Letter in defence of Tr.* 90, p. 99, *et alib.*

it. In the meantime, our established phraseology must be construed as nearly as possible according to the high sense which it is supposed capable of bearing; and the minds of the young must be excited to a state of feeling*, when the concession of the practice of Private Confession, and of the doctrine involved in it, may seem to be naturally and properly required in deference to an existing spiritual demand for it †.

* " It is not our language, but our feelings towards holy rites, which we need to have altered," &c.—*Pusey's Letter in def. of Tr.* 90, p. 39 ; also *Pusey's Serm. on Absol. Pref.* p. 15, and p. 49. In furthering of this object, Jesuit books of devotion, and Manuals of Confession are edited by the author just cited ; and among them is proposed the " Spiritual Exercises " of Ignatius Loyola, the favourite manual of members of the Church of Rome. Persons too are invited to register their names with him ; and are furnished with prayers of " Mutual Intercession" for specific objects; containing directions for applying the Prayers of the Church, in particular the Holy Communion, to such a purpose, " with the prayer that the memorial then made before God of the Sacrifice on the Cross may be accepted in behalf of them ; " recommending also " thrice every day, in honour of the most Holy Trinity, to repeat the Lord's prayer three times, applying it each time to one of the several objects."

† Already it is intimated that there is a great craving for the comfort of Private Confession to a Priest, that there are persons who " long to know how they may be replaced in that condition in which God once placed them" (*Pusey's Sermon on Absolution*, p. 15); *i. e.* how post-baptismal sin, as he views

I would put the young, therefore, on their guard, not to be betrayed by the enthusiasm of religious feeling, into modes of expressing Repentance, and seeking comfort under a sense of sin, such as our own Church, in that simplicity with which it takes up the doctrine of the Cross, is far from sanctioning. Let them look at that artificial system of Repentance which has been set before them, in its true light, as the development of a degenerate age of the Church. Let

it, shall be effaced. Let the following statements also be observed :—

" They hear of the value of habitual Confession of sins before God's ministers, as a means of self-discipline, and of the benefits of Absolution, and know not that our Church suggests it for such as need it, and leaves them at liberty to choose for their Confessor whom they will. In these, and in other ways, it has continually happened that persons have sought in the Communion of Rome, what was laid up for them in their own, more fully, and without corruption, had they but known it; and this valuable class will, of course, be the more secured from wandering, the more the high Catholic doctrines of our Church are developed, and her principles acted on."—*Pusey's Letter in defence of Tract 90*, p. 158.

" There is a greater longing for discipline, for acting under rule, for the comforts of Absolution under a burthened conscience; let the ' ministers of God's Word' be encouraged to train themselves to receive those ' griefs' when others wish to ' open' them, and give them ' the benefit of Absolution ;' and since the godly discipline which our Church yearly laments,

them see it in its perfect form, in the doctrine
and practice of the Church of Rome, together
with its natural evil consequences in the history
of that Church*. Let them indeed never cease
to confess their sins to God, and to pray heartily
for grace to repent truly. But let them not disquiet themselves with desponding fears, or seek
an unscriptural assurance of the forgiveness of
their sins, and reinstatement in their baptismal
purity. Let their daily walk be in the humble

cannot yet be restored, at least let it be extended where it can
and is desired; let not persons have the temptation (I know
such cases) of seeking relief for their consciences in the Roman
Communion, because they look for discouragement if they
apply to ministers in our own."—*Pusey's Letter to the Archbishop of Canterbury*, p. 144.

The consequence here described was naturally to be expected. When persons have had Romanist principles studiously
instilled into them, and are taught to develop every statement
of our Church into some supposed higher doctrine implied in
it, it is but natural that they should go where the way has been
pointed out to them, and realize in their own persons what has
been developed to them in theory.

* Nothing is said here to dissuade any who may feel the
need, from asking spiritual advice of friends competent to give
it, or of such as the Exhortation to the Communion terms
" discreet and learned ministers of God's word." If it be left
as a matter of private feeling, there can be no objection to such
a proceeding. But it is quite another thing to recommend it
as an ordinance of religion and a means of grace.

simple path of Christian duty, as I have before
said, by the light of God's word, and in the
strength of his Holy Spirit, observing all his
commandments and ordinances. Let them watch
and pray that they enter not into temptation; as
knowing, that God will not suffer his servants
"to be tempted above what they are able, but
will, with the temptation, also make a way to
escape that they may be able to bear it;" and
that, though they may be bowed down with a
sense of their own infirmities, they have a great
High Priest in the Heavens ever interceding for
them, ever succouring them with the might of
His Spirit, so that they may be kept in safety
against the great Day.

And how should we all, Brethren, who are in
any station of authority or trust in this place,
this centre of religious teaching and example,
watch at our post to preserve the deposit of the
faith committed to the keeping of our Church!
Let us not be too ready to believe that the danger
is passed away, because some of the more prominent individuals of the recent movement have
cut themselves off from us, and no longer therefore carry on their agitation with the advantage
of place and influence among us. Often the

danger to a state from a faction, is not so much
from those who go over to an enemy's side, and
carry on their warfare from without, as from those
that remain fomenting division within, and in
sympathy, if not in secret communication, with
the enemy. Nor is it very commonly the first
authors of a revolution who effect it in the end;
but rather those who were at first comparatively
of little note, and who, as their leaders move off
the stage, succeed to their place,—who can follow
up and work on an impression which they could
not themselves have made. In factions, too,
there are persons generally found, who, whilst
fully embued with the principles which bind the
party together, are not committed to all the acts
of their leaders, and who obtain for themselves
accordingly the credit of moderation—men, who
watch the signs of the times—ready to advance
or recede as the occasion may serve,—and who,
from that circumstance, are able to rally round
them the discomfited forces, and partly, at least,
retrieve the mistakes or the precipitancy of the
more adventurous. So may it be the case in
parties formed within the Church. Indeed, the
danger here is far greater than in merely poli-
tical factions. For here, they derive a force from

the religious feelings which they enlist on their side, and to which they address themselves. On the strength of these, the weakest instruments become powerful; and the most unworldly in profession,—the humblest and most submissive of men in outward demeanour,—may secretly rule with a despotism the most absolute and imperious*.

Let us not, then, be too confident that the danger is past, because our gates have been closed on this or that leader, or this or that ostensible agitator, with a few of his devoted followers. Let us not, for that reason, lay aside our armour, and cry down those that would keep us on the alert, as vain alarmists ; nor let us listen to those who would soothe us into supineness, while they proclaim a hollow peace. As our whole religion is

* Such is the policy of the Papal power, in professing itself *Servus servorum Dei*. Clarendon gives us a picture of this in his description of the power of the Presbyterian ministers at the time of the Great Rebellion. Describing the strange condescension and submission of the Scottish nobility " to their ignorant Clergy, who were to have great authority, because they were to inflame all sorts of men upon the obligations of conscience," he goes on to say, that the Clergy " had liberty to erect a tribunal, the most tyrannical over all sorts of men, and in all the families of the kingdom : so that the preacher reprehended the husband, governed the wife, chastised the children, and insulted over the servants, in the houses of the greatest

2 M

a warfare with the world, so is our post, as members of that pure form of religion established among us, a state of warfare with all that is of Antichrist,—with all that is corrupt in religious profession. It is our Christian duty, then, not to relax our efforts of resistance. I say not to employ the instruments of worldly warfare,—anger, bitterness, clamour, violence,—but, with Christian plainness of avowal and firmness, to make known, that we will not concede one point of what our Reformers have bequeathed to us, and sealed with the testimony of their blood, either to open assault, or to the sophistry of enticing words of insinuation. The victory of the truth has been gained. Let us watch, that we do not lose it out of our hands.

men. They referred the management and conduct of the whole affair to a committee of a few, who had never before exercised any office or authority in public, with that perfect resignation and obedience, that nobody presumed to inquire what was to be done, or to murmur at or censure anything that was done ; and the General himself, and the martial affairs, were subject to this regimen and discipline as well as the civil; yet they who were intrusted with this superiority, paid all the outward respect and reverence to the person of the General, as if all the power and disposal had been in him alone." ... " This united strength and humble and active temper, was not encountered by an equal providence and circumspection in the King's councils," &c.—*Clarendon's Hist.* B. ii. vol. i. p. 258.

Nor are we without strong warning in the history of our own Church, as well as encouragement to such persevering vigilance. What we have recently experienced, is nothing new in the history of our Church. Not to dwell on the state of things antecedent to the great outbreak of the Rebellion, when such were the tendencies of many of the Clergy to the Church of Rome, that, as the historian observes, " so openly were the tenets of that Church espoused, that not only the discontented Puritans believed the Church of England to be relapsing fast into Romish superstition, but the Church of Rome itself entertained hopes of regaining its authority in this island*;" and when many conversions to Rome took place†;

* Hume's *Hist. of England.* The following remarks of Hume convey an instruction bearing on the present times. " It must be confessed, that, though Laud deserved not the appellation of Papist, the genius of his religion was, though in a less degree, the same with that of the Romish. The same profound respect was exacted to the sacerdotal character, the same submission required to the creeds and decrees of synods and councils, the same pomp and ceremony was affected in worship, and the same superstitious regard to days, postures, meats, and vestments. No wonder, therefore, that this prelate was everywhere, among the Puritans, regarded with horror, as the forerunner of Antichrist."—*Charles I.* vol. vi. p. 287.

† Bishop Hall, censuring the practice of foreign travel as of evil effect in his times on the religion of England, notices some

2 M 2

—to come to times, still nearer, and more outwardly resembling the present, I would refer you
to what Bishop Burnet informs us was the feeling then, in the reign of Queen Anne, the early
part of the last century.

" There appeared at this time," he says, " an
inclination in many of the Clergy to a nearer
approach towards the Church of Rome.   Hicks,
an ill-tempered man, who was now at the head

facts very apposite to the present times.   He thus describes
the state of things then :—"The Society of wilful idolaters
will now down with them, not without ease ; and good mean-
ings begin to be allowed for the clokes of gross superstition.
From thence they grow to a favourable construction of the
mis-opinions of the adverse part, and can complain of the
wrongful aggravations of some contentious spirits ; and from
thence (yet lower) to an indifferent conceit of some more
politic positions and practices of the Romanists.   Neither is
there their rest.   Hereupon ensues an allowance of some of
their doctrines that are more plausible and less important, and
withal a censure of us that are gone too far from Rome. Now,
the marriage of ecclesiastical persons begins to mislike them :
the daily and frequent consignation with the Cross is not to no
purpose.   The retired life of the religious (abandoning the
world, forsooth) savours of much mortification ; and Confession
gives no small ease and contentment to the soul.   And now,
by degrees, Popery begins to be no ill religion. . . . . All this
mischief is yet hid with a formal profession, so as every eye
cannot find it ; in others, it dares boldly break forth to an open
revolt."—*Bp. Hall's Censure of Travel.*   Works, pp. 678, 679.
1624.

of the Jacobite party, had in several books pro-
moted a notion that there was a proper sacrifice
made in the Eucharist, and had on many occasions studied to lessen our aversion to Popery.
The supremacy of the Crown in ecclesiastical
matters, and the method in which the Reformation was carried, was openly condemned : one
Brett had preached a sermon in several of the
pulpits of London, which he afterwards printed ;
in which he pressed the necessity of priestly Absolution, in a strain beyond what was pretended
to even in the Church of Rome ; he said, no Repentance could serve without it ; and affirmed,
that the Priest was vested with the same power
of pardoning that our Saviour himself had *."

Extravagant notions were propagated about the
same time on the subject of Baptism ; and much
pains were taken to give them circulation in
" several little books," as he says, " spread about
the nation."

And what was the result of all this agitation ?
Did it tend to strengthen the Church or to dimi-
nish dissent, or work a religious and moral improvement in the country at large ? The Bishops
indeed exerted themselves to stop the progress of

* Burnet's Hist. of Own Time, vol. vi. 123–125.

such disputations among the Clergy; and happily, though not without some opposition, the evil was checked within the Church. But History is full of complaints of the immorality of those times,— of a corruption of principle and depravation of manners throughout the people, with the spread of infidelity and atheism. And the state of religion became one of deadness; until there arose out of it (the crisis itself forcing its own remedy), a man who,—uniting in his person and character, that high assumption of the dignity of the priestly office which the non-jurors had taught, and the popular spirit craving a more spiritual sustenance than could be obtained generally in the existing condition of the Church,—became ultimately the leader of a schism greater than any which had hitherto rent our Church.

Then, Brethren, if, though we may be thankful for the good which has resulted through the trial and awakening of the Church by the stirring zeal of Wesley, we cannot but deplore the wide schism which has resulted; let us take warning, how we neglect present indications of the like character to those, which preceded the great schism now existing in the Christianity of this country. Let us stand fast against the seductive doctrines, which now are spreading their toils around us; first, on their own account, as being corruptions of the faith ; and then, as naturally leading to a violent re-action, and as unsettling far more in the result than even their advocates may profess to have gained to the Church *.

Consider, then, Brethren, the example set forth to us in the first preaching of the Gospel by the Apostles. Study the provision made by our Lord Himself for the edification of His Church, by the light, which the proceedings of those, to whom it was first communicated, throw

---

* See an article in the *Dublin Review*, No. XL. June 1846, (said to be by Mr. Newman) on Mr. Keble's " *Lyra Innocentium*," in which the like favourable results to the Roman Catholic Church are augured from that publication, to those which the Reviewer traces, not without reason, to Mr. Keble's " *Christian Year.*" That article very justly observes, that it is " by this time abundantly clear" that " the young generation whose pious and serious parents are now teaching them to cross themselves, to fast or abstain, to reverence celibacy, and to say Ave to St. Mary, if they grow up as serious and pious as their instructors, will end in being converts to the Catholic Church."—*Dubl. Rev.* No. XL. p. 457.   It says, also, of Mr. Keble (they are the words of his former associate); that " if there be one writer in the Anglican Church who has discovered a deep, tender, loyal devotion to the blessed Mary, it is the author of the *Christian Year.* The image of the Virgin and Child seems to be the one vision upon which both his heart and intellect have been formed," &c.—*Ibid.* p. 460.

upon it. The Apostles went forth on their mission, without any crucifix in their hands,—
without any relic even of their crucified Lord,—
only with the wonderful story of their Lord on
their lips, and his image in their hearts, to execute his bidding. They had indeed the power of
working miracles in the name of Christ, and declaring his Salvation in every various tongue.
These were the special favours vouchsafed to
their natural feebleness, and inability to achieve
the mighty work on which they were sent, amidst
difficulties appalling to flesh and blood.   Still
look to their mode of going forth on their errand.
Was it not in the unseen strength of the Spirit,
with the word of Salvation, preaching Jesus,
proving Him to be the Christ by the Scriptures,
declaring the whole counsel of God in Him, and
calling sinners to repentance and faith in Him ?
This was the preaching which the Lord " confirmed with wonders and signs following ;" by
this fulfilment of His promise making it evident,
that, by their proceedings, they were rightly discharging the mission with which he had entrusted
them.   And when they had formed the infant
Churches in different parts of the world, do we
find them altering at all the character of their

preaching, or substituting a ritual of Penitence
in the place of the one Gospel with which they
had begun? What say the Acts of the Apostles
generally of their preaching? " Daily in the
Temple and in every house, they ceased not to
teach and preach Jesus Christ*." "Testifying
both to the Jews, and also to the Greeks, repentance towards God, and faith towards our
Lord Jesus Christ†." What say the Epistles of
the same Apostles? " We preach Christ crucified." " I determined not to know anything
among you, save Jesus Christ and Him crucified." The Epistles, as combining refutations of
error with statement and enforcement of the
truth, treat the great heads of the doctrine of
Christ more discursively, or select particular portions of the doctrine for distinct exposition, according to the occasion on which they were
written: but we may say of them still, as of the
several Gospels and the Acts of the Apostles,
that the preaching of Christ Crucified is their
great burthen. Whatever may be their immediate instruction, they send the penitent sinner
for his only ground of hope and relief and comfort, at once to the mercy of God in Christ; ex-

* Acts v. 42.   † Acts xx. 24.

horting believers continually on this ground,—not as bearing Christ Crucified in their own deadened bodies, or as expressing it in the raptures of mystic love*,—but as building on what God in Christ had wrought for them,—that, " as they had received Christ Jesus the Lord, so they would walk in Him, rooted and built up in Him, and stablished in the Faith, as they had been taught, abounding therein with thanksgiving†." So truly was the Holy Spirit to the Apostles a remembrancer of Christ. Like them, let us too go forth ourselves, and send others whom our

---

* " Then truly is the whole man changed into Christ, when detached from himself, and rising above all creatures, he is so wholly transformed into his suffering Lord, as to see nothing and to feel nothing, but Christ Crucified, mocked, railed at, and suffering for us."—*Bonaventura*, quoted by Dr. Pusey in his *Preface to Surin*, p. xxxviii. Such a view of the Atonement (pantheistic as it is) is nothing strange in a mystic writer of the Church of Rome. The strange thing is, that a minister of the Church of England should adopt such a sentiment as his own, and recommend it to others. Dr. Pusey prefers the expression of " Christ Crucified" to that of " the Atonement," or " justification by faith ;" which he regards as " compendious or arbitrary selections, or substitutions of doctrine." (*Ibid.* p. xxix.) That expression, however, naturally recommended itself to him, as being more readily accommodated to that subjective notion of man's Salvation, which he has been employed in developing.

† Col. ii. 6, 7.

instruction and example may reach, in the strength of that mighty Name ; not only professing as our Gospel, that " there is none other Name under Heaven given among men, whereby we must be saved ;" but in every action, and every occasion of our lives,—in all our temptations,—in every fear that casts down the soul,—in every hope that lifts the heart towards heaven, —looking unto Jesus, comforting ourselves in His Name*.

" O that God," I would conclude in the beautiful words of Hooker, " would open the ark of mercy wherein this doctrine lieth, and set it wide before the eyes of poor afflicted consciences, which flee up and down upon the water of their afflictions, and can see nothing but only the gulph and deluge of their sins, wherein there is no place for them to rest their feet ! The God

---

* Admirably does our Church shew of what manner of spirit it is, when it leaves its parting consolation with the sick man, saying to him, " The Almighty Lord, who is a most strong tower to all them that put their trust in him, . make thee know and feel, that there is none other Name under heaven given to man, in whom, and through whom, thou mayest receive health and Salvation, but only the Name of our Lord Jesus Christ."— *Visit. of the Sick.*

of pity and compassion give you all strength and courage every day, and every hour, and every moment, to build and edify yourselves in this most pure and holy faith*."

* Hooker's *Two Sermons* upon part of St. Jude's Ep.

THE END.

PRINTED BY RICHARD AND JOHN E. TAYLOR,
RED LION COURT, FLEET STREET.

Printed in the United States
143653LV00007B/35/A